Herder-Farmer Conflicts in Africa

"This volume lucidly analyses a phenomenon that is one of the serious problems the continent encounters: herder-farmer disputes. This age-old phenomenon representing cooperation, competition and conflict between the two groups, in recent years, driven by multiple factors that include climate change, desertification and droughts has grown causing immense suffering. Omotola and his team employing holistic, multidisciplinary and innovative methodological approaches, mixed data sources and theoretical traditions that span conflict studies, development studies, African studies, gender studies, peacebuilding have provided us invaluable work to increase our understanding, interpretation, analyses, explanation, but most importantly a contribution to resolution of this chronic problem. This work will be of great interest to students of conflict, peacebuilding, climatology, ethnic relations; policymakers, NGOs; all concerned with Africa's wellbeing. I highly recommend it."

—Redie Bereketeab, *Associate professor of sociology and senior researcher at the Nordic Africa Institute, Uppsala, Sweden*

"In this seminal book, the authors explore the phenomenon of herder-farmer conflicts in Africa from the standpoint of selected case studies. The book offers a fresh field-based, theoretically rigorous, and empirically grounded analysis on the historical trajectories as well as contemporary manifestations of the conflicts, against the backdrop of their dynamics over the years. Although there exists a plethora of scholarly and policy-oriented works on the aspects of herder-farmer conflicts in various countries of Africa, there is no foundational book on the subject matter that situates the underpinning issues both comprehensively and comparatively as Omotola's edited volume. This book, therefore, comes handy in providing the much needed nuanced multidisciplinary and transnational perspectives on Africa's herder-farmer conundrum. The insights shared across the variegated thematic facets of the book are profound. I strongly endorse the book as an authoritative source for policymakers, security scholars, students and practitioners."

—Al Chukwuma Okoli, Ph.D, *Department of Political Science, Federal University of Lafia, Nigeria*

"This book arrives at a critical juncture, addressing a significant gap in the literature on peace and security in Africa, and is poised to play an essential role in informing policymakers. It offers a comprehensive exploration of natural resource conflicts—an issue that has plagued the continent for decades and has become a widespread challenge affecting all fifty-four African states. The book illustrates how these conflicts, particularly between herders and farmers, have been largely overlooked or under-analyzed, despite their growing prevalence in regions where pastoralism and agriculture intersect. The authors skillfully unpack how competition over scarce land and natural resources, exacerbated by shifting climate patterns, has intensified these conflicts. The book carefully examines the devastating consequences, including the loss of thousands of lives, large-scale displacement and the widespread disruption of communities. Through rigorous research, it also delves into the multifaceted causes of such conflicts, demonstrating that they stem from a complex interplay of human, environmental, economic and political factors. This work makes a valuable contribution to the field by scientifically demonstrating how Africa, due to its vulnerability to climate change, socio-political instability and economic stressors, is at heightened risk of enduring further conflict. The insights offered in this book not only deepen our understanding of farmer-herder conflicts but also provide a foundation for developing more effective conflict resolution and peacebuilding strategies across the continent."

—Prof. Nsoh Christopher Ndikum, *Specialist in Peace and Security, Academic Registrar, Pan African University Institute of Governance, Humanities and Social Sciences*

J. Shola Omotola
Editor

Herder-Farmer Conflicts in Africa

Perspectives and Lessons for Sustainable Peacebuilding

palgrave
macmillan

Editor
J. Shola Omotola
Department of Political Science
Faculty of Social Sciences
Federal University Oye-Ekiti
Oye-Ekiti
Ekiti State, Nigeria

ISBN 978-3-031-80820-3 ISBN 978-3-031-80821-0 (eBook)
https://doi.org/10.1007/978-3-031-80821-0

Cover illustration: Marina Lohrbach_shutterstock.com

This Palgrave Macmillan imprint is published by the registered company Springer Nature Switzerland AG
The registered company address is: Gewerbestrasse 11, 6330 Cham, Switzerland

This book is dedicated to all individuals, especially women and children, who have suffered losses, no matter how minimal, as a result of herder-farmer conflicts in Africa; and all institutions, formal and informal, local, national or regional, committed to sustainable peacebuilding in Africa.

Foreword

Violent conflicts between herders and farmers in Africa occasioned primarily by struggles over scarce resources and leading to fatal clashes, population displacement and physical, emotional and environmental trauma, have dominated academic discourse in the past few decades. These conflicts have been transformed and aggravated by the insertion of ethnic, communal and religious dynamics, the proliferation of SALW, environmental and demographic changes and (ineffective, flawed or absent) official policies within and across countries and sub-regions. Much has been written on these topics and the publication of yet another volume might seem superfluous to a casual observer. But this volume of essays authored by a new generation of outstanding researchers, and edited by a leading scholar in the field has much to recommend it.

This book is the product of a research sponsored and mentored by the African Peacebuilding Network (APN) of the New York-based Social Sciences Research Council (SSRC). It comprises ten chapters including case studies of herder-farmer conflicts in the African countries of Burkina Faso, Togo, Nigeria, Cameroon and Sudan. This volume is characterised by the following striking features, which underscore its contribution to the literature.

First, its contributors cut across gender, national and disciplinary boundaries. Each brings a critical dimension to the discourse and their respective case studies provide considerable material for insightful comparative analysis, which is captured in the introductory and afterword chapters contributed by the editor. The five case studies are based upon in-depth field research involving direct observations, and engagements with focus groups and key informants.

Second, the chapters demonstrate a common focus on the dynamics of herder-farmer conflicts and subscription to popular, progressive, bottom-up, perpetual and environmental peacebuilding. This is a marked departure from the dominant state-centric, externally induced neo-liberal perspective on peacebuilding which has proven less effective in managing conflicts and their aftermaths.

Third, data collected from field research and secondary sources are anchored on cutting-edge theoretical and conceptual insights in the literature. The authors engage with, and offer illuminating empirical and theoretical insights into, the conjoined issues of gender, class, context, identity politics, the environment and the state while focusing on the changing roles of women, the youth and other emergent (state and non-state) actors. An interesting insight from this book is the exposition on women's roles as protagonists, combatants and enablers of conflict, as opposed to their long-held perception as victims and/or facilitators of peacebuilding.

Finally, beyond filling gaps in the literature, the research findings distilled into this book support robust policy interventions in different contexts. A validation workshop where research encountered policy ensured that this book is based on feedback from the stakeholders in this all-important matter of concern to state and society. As a participant in that workshop and a past member of the Advisory Board of the APN, I derive personal fulfilment from the publication of this volume that demonstrates collaborative capacity for cutting-edge, policy-relevant research by enterprising scholars who overcame various challenges to justify the investment of time and resources on the research project leading to this book.

This volume makes a fresh and insightful contribution to the literature on peacebuilding in Africa. It is highly recommended to scholars and general readers for its illuminating insights into a major many-sided challenge of statecraft, resource management, environmental change, inter-group relations, nation-building and development in contemporary Africa.

October 2024

Ayodeji Olukoju
University Distinguished Professor
of History
University of Lagos
Lagos, Nigeria

Preface

This book critically examines the historical trajectories, complexities, dynamics and nuances of herder-farmer conflicts in Africa, with empirical illustrations from Burkina Faso, Cameroon, Nigeria, Sudan and Togo. These conflicts have their deep-rooted causes in multiple domains, including climate change, environmental scarcities and competition for resources (land and water), demographic changes, historical grievances, environmental mismanagement and socio-political issues. The mismanagement of these conflicts often aggravated the problem, with devastating consequences–financial and economic costs, humanitarian emergencies such as deaths, arson, internal displacements of persons, among others.

Understanding these issues, especially the underlying causes and dynamics of the conflicts is crucial for devising effective management strategies and sustainable peacebuilding initiatives. It also requires the adoption of the comparative method and a multidisciplinary approach, drawing insight from history, law, peace and conflict studies, gender studies, political science and peacebuilding. Basically, these are critical components of what this book has done.

By addressing the geography, history, causes, management, consequences of the conflicts, as well as the lessons for sustainable peacebuilding, mainly but not exclusively from the theoretical prisms of environmental peacebuilding, popular progressive peacebuilding, political ecology, gender and human rights, this book expands the frontier of knowledge on herder-farmer conflicts in Africa. It comprehensively analyses these issues, exploring the diverse roles of state and non-state actors in generating, sustaining and/or managing these conflicts. It also underscores the pertinence of 'local' actors and institutions such as community-based organisations in peacebuilding process. Moreover, the book also engages some topical cross-cutting issues, notably gender, youth, human rights and rule of law in herder-farmer conflicts and sustainable peacebuilding. On the strengths of these and related findings, the book extracts valuable lessons for sustainable peacebuilding. By synthesising these lessons into a cohesive narrative within the book's frame, the book sheds refreshing light on potential pathways towards sustainable management of herder-farmer conflicts and peacebuilding.

Overall, the book fills a critical gap in the literature by providing an analytical framework that addresses the multifaceted nature of herder-farmer conflicts in Africa. Ultimately, this book will not only serve as a pivotal academic resource for scholars and students of African studies, peace and conflict studies, political science, sociology, anthropology, geography, peacebuilding, environmental politics, law and security studies. It also holds significant advocacy ramifications for civil society organisations; as well as practical and policy implications for conflict resolution and peacebuilding initiatives by policymakers and practitioners dedicated to fostering sustainable peace in Africa.

Ekiti State, Nigeria   J. Shola Omotola
October 2024

Acknowledgement

This book would not have been possible without the inestimable and outstanding contributions of certain institutions and individuals. To begin with, the African Peacebuilding Network (APN) of the Social Science Research Council (SSRC), New York, USA, awarded us its flagship research grant—the Collaborative Working Group (CWG) Research Grant in 2019. Without the grant, the research that culminated into the publication of this book project would probably not have been possible. We are deeply indebted to the APN for the grant. We would also like to express our deepest and profound gratitude to APN's Programme Director, Professor Cyril Obi, for his unwavering support and guidance throughout the lifespan of this project. There were turbulent moments along the line. But his deep sense of understanding, peacebuilding skills and experiences and endless patience were pivotal in navigating the troubled waters.

The APN also assigned two distinguished scholars as mentors for the project—Professors Ayodeji Olukoju and Kenneth Omeje. Both of them proved to be invaluable assets, with critical interventions that contributed immensely to the successful completion of the project. Professor Olukoju did not only participate in the research dissemination workshop, but also graciously wrote the foreword to the book. We are extremely grateful to both of them.

We are also deeply grateful to the Federal University, Oye-Ekiti (FUOYE), Ekiti State, Nigeria for serving, creditably, as the host institution for the research. The then Vice Chancellor of the university, Professor Kayode Soremekun, deserves our gratitude. Despite his tight schedules, he demonstrated exemplary academic leadership by fully participating in the methodology workshop of the project hosted by FUOYE in his conference room from the beginning to the end. The Department of Mass Communication, FUOYE, staged a welcome and entertaining play in honour of the research team. I thank my friend, Rev. Sister (Professor) Chika Asogwa for facilitating this.

We would like to register our profound gratitude to the Centre for Democracy and Development (CDD), Abuja, for partnering with us in organising the dissemination workshop at Rockview (Royale) Hotel, Abuja, Nigeria. The Director of CDD at the time, Idayat Hassan, assisted in mobilising key stakeholders for the workshop. The participants, drawn from governmental and non-governmental circles, provided constructive feedback and valuable insights on our research findings and how such connected with their peacebuilding programmes. Notable participants included the Nigerian Ministry of Interior, security agencies, Miyetti Allah, the umbrella socio-cultural organisation of the Fulani herders in Nigeria, Pastoral Resolve, a leading think tank on the issues of pastoralism, Institute for Peace and Conflict Resolution, a leading research and policy think tank under the Nigerian Presidency, relevant civil society organisations, journalists and media practitioners.

We also wish to appreciate all research assistants who helped team members in data collection, transcription and analysis. Again, we must not fail to thank all our colleagues who assisted us to review and provided helpful feedback on the various chapters. We also appreciate Professors Redie Bereketeab, Al Chukwuma Okoli and Nsoh Christopher Ndikum for their generous endorsements for the book.

Finally, every member of the research team deserves special commendation. I cannot but register my deepest gratitude for their support all through. Yes, there were turbulent moments along the line, prolonging the gestation period of the book. But we managed, as conflict and peace-building scholars, to successfully navigate them all. I hope the eventual publication of this book will serve as adequate consolation and reward for all the troubles.

October 2024 J. Shola Omotola, Ph.D.

Contents

List of Contributors

Richard Alemdjrodo School of Law, University of Lome, Lomé, Togo

Abosede Omowumi Babatunde University of Ilorin, Ilorin, Nigeria

Tog-Noma Patricia Emma Bontogho High Institute of Sustainable Development, University Yembila Abdoulaye Toguyeni, Fada NGourma, Burkina Faso

Fatma Osman Ibnouf Development Studies and Research Institute (DSRI), University of Khartoum, Khartoum, Sudan

Aloysius Nyuymengka Ngalim Department of History and African Civilizations, Faculty of Arts, University of Buea, Buea, Cameroon

Akachi Odoemene Department of History and International Studies, Federal University Otuoke, Otuoke, Bayelsa, Nigeria

J. Shola Omotola Department of Political Science, Federal University Oye Ekiti, Oye Ekiti, Ekiti State, Nigeria

List of Figures

List of Tables

PART I

Background and Theoretical Perspectives

CHAPTER 1

Introduction: Dynamics of Herder-Farmer Conflicts in Africa

J. Shola Omotola

Introduction

Across the sprawling savannas and arid plains of Africa, a silent crisis brews—one that intertwines the livelihoods of nomadic pastoralists and settled farmers in a complex dance of cooperation and conflict. For centuries, these groups have shared natural resources, notably land, water and pastures, their lives interwoven through mutual dependence and trade. As pastoralists herded their cattle from one part to the other, across borders in seasonal or cyclical manner and in search of pasture and water, and also to avoid seasonal diseases, they constantly come in contact with farmers along the migratory routes. Also, the pastoralists sometimes settle, develop relationships with farming communities, and function as transhumance pastoralists (Herbert and Birch, 2022; Krätli and Toulmin, 2020a, 2020b; Hussein et al, 1999).

J. S. Omotola (✉)
Department of Political Science, Federal University Oye Ekiti, Oye Ekiti, Ekiti State, Nigeria
e-mail: shoal.omotola@fuoye.edu.ng

J. S. Omotola (ed.), *Herder-Farmer Conflicts in Africa*,
https://doi.org/10.1007/978-3-031-80821-0_1

These relationships have been somewhat interdependent—both provide food and trade with each other, the farms provide grass and crop fodder for the pastoralist's cattle, while the cattle provide manure for the farmer's crops. However, the incremental disruption of this economic interdependence and its replacement by fierce competition for space, power, and resources has often led to tragedy due to threats to and/or violations of each other's means of livelihoods, thus creating a relationship fueled by fear and mutual suspicion (Kendrick and Sanders, 2024; Adams, et al, 2023). These have resulted in huge humanitarian emergencies, including wanton killings and destruction of property worth billions of dollars, denial of means of livelihood, internal displacement of persons, and refugee problems over the past decade (Olumba, et al, 2022; Olumba, 2024; Yakubu, et al, 2021; Odoemene, 2017; Turner, et al, 2011, Turner, 2004).

Conflicts between herders and farmers are not new. In fact, they constitute an old problem that has only gotten worse in contemporary times for many reasons such as the politicization of the relationship between pastoralists and farmers as an extension of national politics, and the failure of leadership in the affected countries (Kendrick and Sanders, 2024; Omotola, 2024a, 2024b). Put differently, relationships between herders and farmers have, historically, been characterized by cooperation, competition, and conflicts. While interdependence promotes close socio-political and economic cooperation, competition fuels conflicts (Hussein, et al, 1999: 402).

Focusing on the problems of herder-farmer conflicts is important in different dimensions. These include:

(a) First of all, these conflicts represent one of Africa's oldest, most historically complex, and very destructive and intractable conflicts that has intensified in contemporary times (Hussein, et al, 1999).
(b) Again, there is a dangerous emotional ethnicization of the crisis, particularly due to the problems of dysfunctional ethnicity (Kendrick and Sanders, 2024; Moritz and Mbacke, 2022; Egwu, 2015; Olaniyan and Omotola, 2015). Thus, it should serve as a wake-up call for the authorities to treat this development as an emergency deserving of pro-active measures/responses.
(c) Moreover, the conflicts are linked to several complex factors, including power, history, citizenship rights, and access to and use of land – all of which are charged and potentially explosive in most

African countries (Nassef, et al, 2023). In other words, the frictions between herders and farmers constitute a potentially destructive factor on the continent.

(d) Furthermore, the crisis between these two 'food-providing' groups underscores the serious threats the development poses to the means of survival and livelihoods of both parties, and what they are tenaciously protecting and projecting, and could as well have implications for national, human and food security in the continent.

(e) In addition, the story of gun-toting herdsmen (freely using AK-47 rifles) should also draw attention to the trafficking and proliferation of small arms and light weapons (SALWs), and ammunition especially by terrorist and criminal gangs operating across Africa (Kwaja and Smith, 2021; IOM, 2017; RMB and Partners, 2021).

(f) Yet, the diverse responses to the conflicts –by States and non-state actors – have often left much to be desired, thus the urgent desire for a way forward. Contentions abound in academic, policy and advocacy circles across Africa as to what constitutes 'appropriate' responses to the problem (Brottem, 2021; Kwaja and Ademola-Adelehin, 2017).

This book advances a fresh understanding of, as well as new knowledge and explanations for the fractured herder-farmer relationships and violent engagement across Africa. It posits that farmer-herder conflicts are not entirely 'new' in Africa, but an old phenomenon. A holistic understanding of the problem in contemporary times, therefore, demands, a deep appreciation of its historical trajectories. This will help to unravel the changing contexts, new dynamics, and expanded actors involved in the processes. Such an approach holds a lot of prospects in identifying progress and setbacks, opportunities and limitations, as well as critical lessons for sustainable security, peacebuilding and development in Africa. Over all, this book offers a fresh perspective by delving into the historical trajectories of herder-farmer relationships, uncovering how past interactions shape present conflicts. By examining these evolving contexts, we aim to identify pathways towards sustainable peace and development in Africa.

The State of the Study: Theoretical, Methodological, and Empirical

The literature on herder-farmer conflicts in Africa is quite vast, each focusing on different aspects of the problem. However, despite these advances, there remains a significant gap—a comprehensive synthesis that unifies old and new studies into a cohesive body of knowledge is lacking. The most comprehensive attempt at doing this, to the best of my knowledge, was a comprehensive review and synthesis, which reviewed empirical studies on farmer–herder conflicts in sub-Saharan Africa, published from 2000 to 2021. After a series of articles' mining and screening using various criteria, the study covered a total 53 empirical studies on farmer–herder conflicts covering nine (9) countries in sub-Saharan Africa (Adams, et al, 2023). This important review highlights most of the salient themes, including geographical coverage, methodology and analytical techniques, theoretical and conceptual frameworks, causes, strategies for prevention, as well as conflict and peacebuilding mechanisms across these studies.

In terms of spatial coverage, the review found that 53 countries were covered majority of which were in West Africa. Not surprisingly, Nigeria dominated with 47% of the publications, Ghana with 25%, Tanzania with 9%, and Mali with 6%. There were a few others in Cameroon, Niger, Kenya, Senegal, and Sudan, suggesting the widespread nature of the problem across Africa. These studies covered 13 main themes, including conflict which accounted for 85% of these studies, with a main emphasis on causes and dynamics (Benjaminsen and Ba, 2021) to the marginalisation of other salient aspects, notably conflict management and peacebuilding (Paalo, 2021; Setrana and Kyei, 2021). Other featured themes include political ecology (21%), livelihood security and agriculture (19%), climate change, conflict management, land tenure, media discourse, local peacebuilding, security and migration (33%), governance, cultural bias and distrust, and livelihood security (see Ahmed and Kuusaana, 2021; Benjaminsen and Ba, 2021; Mbah, et al, 2021, all cited in Adams, et al, 2023).

As noted, most of the extant studies focus on the causes and dynamics of conflicts between herders and farmers. Most studies emphasize ecological and environmental factors—such as resource scarcity, climate change, and desertification—as primary drivers of increased migration and competition over natural resources like land and water (Kendrick and Sanders, 2024; Ahmed, 2022; Hussein, et al, 1999). Some others highlight different other factors as triggers and drivers of the problem. These include the proximity and interaction perspective, which focuses attention on territory as a 'facilitating condition for conflict' (Diehl, 1991),cultural bias (Mahmood and Azuaga, 2020), and tenure problem (Kugbega and Aboagye, 2021), defective policy frameworks, political ecology, population growth and change in land use. Others stress weak state capacity/state, weakness/failure manifesting in the pervasiveness of ungoverned spaces, corruption, violent attacks and regional conflict dynamics (Omotola and Oyewole, 2024; Onwuzuruigbo, 2023; Lenshie, et al, 2020; Mbih, 2020; Eke, 2020; Omotola and Alumona, 2016). Other studies underscore the salience of poor resource governance, privatization and commercialisation of land beyond the reach of herders, stereotyping of herders as jihadists in media outlets to justify ethnic killings, social ostracism, official partisanship, and increased availability of deadly weapons (Kwaja and Ademola-Adelehin, 2017; Chukwuma, 2020; Kendrick and Sanders, 2024; Mohammed, et al, 2021).

Shettima and Tar (2008: 170–174), classified these diverse explanations into: (a) environment-related factors, including climate change; (b) social-related factors such as ethno-religious considerations, (c) political-related factors, especially the seeming political powerlessness of pastoralists in the post-colonial state, including their 'landlessness'.

Irrespective of the causes, a worrisome development is the tendency of herdsmen's unwillingness or refusal to return to their original countries after the official end of the transhumance period. This tendency to 'sit tight' and settle as 'immigrant ethnicity' without attaining 'immigrant incorporation', is defined as the 'shifting of the boundaries of belonging, which has to overcome existing forms of social closure along ethnic lines' (Wimmer, 2009: 245). It seems predominant and remains a major component of the problem in Africa. A relevant representation of this tendency has been found in northern Ghana, particularly Agogo community where related issues have led to the adoption of a policy of expulsion on herders. Bowever, despite a subsisting court order and official efforts to ensure compliance, many herders have refused to honour the eviction order and found means of circumventing its enforcement (see Olaniyan, et al, 2015). In such contexts, violence will increase between Fulani and the local population whose agriculture models cannot coexist year-long with herds of cows. This poses serious legal problems for ECOWAS in terms of a free circulation of people, particularly about legislations of herdsmen's host countries (Ezirigwe, 2023; RBM and Partners, 2021; IOM, 2017).

The methodological and analytical orientations of these studies vary, with a preponderance of the qualitative methods deployed in 58% of the studies. This was followed by studies that used mixed methods (25%) and purely quantitative methods (17%). Data collection methods were also plural across the studies, but also with a dominance of mixed methods of data collection (60%), notably Key Informant Interviews (KII), structured questionnaires, and Focused Group Discussions (FGDs). However, four groups of authors deployed an ethnographic approach. The analytical approach of these studies includes thematic analysis, content analysis, descriptive analysis, discourse analysis, spatial analysis, and statistical analysis. It is important to note that all these studies were single-country case studies, 'suggesting a lack of comparative empirical cases in the literature' (Adams, et al, 2023: 4).

These studies also crisscross several theoretical frameworks of analysis, 21% of which adopted political ecology, focusing on the relationships between political power and environmental dynamics. Others include natural resource issues (19%) such as resource scarcity, access, competition, and relative deprivation, rational choice theory (8%), climate-conflict nexus theory (4%), and peacebuilding framework adopted by only two of the reviewed articles, especially local peacebuilding (Setrana and Kyei, 2021; Adams, et al, 2023).

Extant studies also address issues of adopted strategies for preventing herder-farmer conflicts in Africa. According to the review, three broad categories can be distilled from the literature. These were the aggressive approach such as resorting to carrying weapons for self-defence (self-help strategy), which complicates the proliferation of SALWs, a passive approach that deals with initiatives aimed at avoiding confrontations between the two groups, and the constructive approach, including community organizing for intergroup relations such as education campaigns and the creation of dialogue platforms. In terms of conflict management and peacebuilding, the review identifies three main approaches. These are third-party interventions, litigation, and adjudication including police involvement, as well as compensation and direct herder-farmer negotiations (Adams, et al, 2023).

These conflicts were found to have always had negative consequences for affected countries and/or regions, including human and physical security. International Crisis Group (2017) underscored the humanitarian and economic costs of the conflict to be huge, accounting for about 2500 deaths in Nigeria in 2016 and an annual average casualty figure of about 2000 between 2011 and 2016, making it almost as deadly as the Boko Haram insurgency. Unfortunately, adequate attention has not been paid to the regional and international ramifications of these costs (see Kwaja and Smith, 2021).

Again, studies also show that responses have varied across time and space. Most notable responses include the development of the legal framework, grazing reserve, and policy of expulsion (Okeke, 2014; Omotola, 2017). The African Union (AU) in 2010 developed the Policy Framework for Pastoralism in Africa as the first continent-wide policy initiative that aims to secure, protect, and improve the lives, livelihoods, and rights of African pastoralists. However, most of these responses have not yielded the desired results (Maiangwa, 2017; Olaniyan, et al, 2015; Olaniyan and Uzodike, 2015).

All this calls for new ways of thinking and theorizing about the problem. Ultimately, a much more nuanced and comprehensive interrogation of the subject matter, rooted in a transdisciplinary approach, is required. This represents one of the major contributions of this book.

The Uniqueness of this Book

This book is unique in several ways. It is the first major attempt to holistically understand herder-farmer conflicts in Africa from a multidisciplinary perspective, incorporating African studies, humanities, environmental sciences, peace and conflict studies, development studies, and social sciences. We adopt a comparative approach across five deeply affected African countries—Burkina Faso, Cameroon, Nigeria, Sudan, and Togo—utilizing diverse methodologies such as Key Informant Interviews (KIIs), Focus Group Discussions (FGDs), questionnaires, and desk reviews. This methodological plurality, together with the comparative method, enhances the robustness of the study.

Again, as documented in the preceding section, there is a sizeable number of research outputs on herder-farmer conflicts in Africa. However, a careful reading of these publications reveals some obvious gaps. One, most of the extant studies on the subject focused largely on the causes and consequences of the conflicts. Partial references have been made to the management of the problem (responses), but with greater emphasis placed almost exclusively on the role of the state. Due attention has not been devoted to the role of non-state actors in the process (see for example, Olaniyan, et al, 2015). Yet, non-state (and inter-state-regional) actors are crucial to the understanding of the changing dynamics of herder-farmer conflict in Africa (Omotola, 2024a, Omotola and Hassan, 2015). By its emphasis on the roles of non-state actors in these conflicts, this book fills an important gap in the literature on the subject.

Moreover, the interconnections between these conflicts and security, safety, and development at all levels (regional, national, and local) underscore the urgency and pertinence of this book. This is more so as many conflict resolution and peacebuilding efforts in this regard have failed, thus indicating the intractable nature of the conflicts.

More disturbing, however, is the overwhelming acknowledgment of the very deadly potentials—on diverse fronts—of the herder-farmer conflicts, especially due to their politicization, frequency, and intensity on the continent. Similarly, the effects of the conflicts are no longer local or national; they now have sub-regional and regional implications (Nassef, et al, 2023; Kuna and Ibrahim, 2015). Despite several studies on the herder-farmer conflicts over time, it is clear that there are new issues and dynamics (characteristics and features) –frequency, magnitude, intensity, expanded actors (local, national, regional, and international), and so on–associated with the development, which are yet to be critically examined, understood and properly explained.

Again, the dynamics of the conflicts are equally changing as a result of several factors, including changing contexts—such as new political actors, shifting dynamics of local political economy (such as poverty and unemployment), environmental change and scarcity, changing land rights, new modes of natural resources management, migration, and so on. For instance, on average more such conflicts are recorded in recent times than 10–20 years ago, while the casualty level has equally increased drastically. Also, the use of very deadly weapons—like AK-47—by herders (and the sources of such weapons) has become a serious issue only in recent times. Undoubtedly, these emergent issues and dynamics present fresh challenges to researchers (Nassef, et al, 2023).

The geography and human costs of the problem are troubling. Kratli and Toulmin (2020a: 24) documents that 'over the period 1997–2017, the ACLED records a total of 173,000 civilian fatalities across the three regional clusters', with fatalities related to incidents involving pastoralists accounting for 10,096. Studies have documented these incidents and attendant fatalities across 16 African countries drawn from Central, East, and West Africa. As one source puts it:

> For the 16 countries in our sample, ACLED recorded a total of 5,100 incidents and 13,364 fatalities in the 12 months from May 2019 to May 2020 (all included). Most of these were in Nigeria (1,421 incidents with 4,168 fatalities), Burkina Faso (580 incidents with 2,231 fatalities), Mali (605 incidents with 2,038 fatalities), and Cameroon (783 incidents, with 1,452 fatalities). Violence in CAR appears to have slightly slowed down (164 incidents and 508 fatalities) while it seems to be increasing in Niger (305 incidents and 986 fatalities) and Chad (130 incidents and 731 fatalities). Records for Ghana, Benin and Côte d'Ivoire were respectively 121, 33 and 146 incidents with 50, 43 and 61 fatalities, whereas Togo and Senegal recorded 32 and 8 incidents, with 10 and 2 fatalities respectively. In East Africa, ACLED recorded 191 incidents in Ethiopia with 581 fatalities, 289 incidents in Uganda with 175 fatalities, 271 incidents in Kenya with 293 fatalities and 21 incidents in Tanzania with 17 fatalities. (Krätli and Toulmin, 2020a: 24)

The spatial distribution of the problem in terms of manifestations and fatalities is staggering. It shows the persistence, in fact, escalation of the problem, despite all efforts at taming the monster. Again, no region of the continent is free from the phenomenon; the only difference is in degree. West Africa seems to be the stronghold of the problem where Nigeria, Burkina Faso, and Mali top the ladder as represented in Fig. 1.1.

The financial and economic costs of the problem are also staggering. These include acute loss of vital sources of livelihood (farming and herding) and revenue/income. A report by the UK-based humanitarian organization, Mercy Corps, reveals that herder-farmer conflicts cost Nigeria more than $14bn (£10bn) between 2013 and 2015 (Mercy Corps, 2015: 1). The same report gave further insight into some scenarios depending on the direction of relations between herders and farmers, which can either be stable or otherwise. According to the report:

> Nigeria stands to gain up to $13.7 billion (₦2.3 trillion) annually in total macroeconomic progress if the country is able to maintain peace between farmers and pastoralists in the four states of Benue, Kaduna, Nasarawa, and Plateau alone, which represent up to 2.79% of Nigeria's officially reported Gross Domestic Product (GDP), or 0.8% of the "total economic product"

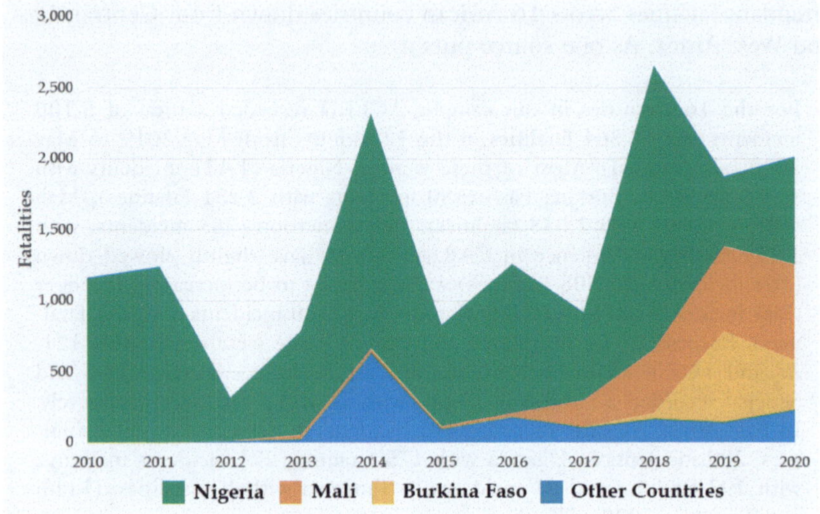

Fig. 1.1 Trends in Farmer-Herder violence in West and Central Africa (*Note* Figures exclude events attributed to violent extremist groups. *Data Sources* Armed conflict location & event data project. *Source* Brottem, 2021: 2)

> of Nigeria, including the informal economy. State revenues suffered significant losses due to farmer-pastoralist conflict, particularly after intense and sustained bouts of violence. The four study states have lost 22-47% of their potential revenue collection, or roughly $719,000 to $2.3 million (₦109-347 million) due to the conflict. In Plateau State—marked by particularly high levels of inter-religious violence—the state government lost up to 75% of potential revenue, demonstrating the imperative of addressing conflict in order to effectively meet other social and economic needs. The average household affected by farmer-pastoralist conflict would experience at least a 64%-- and potentially 210% or higher—increase in income, if these conflicts were reduced to near zero. (Mercy Corps, 2015a; 2015b)

As staggering as these figures are, they are just for one zone, namely the middle belt or north central Nigeria over a very short time period, approximately two years. If the same estimations are made across other parts of the country where the problem has been comparatively equally severe, such as the South West and South East, the figures would become outrageously alarming. Taking a longitudinal view of these costs over

20 years and given the fact that the problem reached its apogee in the post-2015s under the Buhari presidency, the financial and economic costs were gigantic and catastrophic. Extend to the entire continent, then it is arguably one of the most outrageous developmental trappings in Africa.

Also in Cameroon, Ngwoh (2017) noted that between 1946 and 2005, approximately 400,000 farmers and 5,000 graziers lived in the area. Within this span, an estimated 21,074 conflicts were registered making an average of 339 hostilities a year. The highest numbers were recorded in 1973 (150 conflicts), 1981 (175 conflicts), and 2003 (180 conflicts) in Wum; in Esu, the highest figures were 150 conflicts in 1966, 210 conflicts in 1988, and 195 conflicts in 1993. Yet, there are social dimensions of the problem, most notably concerning social cohesion and nation-building.

Furthermore, the extant literature on the subject has been largely dominated by single-country case studies, with a very limited focus on the comparative approach (Adams, et al, 2023). Consequently, the transnational and regional character/dimensions of the problem have been underexplored, if not neglected. By adopting a comparative approach spanning four countries, our study seeks not only to fill the gap but also expand the frontier of knowledge on the subject, exploring important cross-cutting issues such as human rights, rule of law, gender, and youth across its various sub-themes.

Again, the gender and youth dimensions of the conflicts have occupied the margins of mainstream literature, or at least mischaracterized. In most instances, they have been largely neglected all together. In a review of literature on the subject, Nassef et al (2023: 4) found that 'women are mentioned in relations to conflict in only 28% of the studies, primarily as victims and less frequently as instigators of conflict or peacemakers. While young people were found to be more frequently mentioned, specifically in 43% of the studies, they were often portrayed as 'primarily as participants in conflict'. While this claim may be valid, there are many other ways in which youth agency manifests in these conflicts. Beyond their agency, young people are also victims of these conflicts. Yet, anecdotal evidence reveals that these conflicts have had severe impacts on women and young people, not only in terms of victimhood as the dominant scholarly narrative relating to women in conflicts and civil wars tends to suggest, but also their agency (Flintan, et al, 2024). Our book pays significant attention to these tendencies in almost equal measures, but most notably by J. Shola Omotola, Abosede Babatunde, Fatma OsmanIbnouf, the last two focusing exclusively on the gender ramifications of these conflicts in Nigeria and Sudan respectively.

Also of crucial importance is the management of conflicts. In this respect, both state and non-state actors have been engaged. However, the former seems to have been far ahead of the latter in managing herder-farmer conflicts. This trend may have largely been responsible for the almost exclusive focus on the state actors —government agencies, the military, police, etc- in the literature to the exclusion of non-state actors. Yet, non-state actors such as civil society organisations (SCOs)/Non-Governmental Organisations (NGOs) of various persuasions: community-based associations, traditional institutions, vigilante groups, and religious institutions, as the entries in this book reveal almost across the board, are found to be increasingly involved in the management of the crisis (Omotola, 2024a, Omotola, et al, 2019). This book is unique in capturing this important aspect of the management of herder-farmer conflicts in Africa.

The book also explores important cross-cutting issues such as human rights, the rule of law, gender, and youth across its various sub-themes. Moreover, by exploring the historical trajectories of the problem, the book helps in unraveling the changing contexts, new dynamics, and expanded actors involved in the processes. This in turn helps in identifying progress and setbacks, opportunities and limitations, as well as critical lessons for security, development, and peacebuilding in Africa.

Above all else, the emphasis on lessons for peacebuilding stands the book out in many ways. At the risk of repetition, extant studies have marginalized, indeed, almost excluded the important theme of peacebuilding. It is such that of the 53 articles reviewed by Adams, et al (2023: 9), only two (2) adopted peacebuilding framework, especially local peacebuilding. Our emphasis on peacebuilding, including environmental and local peacebuilding comes across as one of the strongest selling points of this book.

The book also has crucial policy relevance in many respects. Farmers and herders play a critical role as food providers, which is a basic human need that is essential to the social and economic well-being of the people. It is also an important component of human security. Africa has been facing a serious food crisis in recent times, which has been worsening because of the protracted conflict between farmers and herders that has remained intractable without adequate responses from the African government, and sub-regional and regional organizations. This book advances the debate and discourses, as well as produces reliable data on diverse peacebuilding efforts—both in practice and policy—to contain one of Africa's oldest, most complex intractable, and very destructive conflicts. This will help development partners and African governments to develop the most appropriate strategies for curtailing the destructive conflict that continues to undermine national and human security in Africa.

Focus and Contribution of the Book

The overarching goal of this book is to critically explore the historical trajectories, changing contexts, new dynamics, and expanded actors involved in the entire gamut of farmer-herder conflict in Africa. This is done to identify progress and setbacks, opportunities and limitations, as well as critical lessons for sustainable security, peacebuilding and and peacebuilding in Africa. In addressing these concerns, we emphasize several cross-cutting issues: human rights, gender, youth, etc. We also explore official and unofficial responses to the problem (management of the problem by State and non-state actors) and lessons for sustainable peacebuilding.

The book makes some modest contributions to the understanding of herder-farmer conflicts in Africa. Theoretically, the book situates the problem within the theoretical insights offered by the peacebuilding perspective. Here, a distinction is made between post-conflict neoliberal peacebuilding and popular progressive peacebuilding. By popular progressive peacebuilding, we mean long-term efforts geared towards 'the gradual construction of the socio-economic and political institutions of societies' (Bereketeab, 2021: 35). Such peacebuilding holds the prospects for suitable security and development, both in pre-and post-conflict settings. Popular progressive peacebuilding draws on 'proven domestic institutions, mechanisms, and authorities', thereby deepening its societal connections, penetrations and legitimacy. It is coterminous with what Paffenholz (2021: 367) calls 'perpetual peacebuilding', which envisioned peacebuilding 'as an ever-developing process manifested in a series of (re-)negotiations of the social and political contracts'. The is the approach that is most suitable for African countries, not just because of the plural character of most of them, but also as a result of deep historical and cultural ties, the destruction of which lies at the heart of most of the crisis and contradictions of governance and development afflicting the continent.

This contrasts sharply with neoliberal peacebuilding, whose emphasis is on the state as the primary, if not the sole actor. It is also externally-driven and largely disconnected from local realities. These dysfunctions were well articulated thus: 'it is an external imposition and fails to cohere with the specific social, cultural, historical, economic, political, and ethnic realities of the particular society' (Bereketeab, 2021: 36). It is basically the antithesis of popular progressive peacebuilding, usually short-term in focus, and limited societal penetration and legitimacy. It is, certainly, not sustainable in Africa. Apart from the aforesaid factors of pluralism, history and culture, neoliberal peacebuilding in Africa has a pervasive history of monumental failure across the continent (Zambakari, 2016; Caffentzis, 2002).

A critical component of popular progressive or perpetual peacebuilding, with specific reference to herder-farmer conflicts, is environmental peacebuilding. Dresse, et al, (2018: 104) define environmental peacebuilding as 'the process through which environmental challenges shared by the (former) parties to a violent conflict are turned into opportunities to build lasting cooperation and peace'. According to Bruch, et al, (2022), it 'comprises efforts to prevent environment-related conflicts, to build trust and establish shared identities, to facilitate integration between conflict parties, and to build capabilities for resilient and sustainable livelihoods' (Chapter 2 by Omotola sheds more illuminations on both concepts). The incorporation of popular progressive peacebuilding and environmental peacebuilding as an analytical framework stands this book out in comparison to the extant studies on the subject matter in Africa.

Methodologically, the book is multidisciplinary in orientation, drawing from important analytical lenses from the humanities (history, law, and philosophy), social sciences (political science, peace, conflict, and strategic studies), and environmental sciences (climate change and water resources governance), among others. While each chapter adopts the case study approach, the book is also comparative, with geographical coverage spanning five African countries: Burkina Faso, Cameroon, Nigeria, Sudan, and Togo. Empirically, the book is well illustrated, drawing on primary data from extended field works across different study areas of the various chapters. This is a rare feat by the standard of the current state of study on the subject matter in Africa.

Overall, these distinct contributions along the theoretical, methodological, and empirical lines serve to fortify the strengths of the book. Apart from exposing us to the current state of debates and knowledge on the subject matter, the book also makes modest contributions in highlighting the gaps in the literature, as well as a bold attempt to contribute towards filling the identified scholarly gaps. The book also highlights the research and policy implications of its major finding, teasing out critical lessons for sustainable peacebuilding, security, and development.

Data and Methods

The study adopts multidisciplinary and comparative approaches, together with historical cum descriptive method of research, both qualitatively and quantitatively. It deploys triangulation in data collection, exploring both primary and secondary sources. Primary data were collected using structured and semi-structured in-depth interviews, Focus Group Discussions (FGD), Key Informant Interviews (KII), direct observation, and questionnaire administered to purposefully selected respondents and stakeholders in the selected communities in the study areas. These include state and non-state actors such as government officials, farmers, herders, and their associations (such as Miyetti Allah Cattle Breeders Association (MACBAN), being the umbrella socio-cultural group of the Fulani's herders in Nigeria; and the All Farmers Association of Nigeria (AFAN), traditional institutions, community-based associations, vigilante groups, youth, and women in the selected communities in these countries. Other targets include security establishment and personnel, as well as community-based organisations (CBOs). Key considerations in the selection of the cases and sample population include scope and intensity of the conflicts, relevance –participants understanding of the issues- and availability.

The research team held a series of workshops in the course of the study. These includes a two-day methodology workshop held at the Federal University, Oye Ekiti, Ekiti State, Nigeria, the host institution for the study in 2019 to design and fine-tune the methodological frames of the study. This was followed by dissemination cum validation workshop held at Rockview Royale Hotel, Abuja to subject the research outputs to scrutiny by experts and practitioners with extensive involvement and knowledge of the subject. Participants were careful selected across various stakeholders' constituencies, including academia, relevant government agencies such as Ministries of Agriculture, Defence and Interior, office of the National Security Adviser, security agents, CSOs, media, and herder and farmers associations.

Secondary data were derived from archival sources, books, journals, newspapers, and the internet. Analytically, the study draws from descriptive analysis, interpretative analysis, thematic analysis, content analysis, discourse analysis, spatial analysis, and statistical analysis using tables, graphs, bar-charts, frequency distribution and simple percentages. Together, the approaches.

Organisation and Structure of the Book

Organised into three sections, the book contains 10 chapters. The first section contains two chapters, both of which were written by J. Shola Omotola, the editor of the book. The Section addresses important background issues, notably conceptual, theoretical, and methodological framings. Specifically, Chapter 1 provides a general introduction to the book. It problematizes the phenomenon of herder-farmer conflicts in Africa, highlighting its history, geography, trends, intensity, and consequences to underscore why this book matters at this point in time. It also highlights the central arguments of the book and those of each chapter, showing the intersections not just across some cross-cutting issues (human rights, gender, youth, etc.), but also cross-national comparison.

Chapter 2 situates the book within an appropriate theoretical framework, with particular emphasis on peacebuilding perspectives to the understanding of herder-farmer conflicts in Africa. The chapter critically engages with various theoretical perspective herder-farmer conflicts in Africa, including the role of climate change and attendant scarcity of resources and migration (both internally within countries and across borders), weak state/declining state capacity, citizenship and politicized ethnicity, etc. The chapter also reflects on the contending perspectives on peacebuilding, notably the neoliberal and popular progressive arguments, showing the strengths and weaknesses of each of these perspectives. It also underscores the pertinence of environmental peacebuilding as a critical component of the latter.

Section 2 presents a series of critical case studies across multiple regions, each providing unique insights into the complexities and localized dynamics of herder-farmer conflicts on the continent. Arranged in alphabetical order, Tog-Noma Patricia Emma BONTOGHO in Chapter 3, the first in the section, focuses on Natural Resource Scarcity and its Implication on Farmers Herders Conflict in Burkina Faso. The geographic scope of the study covers the three climatic zones of the country from which cases were selected for in-depth investigation. These were Pama (Sudano Sahelian zone), Manga (Sudanese zone), and Thiou (Sahelian zone). The chapter examines the trends of herder-farmer conflicts in Burkina Faso, highlighting their manifestations, causes, consequences, management strategies, and key lessons for sustainable peacebuilding and development. The chapter approaches these issues from the perspective of natural resource availability and management, particularly land use. In doing so, the chapter relies on changes in land uses/land cover (LULU) derived from remotely sensed satellite imagery over a period of time. Specifically, multi-date images including historical satellite imageries for 1990, 2002, and 2015 were retrieved from Landsat Thematic Mapper (TM) and OLI-TIRS to determine both landscape features. Data from these sources indicate variations in LULU across time and space. It argues that understanding the dynamics of land use and land cover is essential for advancing the debates on farmer-herder conflicts. This, in the arguments of the author, can contribute to finding sustainable solutions to the problem, particularly concerning food and human security.

In Chapter 4, Aloysius Ngalim explores the problem in Cameroon, with illustrations from the conflicts in Donga Mantung Division of the North West Region of the country. The chapter highlights how herder-farmer conflicts threaten peace and security in the country due mainly to competition for scarce resources between herders and farmers, leading to recurrent and growing violence. The conflicts, according to Ngalim, intensify in terms of theirfrequency, intensity, and geographical scope. They were also complicated by ethnic, cultural, land, and other natural resource issues. The chapter also underscores the salience of the intersectionality of herder-farmer conflicts with other forms of conflicts, namely communal conflicts and secessionist militias. This was in addition to many other explanations for the conflicts such as environmental factors, securitization, identity politics, the politicization of the conflicts and criminalization, and the economy of war, including the role of conflict entrepreneurs feeding fat on the problem, The conflicts have had devastating consequences such as deaths including pregnant women and children, rape, arson (burning of churches in several places), kidnapping of people in their farms and forced migration, among others. While the government and other stakeholders have always sought ways of mitigation through various management mechanisms, such responses have not been able to produce the desired results. His findings resonate with most others, especially in terms of the causes and consequences of the conflicts, as well as cross-cutting issues.

As arguably one of the most affected countries by herder-farmer conflicts in Africa, Nigeria has three case studies, the first of which comes up in Chapter 5, which examines the problem in Benue state. In this chapter, Akachi Odoemene critically interrogates how to better understand and properly articulate the problem - causes, dynamics, consequences, management, and lessons for peacebuilding - in Benue State. It opens with the important assertion that the problem is old and longstanding, but radiating several new dimensions in its contemporary manifestations, which were adequately illustrated. It also highlights the remote and immediate causes of the problem. While the former includes resource scarcity, social differences, population growth, extinction of grazing routes, and failure of the state; the latter encompasses issues such as land rights (ownership, use, and grabbing tendencies), threats to livelihood, cultural intolerance, mutual suspicion, and competing victimhood. The problem has come at a high cost, including attacks, deaths, displacement of persons, destruction of properties, and so on.

One of the salient arguments by Odoemene in the chapter is that despite widespread criticisms against the Federal Government over the farmer-herder conflicts in Benue State, the government should still be commended for its various and longstanding interventions in the problem. He highlighted a few of such efforts which sought "to mediate, contain, manage and/or resolve the conflicts", including the creation of Grazing Reserves in 1965, which was meant to keep the herders away from farmlands, thus reduce the incidents of conflicts; and the establishment of the National Commission for Nomadic Education (NCNE) in 1989, to integrate the pastoralists into the society and national life through mobile basic education and skill acquisition training as some of the earliest strategies by the federal government. These were apart from other recent measures by the federal and Benue state governments, as well as non-governmental actors, including traditional institutions, faith-based organisations, and others. The chapter concludes with several important lessons for sustainable peacebuilding in the state.

This is closely followed by the case of Nasarawa state authored by J. Shola Omotola in Chapter 6. The chapter attempts a holistic understanding of herder-farmer conflicts in the state, with emphasis on several critical issues, like others: historical trajectories and manifestations, actors, causes, and consequences, as well as critical lessons for security, development, and peacebuilding. The chapter critically engages these and related issues in the state being one of the leading epicenters in the transformation of herder-farmer conflicts in Nigeria in recent times. The chapter located the conflicts in the state in different sources, including environmental factors such as climate change, resource scarcity, migration, contradictions in the roles of some actors, notably security agents, traditional institutions and the media. Security agents often exhibit poor professionalism in their official responses such as failure to heed early warning signals/reports and act proactively, late and inadequate deployment of personnel, corruption and extortion of the 'locals' in the name of peacekeeping, and gale human rights violations. Traditional institutions were accused of selling ancestral lands to herders to settle in some parts of the state. Media were alleged of underreporting of incidents and fatalities, thereby downplaying the severity of the problem and attendant official responses. The passage of the anti-open grazing law in neighbouring Benue state also contributed because most of the fleeing herders migrated to Nasarawa, greatly increasing the number of herders in the state and thus, fueling heightened competition for already scarce natural resource. The proliferation of SALWs also complicated the matter.

The chapter also shows that these conflicts have had devastating consequences on both state and society. Specifically, conflicts in the state have negative impact on human and food security, education, health, and social capital. They have also led to humanitarian emergencies, including deaths and displacement of persons, as well as rise in crime rates in the state. Women, girls and young people also suffered from the conflicts: rape, loss of pregnancy and miscarriages. State and non-state actors have intervened in diverse ways: deployment of security personnel, peace education, humanitarian assistance such as the provision of relief materials and the safe return, rehabilitation and resettlement of IDPs. However, these responses, as the chapter reveals, were largely seen as inadequate or ineffective for various reasons such as the dominance of state actors, politicization or political interference, ethnicisation, poor management natural resources and of IDP camps, among others. The peacebuilding implications of these findings were reflected in the chapter.

In Chapter 7, Abosede Babatunde examines the gender dimensions of the problem in Nigeria, with empirical illustrations from Plateau state, also of the North Central or Middle-Belt of Nigeria. Titled "Women in the Shadow of the Conflict in the Farming and Herding Communities in Plateau State, Nigeria", the chapter underscores the intensified contestations for land and water resources between the farming and herding communities. Anchored on the theoretical insight provided by feminist political ecology, an environmental perspective that focuses on the politics of access and control over natural resources and their implication for the environment, the chapter recognizes the significance of elite behavior, including the national questions around which they can build consensus. It also highlights the interconnection between political ecology factors and other explanatory variables such as class, ethnicity, and culture, illustrated by the fact that such conflicts tend to escalate during ethno-religious and political crises, as well as during planting and harvesting seasons in the state. It is, therefore, hardly surprising to note one of the findings of the study that both herders and farmers act as aggressors in these conflicts depending on the case under review.

The chapter then devotes attention to the form and character of women's involvement in the conflicts in the state. The central argument of the chapter is that women in the state have played major roles as actors in the conflict, including such negative tendencies as undermining the peace process in diverse ways. The chapter deviates from the dominant narratives in the literature that tend not only to portray women as mainly victims of conflicts but also underscores masculinity in the profiling of actors of violence in general and herder-farmer conflicts in particular. Though Babatunde still recognized how women have been brutalised, victimized, and dehumanized because of these conflicts, she pushed the narratives further by underscoring the roles of women, beyond victimhood and peacemakers, as combatants and agents of logistics support for men fighters. They also provide a shield (escape route or safe haven) for men who have committed various atrocities in the conflicts. Yet, as the chapter reveals, women also prompt or instigate men into fighting through encouragement and shaming for failure to heed the prompting. However, they managed to conceal such involvement (agency), which remains largely invisible. As she puts it, women are the 'unseen and invisible actors in the violence perpetuated by men'. The complicated role of women in these conflicts partly accounts for the underwhelming performance of both governmental and nongovernmental interventions in these conflicts.

Fatma Osman Ibnouf extends the gender dimensions of the problem in Chapter 8, with insights from the Sudanese experience. Focusing on Darfur, western Sudan, and anchored on the gendered approach to peacebuilding, the chapter demonstrates, ab initio, the fact that farming and pastoralism have been the main livelihood production systems in the region; and that people of the region have lived harmoniously until recently, precisely the 1980s when increasing frequency and severity of drought became a major environmental challenge. The attendant environmental scarcities (land, vegetation, water) transformed the once stable relations between farmers and herders who now engaged in fierce competition for these resources. This challenge, according to Ibnouf, has been complicated by many other factors, notably the weakening of customary/traditional institutions, poor governance, and proliferation of small arms and light weapons due to conflicts in neighbouring countries such as the Central African Republic, Chad, and Libya, securitization (treating the problem as a security problem), creation of tribal militias, among other. The result was the failure to attain any form of peace –even negative peace in the region. This failure, according to Ibnouf, is not unconnected to the fact that peace initiatives were largely disconnected from the 'ground realities'. One of the most critical errors of omissions, as the chapter argues, relates to the marginalization, if not outright exclusion of the gender dimensions of the problem.

Basically, the chapter emphasizes the need for all actors to critically reexamine the factors that have undermined all peace efforts with respect to the problem. These factors were identified as lack of or poor inclusivity, failure to pay attention to local peculiarities, and exclusion of traditional conflict resolution mechanisms. The chapter then singled out the gender dimension as a very critical component of inclusivity. It argues in favour of the imperative of accommodating the voices of the most affected people, or better still victims of these conflicts as the surest way to sustainable peacebuilding. For Ibnouf, women constitute the most significant constituency in this respect. This is because these conflicts have not only had devastating socio-economic impacts on women, but they have also had to endure diverse forms of deprivations as a result of cultural barriers, assigned roles, and socially constructed/determined gender activities. The difference between Ibnouf and Babatunde seems to be that while the former portrays women as victims of these conflicts, not as legitimate actors, the latter accommodates both, considering women as both victims and actors. In the final analysis, Ibnouf calls for increasing attention and spaces for popular voices, participation, and local ownership of the conflict resolution processes by all, especially women.

In Chapter 9, Richard Alemdjrodo engages the problem in Togo. The chapter adopts largely a legalistic approach, with main insights from the ECOWAS Protocol and other official responses. The emphasis on the ECOWAS Protocol is predicated upon the fact that ECOWAS prioritises transhumance as a critical component of the drive for sustainable agriculture, food security, and poverty reduction strategy in the subregion. The chapter also highlights some of the critical interventions of the government aimed at managing the conflicts. These include initiatives by the' Togolese authorities for strengthening cooperation with countries of origin to enforce the periods of transhumance (January 15–May 15)'; as well as 'the redefinition of entry points on the territory and specified authorized transit and grazing corridors'. The chapter underscores resource scarcity and its governance, particularly the poor distribution of resources between herders and farmers on the one hand; as well as the shortcomings inherent in official responses to the problem as two main explanations for the problem in the country. These are in addition to the disconnect between national laws and community regulations, as well as contradictions inherent in ECOWAS Protocols, including poor linkage between ECOWAS and other Regional Economic Communities (RECs). Yet, the tendency of transhumant herders to get closer and closer to the coast and, above all, to the capital Lomé and to stay in its surroundings beyond the date of the end of the transhumance period, as the author argues, has tended to complicate the problem. Not even the threats or actual issuance of decrees asking pastoralists—mostly from the Fulani tribe—to leave the country had carried sufficient weights of deterrence against the herdsmen. It concludes with some policy recommendations for addressing the challenge, notably policy reforms and greater involvement of civil society.

In Chapter 10, J. Shola Omotola provides some concluding reflections. Titled "Conclusion: Matters Arising in Herder-Farmer Conflicts and Lessons for Sustainable Security, Development and Peacebuilding", this chapter teases out the major findings of the various chapters, highlighting convergences and divergences. It does this by critical reflections based on inferences from the various subthemes of the study, notably trends, causes, consequences, management, and lessons for sustainable peacebuilding. The chapter thus provides a basis for cross-national comparisons and generalizations.

References

Adams, E. I., Thill, A., Kuusaana, E. D. and Mittag, A. 2023, 'Farmer–herder conflicts in sub-Saharan Africa: Drivers, impacts, and resolution and peacebuilding strategies', *Environmental Research Letters,* 18 (12), pp. 1–18. https://doi.org/10.1088/1748-9326/ad0702.

Ahmed, A. 2022, 'Farmer-herder conflicts in Northern Ghana amid climate change: Causes and policy responses', *Megatrends Africa Policy Brief 09*, December.

Ahmed, A. and Kuusaana, E. D. 2021, 'Cattle ranching and Farmer-Herder conflicts in sub-Saharan Africa: Exploring the conditions for successes and failures in Northern Ghana', *African Security*, 14, pp. 132–55.

Benjaminsen, T. A. and Ba, B. 2021, 'Fulani-Dogon killings in Mali: Farmer-herder conflicts as insurgency and counterinsurgency', *African Security*, 14, pp. 4–26.

Benjaminsen, T. A., Maganga, F. P. and Abdallah, J. M. 2009, 'The Kilosa killings: Political ecology of a farmer–herder conflict in Tanzania', *Development and Change*, 40, pp. 423–45.

Bereketeab, R. 2021, 'Peacebuilding in Africa: Popular progressive versus neoliberal peacebuilding', in Adetula, Victor, Bereketeab, Redie and Obi, Cyril. Eds. *Regional Economic Communities and Peacebuilding in Africa: Lessons from ECOWAS and IGAD.* London and New York: Routledge, pp. 35–54.

Brottem, L. 2021, 'The growing complexity of Farmer–Herder conflict in West and Central Africa', *Africa Security Brief* 39. Washington, DC: Africa Center for Strategic Studies.

Brottem, L. V. 2016, 'Environmental change and farmer-herder conflict in agro-Pastoral West Africa', *Human Ecology*, 44, pp. 547–563.

Bruch, C., Weinthal, E., Johnson, M. and Ide, T. 2022, Towards a definition of environmental peacebuilding, Ecosystem for Peace. Available at https://www.ecosystemforpeace.org/compendium/towardsadefinitionofenvironmentalpeacebuilding (accessed on 30 April, 2024).

Bukari, K. N. and Schareika, N. 2015, 'Stereotypes, prejudices and exclusion of Fulani pastoralists in Ghana', *Pastoralism,* 5, pp. 1–12.

Caffentzis, G. 2002, 'Neoliberalism in Africa, Apocalyptic failures and business as usual practices', *Turkish Journal of International Affairs*, 1 (3), pp. 80–103.

Chukwuma, K. H. 2020, 'Constructing the Herder–Farmer conflict as (in)security in Nigeria', *African Security*, 13 (1), pp. 54–76. https://doi.org/10.1080/19392206.2020.1732703.

Diehl, D. F. (1991), Geography and War: *A Review and Assessment of Empirical Literature*, International Interaction, 17(1) 11-27.

Dresse, A., Fischhendler, T., Nielsen, J. O. and Zikos, D. 2018, 'Environmental peacebuilding: Towards a theoretical framework', *Cooperation and Conflict*, 54 (1), pp. 99–119.

Egwu, S. G. 2015, 'The political economy of rural banditry in contemporary Nigeria', in M. J. Kuna and J. Ibrahim, Eds. *Rural Banditry and Conflict in Northern Nigeria, Abuja: Centre for Democracy and Development (CDD)*, pp. 14–68.

Eke, S. 2020, "'Nomad savage' and herder–farmer conflicts in Nigeria: The (Un) making of an ancient myth', *Third World Quarterly*, 41, pp. 745–763.

Ezirigwe, J. 2023, 'ECOWAS rules to protect pastoralists discourage investments in modern livestock farming', *The Conversation*, 8 October, https://theconversation.com/ecowas-rules-to-protect-pastoralists-discourage-investments-in-modern-livestock-farming-213493.

Flintan, F., Suleiman, H. M., Eba, B. and Nassef, M. 2024, 'Farmer-herder conflicts in Africa—dynamics and potential solutions', *Rural: The International Journal for Rural Development*, 58 (2).

Herbert, S. and Birch, I. 2022, *Cross-border pastoral mobility and cross-border conflict in Africa—patterns and policy responses. XCEPT Evidence Synthesis.* Birmingham, UK: GSDRC, University of Birmingham (https://csf-sudan.org/wp-content/uploads/2023/01/gsdrc-pastoralist-mobility.pdf).

Hussein, K., Sumberg, J. and Seddon, D. 1999, 'Increasing violent conflict between Herders and Farmers in Africa: Claims and Evidence', *Development Policy Review*, 17, pp. 397–418.

International Crisis Group, 2017, Herders against farmers: Nigeria's expanding deadly conflict. https://www.crisisgroup.org/africa/westafrica/nigeria/252-herders-against-farmers-nigerias-expanding-deadlyconflict.

International Organization for Migration (IOM), 2017, *Regional policies and response to manage pastoral movements within the ECOWAS region*, Abuja: IOM (https://environmentalmigration.iom.int/sites/g/files/tmzbdl1411/files/documents/2023-09/regional-policies-and-response-to-manage-pastoral-movements-within-the-ecowas-region-2019.pdf).

Kendrick, C. and Sanders, L. 2024, Don't call it Farmer-Herder Conflict, The SAIS review of international affairs, 9 February. Available at https://saisreview.sais.jhu.edu/dont-call-it-farmer-herder-conflict/.

Krätli, S. and Toulmin, C. 2020a, Farmer-Herder conflict in sub-Saharan Africa, International Institute for Environment and Development (IIED). Available at https://www.iied.org/sites/default/files/pdfs/2021-01/10208IIED.pdf.

Krätli, S and Toulmin, C. 2020b, 'Farmer–Herder conflict in Africa: Re-thinking the phenomenon?', *Briefing IIED*. https://pubs.iied.org/17753IIED/.

Kugbega, S. K. and Aboagye, P. Y. 2021, 'Farmer-Herder conflicts, tenure insecurity and farmer's investment decisions in Agogo, Ghana', *Agriculture, Food and Economics*, 9, pp. 1–38.

Kuna, M. J and Ibrahim, J. 2015, eds. *Rural banditry and conflict in Northern Nigeria*, Abuja: Centre for Democracy and Development (CDD), pp. 217–256.

Kuusaana, E. D. and Bukari, K. N. 2015, 'Land conflicts between smallholders and Fulani pastoralists in Ghana: Evidence from the Asante Akim North District (AAND)', *Journal of Rural Studies*, 42, pp. 52–62.

Kwaja, C. M. and Ademola-Adelehin, B. I. 2017, The Implications of the open grazing prohibition and ranches establishment law on farmer–herder relations in the Middle Belt of Nigeria, Washington, DC: Search for Common Ground. Available at www.sfcg.org/wp-content/uploads/2018/02/Open-Grazing-Prohibition-Law-in-BenueState-December-2017.pdf.

Kwaja, C. M. A. and Smith, K. 2021, Transnational dimensions of conflict between farmers and herders in the Western Sahel and Lake Chad Basin. Search for Common Ground. https://www.sfcg.org/wpcontent/uploads/2020/04/SFCG_Policy_Brief_Transnational_Dimension_to_FH_Conflicts.pdf.

Lenshie, N. E., Okengwu, K. Ogbonna, C. N. and Ezeibe, C. 2020, 'Desertification, migration, and herder-farmer conflicts in Nigeria: Rethinking the ungoverned spaces thesis', *Small Wars and Insurgency*, 32, pp. 1221–1251.

Mahmood, H. U. and Azuaga, C. I. 2020, 'Perceptions of the relationship between cultural biases and Farmer-Herder conflicts in Taraba State, Nigeria', *Journal of Agricultural Extension*, 24, pp. 104–111.

Maiangwa, B. 2017, '"Conflicting Indigeneity" and Farmer–Herder Conflicts in Postcolonial Africa, *Peace Review 29*, no. 3, pp. 282-288.

Mbah, P. O., Iwuamadi, K. C., Udeoji, E., Eze, M. and Ezeibe, C. C. 2021, 'Exiles in their region: Pastoralist-farmer conflict and population displacements in North Central, Nigeria', *African Population Studies*, 35.

Mbih, R. A. 2020, 'The politics of Farmer–Herder conflicts and alternative conflict management in Northwest Cameroon', *African Geographic Review*, 39, pp. 324–344.

Mercy Corps. 2015, The economic costs of conflict and the benefits of peace: Effects of farmer-pastoralist conflict in Nigeria's middle belt on households. Available at https://www.mercycorps.org/sites/default/files/Mercy%20Corps%20Nigeria%20Household%20Costs%20%20of%20Conflict%20Policy%20Brief%20July%202015.pdf.

Mercy Corps, 2015a, The economic costs of conflict and the benefits of peace: Effects of farmer-pastoralist conflict in Nigeria's Middle Belt on households. Available at https://www.mercycorps.org/sites/defaultfiles/2019-11/Mercy%20Corps%20Nigeria%20Household%20Costs%20of%20Conflict%20Policy%20Brief%20July%202015.pdf

Mercy Corps, 2015b, The Economic Costs of Conflict and the Benefits of Peace: Effects of Farmer-Pastoralist Conflict in Nigeria's Middle Belt on State, Sector, and National Economies; available at https://www.mercycorps.org/sites/default/files/2019-11/Mercy%20Corps%20Nigeria%20State%20Costs%20of%20Conflict%20Policy%20Brief%20July%202015.pdf

Moritz, M. and Mbacke, M. 2022, 'The danger of a single story about Fulani pastoralists', *Pastoralism* 12, 14, pp. 1–10.

Mohammed, M., Ekhmheye, S. and Ibrahim G. M. 2021, 'The impact of Herders and Farmers conflicts on agricultural activities in Nasarawa state', *International Journal of Advanced Academic Research*, 7 (10), pp. 319–335.

Nassef, M., Eba, B., Islam, K. Djohy, G. and Flintan, F. 2023, *Causes of Farmer–Herder conflicts in Africa: A systematic scoping review*, Report by Supporting Pastoralism and Agriculture in Recurrent and Protracted Crises (SPARC).

Ngwoh, V. K. (2017). 'Cameroon: Endemic Agro-pastoral Conflicts in Menchum', *Conflict Studies Quarterly*, Vol. 19, pp. 23-42.

Nnoko, J. 2018, Farmer-Herder conflicts on the rise in Africa, Human Rights Watch. Available at https://www.hrw.org/news/2018/08/06/farmer-herder-conflicts-rise-africa.

Odoemene, A. 2017, Fulani Herdsmen and the threat to grassroots security and stability in rural Nigeria, Paper presented at the 5th faculty of humanities and social science seminar series, Federal University Otuoke, Bayelsa State, Nigeria (19 June).

Okeke, Okechukwu E. 2014, 'Conflicts between Fulani Herders and Farmers in central and Southern Nigeria: Discourse on proposed establishment of grazing routes and reserves', *AFRREV—International Journal of Arts and Humanities*, 3 (1) January, pp. 66–84.

Olaniyan, A. and Okeke-Uzodike, U. 2015, 'Desperate guests, unwilling hosts: Climate change-induced migration and farmer-herder conflicts in Southwestern Nigeria', *Conflict Studies Quarterly* 10, January, pp. 23–40.

Olaniyan, A., & Omotola, S. (2015). Ethnic crises and national security in Nigeria. Defense & Security Analysis, 31(4), 303–318. https://doi.org/10.1080/14751798.2015.1087104

Olaniyan, A., Francis, M. and Okeke-Uzodike, U. 2015, 'The cattle are "Ghanaians" but the herders are strangers: Farmer-Herder conflicts, expulsion policy, and pastoralist question in Agogo, Ghana', *African Studies Quarterly*, 15 (2), March, pp. 53–67.

Olumba, E. E. 2024, 'The politics of eco-violence: Why is conflict escalating in Nigeria's middle belt?' *Terrorism and Political Violence*, 36 (2), pp. 180–197.
Olumba, E. E., Nwosu, B. U., Okpaleke, F. N. and Okoli, R. C. 2022, 'Conceptualising eco-violence: Moving beyond the multiple labelling of water and agricultural resource conflicts in the Sahel', *Third World Quarterly*, 43 (9), pp. 2075–2090.
Omotola, J. S. and Hassan, I. 2015, '"Herders and Farmers" associations and social conflicts in Northern Nigeria', in: M. J. Kuna and J. Ibrahim, Eds. *Rural Banditry and Conflict in Northern Nigeria*, Abuja: Centre for Democracy and Development (CDD), pp. 217–256.
Omotola, J. S. and Alumona, I. M. eds. 2016, *The state in contemporary Nigeria: Issues, perspectives and challenges (Essays in Honour of Professor Ben Nwabueze),* Ibadan, NG: John Archers Publishers.
Omotola, J. S., Odoemene, A., Babatunde, A., Alemdjrodo, R., Ibnouf, F., Ngalim, A. and Bontogho, P. 2019. Herder-farmer conflicts in Africa: Historical trajectories, "New" issues, responses and lessons for peacebuilding, *research report of the collaborative working group research grants*, 2018–2020 Submitted to the African Peacebuilding Network (APN) of the Social Science Research Council (SSRC), New York.
Omotola, J. S. 2017, 'Cattle herding in Nigeria: Problems and prospects', Commissioned lead paper presented at the annual national conference of Nigerian society of animal production, Landmark University, Omu-Aran, Kwara State, July 2017.
Omotola, J. S. 2024a. 'Traditional institutions and the management of Herders-Farmers conflicts in Nasarawa State, Nigeria', in Ehrhardt, D, Umar, S. and Alao, D, Eds. *Traditional Authority and Security in Contemporary Nigeria*. London: Routledge, pp. 169–190.
Omotola, J. S. 2024b, 'SADC and peacebuilding in the southern african region', in Bereketeab, R. Ed. *Supranational Institutions and Peacebuilding in Africa: The African Union and Regional Economic Communities*, London: Routledge, pp. 171–186. https://doi.org/10.4324/9781003473619-18.
Omotola, J. S. and Oyewole, S. eds. 2024, *'The political economy of kidnapping and insecurity in Nigeria"*, Cham, Switzerland: Springer.
Onwuzuruigbo, I. 2023, 'Citizenship, indigeneity and the management of Herders and Farmers conflicts in Ghana and Nigeria', *Nationalism and Ethnic Politics*, 29 (3), pp. 352–370. https://doi.org/10.1080/13537113.2023.2211448.
Paalo, S. A. 2021, 'The politics of addressing Farmer-Herder conflicts in Ghana', *Peacebuilding*, 9, pp. 79–99.

Paffenholz, T. 2021, 'Perpetual peacebuilding: A new paradigm to move beyond the linearity of liberal peacebuilding', *Journal of Intervention and Statebuilding*, 15 (3), pp. 367–385. https://doi.org/10.1080/17502977.2021.1925423.

Réseau Billital Maroobé (RBM). and Partners, 2021, 'Listening to Herders in West Africa and the Sahel: What is the future for pastoralism in a context of rising insecurity?', Synthesis report, Réseau des Organisations d'Eleveurs et Pasteurs de l'Afrique (https://www.maroobe.com/images/DOCS/Synthetic%20Report-Patoralism%20and%20Insecurity%20in%20the%20Sahel%20and%20West%20Africa-%20RBM.pdf).

Setrana, M. B. and Kyei, J. R. K. 2021, 'Migration, Farmer-Herder conflict and the challenges of peacebuilding in the Agogo traditional area, Ghana', *Journal of Geography*, 13.

Shettima, A. G. and Tar, U. A. 2008, 'Farmer-pastoralist conflict in West Africa: Exploring the causes and consequences', *Information, Society and Justice* 2 (1), pp. 163–184.

Turner, M. D. 2004, 'Political ecology and the moral dimensions of "resource conflicts": The case of Farmer–Herder conflicts in the Sahel', *Political Geography*, 23 (7), pp. 863–889.

Turner, M. D., Ayantunde, A. A., Patterson, K. P. and Patterson, E. D. 2011, 'Livelihood transitions and the changing nature of Farmer–Herder conflict in Sahelian West Africa', *Journal of Development Studies*, 47 (2), pp. 183–206.

Wimmer, A. (2009). Herder's Heritage and the Boundary-Making Approach: Studying Ethnicity in Immigrant Societies. *Sociological Theory*, 27(3), pp. 244-270. https://doi.org/10.1111/j.1467-9558.2009.01347.x

Yakubu, S. M., Musa, M. W., Bamidele, T. E., Ali, M. B., Bappah, M. T., Munir, R. T. and Manuwa, A. 2021, 'Effects of Farmer-Herder conflicts on rural households food security in Gombe State, Nigeria', *Journal of Agricultural Extension*, 25 (1), pp. 11–20.

Zambakari, C. 2016, 'Challenges of liberal peace and statebuilding in divided societies', *Conflict Trends*, 4.

CHAPTER 2

Peacebuilding Perspectives and Herder-Farmer Conflicts in Africa

J. Shola Omotola

Introduction

This chapter proposes a peacebuilding approach to the management of herder-farmers conflicts in Africa. It opens with a clarification of the central concept of the book, herder-farmer conflicts. As simplistic as it appears, the concept means different things to different people, with some questioning its relevance and applicability to the issues in contention. It then proceeds to offer a panoramic overview of some of the theoretical perspectives on peacebuilding relevant to the understanding and sustainable resolution of herder-farmer conflicts in Africa.

Specifically, the chapter reflects on the contending perspectives on peacebuilding, notably the neoliberal and popular progressive arguments. It also emphasizes the pertinence of environmental peacebuilding as a critical component of the latter. Finally, the chapter highlights other salient components of progressive peacebuilding that are critical to the sustainable resolution of herder-farmer conflicts in Africa. These include the

J. S. Omotola (✉)
Department of Political Science, Federal University Oye Ekiti, Oye Ekiti, Ekiti State, Nigeria

J. S. Omotola (ed.), *Herder-Farmer Conflicts in Africa*,
https://doi.org/10.1007/978-3-031-80821-0_2

gender dimensions of peacebuilding, the role subnational and local peacebuilding initiatives/institutions, and the pivotal position of both formal and informal actors in the peace process. These and related salient themes came out very strongly across the various case studies in the book, from which critical lessons for sustainable peacebuilding were drawn in the concluding chapter of the book.

Herder-Farmer Conflicts: A Clarification

The concept of herder-farmer conflicts, on the surface, looks simplistic without much complication. But that innocuous look may be deceptive, concealing under its cloak a number of contentious and controversial issues that make the term essentially contested. The contestations over its meaning are multidimensional. It is therefore apposite to begin by defining this concept because it is used in different and often ambiguous ways. This section attempts a clarification of certain contentions surrounding this concept. After highlighting some of the controversies, the section critically evaluates some of the extant definitions in the literature. It also proposes a much more nuanced definition of the concept that is both holistic and specific.

First, different narratives have been developed around the phenomenon across time and space in Africa. In the Nigerian context, for instance, Adigun (2022) documents different dimensions of such narratives, which hardly depict the true picture of the problem. For example, he narrated how overgeneralization in media reportage, especially in the absence of disaggregated data on pastoralist conflicts, constituted one of the dominant narratives. In the circumstance, even conflicts that have little or no direct connections to herders and farmers, probably because they occur in herder-farmer communities are usually labeled as herder-farmer conflicts.

Second, most of the databases invested in the gathering and storage of such data, including the ACLED, hardly disaggregate such data in ways that allow for neat classifications. By logical extension, most of those databases are often guilty of disregard for joint exhaustiveness and mutual exclusivity of the entire domain of violence generally, and pastoralist conflicts in particular. In contexts where political violence, ethno-religious and communal conflicts have been deeply rooted, escalating by the day under various strands of authoritarian democracy in most African countries (Adenuga, et al., 2023), labelling all pastoralist conflicts as herder-farmer conflicts may be inaccurate and misleading. As Adigun (2022) puts it in the Nigerian case, while 'farmer-herder conflicts could have developed criminal aspects, such as kidnapping, armed robbery, cattle rustling, etc., reporting all these as relating to the farmer-herder conflicts is a gross exaggeration'.

Again, the menace of what is generally categorized as herder-farmer conflicts has not been static, constantly evolving and changing in its complexions. The expanded geography, manifestations, frequency, weapon used, actors involved and intensity of the conflicts have always changed in form and character. Such conflicts are also, in some cases, interwoven with other preexisting forms of violence such as ethno-regional, religious and communal conflicts. Reducing all such conflicts to herder-farmer conflicts tends to oversimplify the issues. It is tendencies of this nature that allows for the criminalization, or better still, ethnic profiling or labelling of herdsmen, usually Fulani, as terrorists who must be so labelled and treated (Brottem, 2021).

Moreover, studies have also raised some concerns about the tendency to forge a distinction between farmers and herders as if they are entirely distinct groups. Such a distinction may be a facade because of the existence of different layers of interdependence between the two groups right from the precolonial days. Intragroup multitasking also exists, for instance, with herdsmen who also engage in farming, and farmers who deal in livestock herding through proxies, usually the herdsmen (Kendrick and Sanders, 2024).

Nevertheless, the famed concept of 'herder-farmer conflicts', is often used as 'an umbrella term for a range of interactions, typically describing resource competition between pastoralist herders and sedentary farmers' (Kendrick and Sanders, 2024: 1). The challenge though, is that these studies hardly clarify or define the types of conflicts in question. Such a clarification is important, given that conflict is multidimensional, including conflict of interests that can lead to competition, as well as non-violent and violent conflicts, each with varying ramifications (Hussein et al, 1999). Conflicts can also be intergroup, intragroup, and interpersonal, meaning that such conflicts can take place within farmers or herders, and between the two groups. The import of this is that we need more clarity about the types of conflicts in question when we speak about herder-farmer conflicts.

For these and related concerns, some scholars have argued that the term required a new description. Olumba, et al (2022) and Olumba

(2024) argued in favour of the term ‘eco-violence’, which they defined as ‘conflicts in which competition for water and agricultural resources occurs within or between social groups or state actors’. For them, ‘such conflicts are made worse by state failure to address resource redistribution challenges, institutional failures, and environmental and social injustice’. More radical scholars advocate for a total rejection of the term ‘herder-farmer conflicts’ as a misrepresentation of the problematics (Kendrick and Sanders, 2024).

In the light of the foregoing, it is pertinent to clarify out usage of the term herder-farmer conflicts in this book. Our definition is both generic and specific. At a general level, it encompasses violent conflicts that directly involve herders and farmers resulting from various factors such as environmental scarcity, climate change, migration, resource completion (land, vegetation and water) and the mal-governance of these issues. Considered this way, herder-farmer conflicts may and may not be pastoralist in orientation and/or outlook. While pastoralist conflicts can embrace aspects of pastoralism, not all pastoralist conflicts are entirely herder-farmer conflicts. Anything beyond this risks falling into the pitfall of conceptual stretching, accommodating all varieties of conflicts that occur in herding and farming communities.

At a more specific level, our usage of herder-farmer conflicts emphasizes violent conflicts between herders and farmers as the primary actors, with several other secondary and even tertiary actors. More definitively, herder-farmer conflicts in the context of this book pay specific attention to the following key elements:

(a) Multiple Actors: herders, farmers and government (federal, state and local) as the primary actors, with several non-state actors (civil society organization, community-based organizations, religious organizations, etc.).
(b) Level of conflicts: which can either be local, state, regional or national
(c) Scale of conflicts: defined in terms of increasing frequency of conflicts or intensity of existing conflicts.
(d) Intensity: defined by weapons used and consequences such as the number of casualties and destruction of properties including farmlands, killing of cows, etc.

Enters the Peacebuilding Perspectives

Peacebuilding is considered as a critical component of security and development (Smoljan, 2003). Omotola (2024a, 2024b) highlights some of these interconnections when he emphasizes the significance of expanding the definition of security beyond its traditional, state-centric, military approach as state security, to accommodate non-military elements, particularly human security. Moreover, he also posits out that development is unthinkable in the absence of security. Both development and security are equally unsustainable in the absence of adequate investment in progressive peacebuilding; and that all major players and critical stakeholders in the development circle, at the global, regional, sub-regional, national and local levels, formal and informal, now pay critical attention to these multiple dimensions of security, both in theory and practice.

Broadly defined, peacebuilding encompasses institutions and processes aimed at addressing the underlying causes of conflict, conflict resolution and building sustainable foundations for sustainable peace and stability - preventing future violence. Understood this way, peacebuilding should be seen as a long-term and gradual process of establishing and consolidating the peace process. It is predicated upon certain principles, notably inclusivity, impartiality, transparency, and local ownership, recognizing the importance of engaging all stakeholders, the high and the low, including marginalised groups, in the peace process (Gawerc, 2006). Boutros-Ghali (1992) defines it as a post-conflict activity involving 'action to identify and support structures which will tend to strengthen and solidify peace in order to avoid a relapse into conflict'. More broadly defined, however, peacebuilding entails 'action before, during, and after violent conflict, to address root causes of conflict that include transforming relationships and structures' (see Lederach and Appleby, 2010, quoted in Neufeldt, 2024).

Two main theoretical approaches to peacebuilding have been established in the literature: short-term peacebuilding and long-term peacebuilding (Bereketeab, 2021: 35). On the one hand, short-term peacebuilding usually follows after a war and to that extent mainly reactive. Its primary focus seems to be the absence of war, what Johan Galtung (1967) refers to as negative peace which, as studies and experiences have shown over the decades, hardly guarantees sustainable peace. Peace, in such contexts, equals stability but hardly address its preconditions such as inequality, exploitation, exclusion and other forms of injustices.

Long-term peacebuilding, on the other, 'relates to the gradual construction of the socio-economic and political institutions of societies'. This is a multipronged approach to peacebuilding, covering the past, present and future. Nevertheless, it should be noted that that peacebuilding has both short-term and long-term agenda. By implication, a holistic peacebuilding framework is one that encompasses both the short and long-term components.

In the African context, studies have highlighted two types of peacebuilding. The first is the post-conflict neoliberal peacebuilding, whose primary objective has been about shaping and reshaping African societies along the Western model of societal formation. Because such an approach often disconnects societies from their historical and social foundations, it has most often been counterproductive. Instead of producing peace, it tends to generate more conflicts and instability (Bereketeab, 2021; Lemay-Herbert, 2013). This is because it is usually externally-driven and largely disconnected from local realities, without due attention to 'the specific social, cultural, historical, economic, political, and ethnic realities of the particular society' (Bereketeab, 2021: 36). As the antithesis of popular progressive peacebuilding, it is usually short-term in focus, and limited societal penetration and legitimacy. Its history in Africa is replete with catastrophic failure, leaving in its trails disastrous results (Zambakari, 2016; Caffentzis, 2002).

The second is the popular progressive peacebuilding, which is said to be 'historical, contemporary, and futuristic' because it 'strides along the past–present–future continuum'. It deals with the evolutionary construction and reconstruction of society' politically, economically and socially. Paffenholz (2021: 367) calls it differently as 'perpetual peacebuilding', which envisioned peacebuilding 'as an ever-developing process manifested in a series of (re)negotiations of the social and political contracts'. Drawing on 'proven domestic institutions, mechanisms, and authorities', thereby deepening its societal connections, penetrations and legitimacy, popular progressive peacebuilding holds better prospects for suitable security and development both in pre-and post-conflict settings. It is the approach that is most suitable for African countries, not just because of the plural character of most of them, but also as a result of deep historical and cultural ties, the destruction of which lies at the heart of most of the crisis and contradictions of governance and development afflicting the continent. The key defining elements of popular progressive peacebuilding, as articulated by Bereketeab (2021: 35–36) include:

> The basic premises of popular progressive peacebuilding are the embracing of holistic, national, regional, and local ownership; indigenous institutions, authorities, and mechanisms; and inclusive bottom-up and top-down strategies ... Local ownership of the agendas, processes, solutions, long-term institution-building, negotiations, bargaining, compromises, reconciliation, participation, and transformation are mother aspects of popular progressive peacebuilding. It is a domestic process, home-grown, not oriented towards a winner or loser outcome. These are fundamental prerequisites for functional and sustainable peace. Peacebuilding from this perspective is exclusively domestic or home-grown ... Any external involvement could only serve as an additional supporting toolkit. In other words it is culture and context-contingent. ... It aims at restoring the balance; the equilibrium ... The focus is a restorative instead of a retributive peace.

The Imperative of Environmental Peacebuilding

The environmental dimension of insecurities and sustainable peacebuilding is critical. International organisations such as the United Nations have long realized the significance of environmental peacebuilding and made huge investments in environmental programmes and knowledge creation for environmental peacebuilding (Dalmer, 2021). This is hardly surprising because environmental considerations have always been fingered in conflict and security dilemmas broadly defined, and more particularly about herder-farmer conflicts. Moreover, environmental peacebuilding has since emerged as a powerful interdisciplinary field of research and practice in environment, security, conflict, peace, governance and development studies (Ide, et al, 2021a, 2021b; Bruch, et al, 2019; Hardt and Scheffran, 2019).

What then is environmental peacebuilding all about? In the view of Ide, et al (2021a: 2–3), environmental peacebuilding 'comprises the multiple approaches and pathways by which the management of environmental issues is integrated in and can support conflict prevention, mitigation, resolution and recovery'. According to these scholars, environmental peacebuilding works in three dimensions. These are:

> ***Security,*** predicated on the assumption that 'inclusive and sustainable management of natural resources can help avoid conflicts about or linked to these resources' - land, water, fish and other resources,

as well as their governance, including in/equitable allocation of the benefits of natural resources;

Livelihoods and economy, based on the assumption that 'livelihood insecurity and weak economic performance serve as key predictors of violent conflict and peacebuilding failure', which can increase the grievances of affected populations and provide incentives for joining and participating in violent groups; and.

Politics and social relations, based on the assumption that shared environmental challenges are potential entry points for cooperation between groups, even if their relations are hostile or characterized by mistrust because such 'challenges offer opportunities for cooperation because they transcend political boundaries, may be less sensitive politically than other topics, and may stimulate actors to consider longer time horizons' (Ide, et al, 2021a: 3).

For Dresse, et al, (2018: 6), it is 'the process through which environmental challenges shared by the (former) parties to a violent conflict are turned into opportunities to build lasting cooperation and peace'. They proceed to discuss the initial conditions, mechanisms and outcomes of environmental peacebuilding. These outcomes include direct benefits such as the reduction of environmental problems, uncertainty or resource inequality; repeated interaction between conflict parties, which can foster a habit of cooperation and build trust; and that environmental cooperation, can reduce perceived inequalities related to natural resource access and distribution, thereby laying the roots of sustainable peace (Dresse, et al,2018: 8–10; Carius, 2006). This position is in tandem with that of Bruch, et al (2019: 10144) who content that environmental peacebuilding:

> Ultimately focuses on the mix of renewable and nonrenewable natural resources available to a country that can support stabilization, reconstruction, and development'. This, according to the authors, 'can in turn generate peace dividends: as natural resources are managed more effectively and resource benefits shared more equitably, the state-society compact is strengthened and there is often increasing confidence that peaceful long-term development is possible.

The relevance and applicability of environmental peacebuilding to harder-farmer conflicts in Africa is clear from the above. The most obvious connection can be located in the fact that most of these conflicts are directly or indirectly connected to environmental challenges such as climate change, resource scarcity, climate-induced migration and attendant heightened competition for resources. Managing such environmental concerns requires the kind of frameworks espoused by environmental peacebuilding.

The Gender Dimensions of Peacebuilding

Peacebuilding is also a gendered process in many ways. In fact, some have argued that involving women and taking a gender perspective on peacebuilding activities 'are essential for democratic inclusiveness, sustained economic growth and human and social capital recovery'; and that peacebuilding 'may well offer the single greatest opportunity to redress gender inequities and injustices of the past while, setting new precedents for the future' (Lemay-Herbert and Toupin, 2011: 13). This is why any successful peacebuilding initiative must pay attention to the gender aspects of peacebuilding (Wilén, 2022; Yoshida and Céspedes-Báez, 2021; Owonikoko, 2020; Rey and McKay, 2006). These include issues of women as victims of violence/conflict, as actors and their agency in conflict and peacebuilding, both the visible and invisible, including serving as arms traders, bearers, transporters and keepers, providing shields for men escaping from conflicts, as well as their roles as peacekeepers and peacemakers.

McKay and Mazurana (2007) argue that feminist analysis contributes to a more comprehensive meaning of peacebuilding than a non-gendered analysis. Such an approach focuses on 'women's specific concerns about peacebuilding, approaches peacebuilding from women's perspectives, and welcomes pluralistic voices and diverse methods'. It also entails the extent of women's involvement in decision making. According to McKay and Mazurana (2007), feminist analysis addresses critical questions about peacebuilding such as: what does building peace mean to women across cultures? Who are the women talking to about peacebuilding? Do their perspectives and practices about peacebuilding coincide with extant definitions by state and non-state actors? To what extent do key actors emphasize in their peacebuilding human processes such as reconciliation and restoration of relationships, as compared with institutional and structural rebuilding? These and related issues underscore the imperative of gender consideration in peacebuilding.

Relevance of Subnational and Local Peacebuilding Initiatives

The place of the 'local' in the peacebuilding process has also received considerable scholarly attention (Hirblinger and Simons, 2015). Pervasive but contentious, dividing opinions as it does, the question of the 'local' in peacebuilding, though longstanding, remains largely unresolved and problematic. In fact, its meaning remains contested, with multiple interpretations. Arguably because of the contentions built around the subject, Hirblinger and Simons (2015: 1) argue that 'the 'local' haunts peacebuilding'. It does so in the several ways it is invoked in peacebuilding discourses and scholarships. Emah and Kwaja (2020: 88–93) reflect on these contending perspectives and came to the conclusion that "what and/or who constitutes 'the local'" is complex and contested, which has 'created a multiplicity of definitions'. Following the lead of Hughes, et al. (2015), they noted that 'the local is inherently defined through relationships to other political scales and spheres, primarily the national and the global'. They noted further that it comprised of 'codified relationships, practices and sites that are somehow below the level of the national state'. They also argued that the local can also be an ideology formed to resist hegemonic systems that constrain the possibilities of increasing or achieving social change, alluding to 'the existence of a concrete presence of powerful actors or groups within specific territories, each having distinct boundaries, languages and structures of authority as well as political, economic and social influence'.

While the debate remains lively and ongoing, the conversations about the local in peacebuilding encompasses pertinent issues of 'local ownership, civil society, 'traditional' institutions, hybridity, or resistance against international intervention', among others. Essentially, the idea of the 'local' in peacebuilding conveys diverse meanings such as:

> Local actors, populations, and institutions; as that which is at the 'bottom', 'on the ground', or works from the 'bottom-up', and thus largely in relation to scale; as a spatial characteristics, associated with distinctive places where actors, institutions, and practices relevant for peacebuilding are located, or in terms of a confined administrative and spatial entity, such as a province. (quoted in Hirblinger and Simons, 2015: 2)

The advantages of the 'local' in peacebuilding are numerous. Studies and experiences have demonstrated that 'local communities are frequently successful in managing natural resources and mitigating or managing environmental conflicts'. Moreover, bottom-up approaches have also been credited with empowering 'marginalized and vulnerable communities who lack seats at decision-making tables and suffer from the 'slow violence' of rampant destruction of their livelihoods and ecosystems'. Again, their failure for different reasons such as 'local circumstances, misguided or manipulative external involvement, or political interference' has been noted to be very catastrophic, including 'resource exploitation, livelihood insecurity and communal conflict' (Ide, et al, 2021a: 8). Other limitations of the 'local' in peacebuilding include 'the complexity, politics, oppression, resistance and variability that exist within different locals, which in turn significantly influences the outcomes and effectiveness of peace-building' (Emah and Kwaja, 2020: 88).

Irrespective of the qualifications of the 'local', one man criticism of peacebuilding has been the total lack or inadequacy of local contents, including voices from below or community voices (Medina, et al, 2024; Ide, et al, 2021b; Hachmann, et al, 2023). The marginalization or exclusion of the 'local' in peacebuilding meant that in most cases the process is top-down, instead of bottom-up. This development should not be entirely surprising as it mirrors a broader issue of exclusion in power dynamics at various levels –international, regional, national and subnational. The results, as studies have shown, is the 'low-quality or stalled peace... that suffers from deficits in the areas of local empowerment, local ownership, and legitimacy' (Funk, 2012: 395).

What the foregoing suggests is that sustainable peacebuilding, one that will not only yield high quality peace, but also endures, must by deliberate design and implementation, pay sufficient attention to the 'local', including grassroots peacebuilding initiatives (Allouche and Zadi, 2022; Huda, 2021). This is supported by extant studies, which tease out some of the emerging themes in the ongoing agenda for localizing peace. Such an agenda seeks to ensure that 'peace promoting activities are conducted as much as possible with local materials and resources, and in a manner that activates latent cultural energies, creates a genuine sense of ownership and empowerment, and heightens prospects for sustainability' (Funk, 2012: 398). Like the popular progressive peacebuilding, localizing peace and peacebuilding demands that we understand 'peace as a locally constructed reality, viewing culture as a resource rather than as a constraint or afterthought, and recognizing that outsiders are most likely to make positive contributions when they act as facilitators or midwives rather than headmasters'. Peacebuilding can easily be compromised when these salient elements are missing (Barnett, et al, 2014). These salient themes run through most of the chapters in the book.

Formal vs Informal Institutions

There have also been lively conversations regarding the relationships between formal and informal institutions in peacebuilding. For clarity, formal institutions are state institutions established formally by the governments at different levels (federal, state and local); informal, non-state institutions often emerge from the traditional and cultural institutions of society, including ethnic and religious communities, as well as from Non-Governmental Organisations (NGOs) working in peacebuilding (Ebiede and Kwaja, 2024). When unpacked, informal institutions of peacebuilding extend to specialist interest groups, faith-based organisations, traditional and community groups (youth, women, vigilante, etc.), researcher and research institutions, humanitarian and development service delivery organisations, human rights and advocacy organisations, business associations involved directly or indirectly in the peacebuilding process (Paffenholz, 2015: 108–109).

The debate about formal and informal institutions of peacebuilding sits at the intersections of state-society relations and citizenship in situations of conflict and fragility. Contending perspectives abound about the form and character of relations between the two. While some argue in support of interdependence, where both actors work synergistically to complement each other and reinforce the peacebuilding process, others prefer institutional autonomy, with both institutions competing with each other over the same space for relevance and delivery; and in the extreme may even struggle to outdo or undermine each other (Haider and Mcloughlin, 2016).

The arguments in support of formal state institutions are many. Among others, they are reputed to have strong capacity, including better resources – human, material and financial- over and above what formal institutions can ever mobilise. Nevertheless, the other side of it is that formal state institutions ' may be weak or deemed illegitimate in fragile and conflict-affected contexts', thereby limiting their reach. It has long been realized by different actors that the exclusion of non-state, informal institutions is problematic and could end up being counterproductive (Westerwinter, 2013). These and related criticisms have been escalated by other scholars to advance the argument in support of informal, non-state institutions in peacebuilding.

There are many arguments in support of the involvements of informal, non-state actors in peacebuilding. These include the position that such institutions tend to find a way to persist and retain legitimacy, against all odds. Moreover, they are said to be diverse, with extended local knowledge and network. Their legitimacy also derives from the realization that informal institutions represent local culture and practices, which can provide a bridge between state and society. They are also credited with capability to improve public service delivery, help stimulate investment, facilitate the transition to more inclusive, rules-based governance, and promote social reconciliation in situations of conflict. Taking together, informal institutions are said to be imbued with capacity for all or some of the following: protection, monitoring, advocacy, socialization, intergroup social cohesion, facilitation and mediation and service delivery (Paffenholz, 2015: 110–113). In this light, Westerwinter (2013: 61) submits that 'the frequency, scope, and depth of non-state-actor involvement has changed, ranging from assistance in the implementation of projects to participation in decision-making and monitoring'. Little wonder that various actors have continued to devote substantial efforts and resources 'towards building and strengthening the capacities of civil society actors, and harnessing their potential as peace actors' (Paffenholz, 2015: 108).

Despite the positive representation of informal institutions in peacebuilding, they are often confronted with some challenges, which limit their effectiveness. Critics have also argued that informal institutions can, in some cases, undermine norms of governance and citizenship, hijacked, politicized and may not necessarily function better than the state and can in some cases be discriminatory, particularly towards women and youth. They also suffer from resource constraints, political interferences, security threats, and lack of social cohesion in communities (Ebiede and Kwaja, 2024; Haider and Mcloughlin, 2016).

Both formal and informal institutions have their strength and weaknesses. This explains why synergy between the two is pivotal and has been advocated by many scholars (Burki and Guillermo, 1998; Evans, 1996). Both can collaborate and play 'an important role in cultivating institutional reconciliation, interpenetration, and integration between macro-level government structures and subnational social institutions' (Ogbaharya, 2008: 395). This perspective permeates several chapters of this book.

Concluding Reflections: Crosscutting Themes in Peacebuilding

This chapter has analysed different theoretical perspectives on peacebuilding. Given the focus of the book on herder-farmer conflicts, we have laid greater emphasis on themes that we consider to be most relevant and applicable to the subject of study. In doing this, we opened with a clarification of the contentious concept of 'herder-farmer conflicts', showing the various perspectives and controversies that surround the concept. We then offered a working definition of the concept as used in this book. The chapter also highlighted two broad approaches to peacebuilding, namely the short-term and long-term, showing why the latter offers better prospects of sustainable peacebuilding. In the African context, post-conflict neoliberal peacebuilding and radical progressive peacebuilding were highlighted, underscoring why the latter is much more applicable to the African situation. The chapter then dovetails to environmental peacebuilding, showing its salient elements and applicability to herder-farmer conflicts since environmental issues are deeply implicated in these conflicts. Other issues addressed in the chapter include the gender dimensions of peacebuilding, the relevance of subnational and local peacebuilding initiatives, and the place of formal and informal institutions of peacebuilding.

From the analysis, a number of crosscutting themes are discernible. One is the dominance of environmental concerns in peace, conflict and post-conflict peacebuilding. Across board, there seems to be convergences and divergences, including the cohabitation in the same space, between a number of peacebuilding institutions and processes, most notably the national and local institutions, as well as formal and informal. This connects to be question of hybridity or synergy and autonomy of these institutions in peacebuilding. Gender issues also overlap with social inclusion, including the possible roles of young people, people with disability in the conflict and peacebuilding process. Across these broad spectrums are underlying issues of human rights often generated by the dynamics of conflicts and peacebuilding. Yet, the relationships between development and peacebuilding remain unresolved. Though they differ in meaning, they are also similar in some respects. In the least, development and peacebuilding operate in overlapping spaces (Stauffer, 2022; Brinkerhoff, 2005). This raises the question of what the appropriate interventions should be in post-conflict settings – development or peacebuilding. But both are intricately interconnected and can hardly be detached from each other. Ordering them in a particular sequence can also be problematic. They ought to be pursued simultaneously. Logically, development is peacebuilding and vice versa.

References

Adenuga, G., Olajubu, A., Oyewole, S., and Omotola, J. S. (2023). Ethno-religious Conflicts and the Challenges of National Security in Nigeria's Fourth Republic. *South African Review of Sociology*, *53*(2), 130–149. https://doi.org/10.1080/21528586.2023.2233462

Adigun, O. W. 2022. Analysing the Patterns and *Dominant Narrative(s) of Nigeria's Farmer-Herder Conflicts*, ACCORD Policy and Practice Brief, 14 July; available at https://accord.org.za/publication/analysing-the-patterns-and-dominant-narratives-of-nigerias-farmer-herder-conflicts/#

Allouche, J. and Zadi, P. Z. 2022, 'Local peacebuilding: The reflexive encounter between a subaltern view and a practitioner in Côte d'Ivoire', in Charbonneau, B. and Ricard, M. Eds. *Routledge Handbook of African Peacebuilding*. London: Routledge.

Barnett, M., Fang, S. and Zurcher, C. 2014, 'Compromised Peacebuilding', *International Studies Quarterly*, 58 (1), pp. 608–620.

Bereketeab, Redie. 2021, 'Peacebuilding in Africa: Popular progressive versus neoliberal peacebuilding', in Adetula, Victor, Bereketeab, Redie and Obi, Cyril. Eds. *Regional Economic Communities and Peacebuilding in Africa: Lessons from ECOWAS and IGAD*. London and New York: Routledge, pp. 35–54.

Boutros-Ghali, B. 1992, *An agenda for peace: Preventive diplomacy, peacemaking and peace-keeping*. United Nations.

Brinkerhoff, D. W. 2005, 'Rebuilding governance in failed states and post-conflict societies: core concepts and cross-cutting themes', *Public Administration and Development*, 25 (1), pp. 3–14.

Brottem, L. 2021, 'The growing complexity of Farmer–Herder conflict in West and Central Africa', *Africa Security Brief* 39. Washington, DC: Africa Center for Strategic Studies.

Bruch, C., Jensen, D., Nakayama, M., and Unruh, J. 2019, 'The changing nature of conflict, peacebuilding, and environmental cooperation', *Environmental Law Report: News & Analysis*, 49.

Burki, S. J., and Guillermo, E. P. 1998, *Beyond the Washington consensus: Institutions matter*. Washington, DC: World Bank.
Caffentzis, G. 2002, 'Neoliberalism in Africa, Apocalyptic failures and business as usual practices', *Turkish Journal of International Affairs*, 1 (3), pp. 80–103.
Carius, A. 2006, 'Environmental peacebuilding: conditions for success', *Environmental Change and Security Program Report*, 12, pp. 59–75.
Conca, K. 2024, 'Environmental peacebuilding: Yesterday, today, and tomorrow', *The Journal of Social Encounters*, 8 (1), pp. 4–12.
Dalmer, N. 2021, 'Building environmental peace: The UN environment programme and knowledge creation for environmental peacebuilding', *Global Environmental Politics*, 21 (3), pp. 147–168.
Dresse, A., Fischhendler, I., Nielsen, J. Ø., and Zikos, D. 2018, 'Environmental peacebuilding: towards a theoretical framework', *Cooperation and Conflict, 001083671880833*. https://doi.org/10.1177/0010836718808331
Eade, D. and Afshar, H. 2003, *'Development, women and war: feminist perspectives'*. Oxford: Oxfam.
Ebiede,T. M. and Kwaja, C. M. A. (eds.). 2024, Policy levers for peace: sub-national and local peacebuilding mechanisms in Nigeria. Conflict Research Network West Africa.
Emah, E. B. and Kwaja, C. M. A. 2020, 'The effectiveness of peace-building efforts and the legitimacy of actors: an exegesis and reflection of "The Local" in Myanmar and Nigeria', *Journal of African-Centered Solutions in Peace and Security*, 3 (1), pp. 86–126.
Evans, P. 1996, 'Government action, social capital and development: reviewing the evidence on synergy', *World Development*, 24 (6), pp. 1119–32.
Funk, N. C. 2012, 'Building on what's already there valuing the local in international peacebuilding', *International Journal*, Spring, pp. 391–408.
Galtung, J. (1967). Theories of Peace: *A synthetic approach to peace thinking. Oslo: International Peace Research Institute.*
Gawerc, M. I. 2006, 'Peace-building: theoretical and concrete perspectives', *Peace and Change*, 31 (4), pp. 435–478.
Gizelis, T. 2011, 'A country of their own: women and peacebuilding', *Conflict Management and Peace Science*, 28 (5), pp. 522–42.
GSDRC. 2016, State-society relations and citizenship in situations of conflict and fragility.
Hachmann, S., Löhr, K., Morales-Muñoz, H., Eufemia, U., Sieber S., & Bonatti, M. 2023, 'Conceptualizing community-based environmental peacebuilding in Cesar, Colombia', *Human Ecology*, 51, pp. 221–235.
Haider, H. and Mcloughlin, C. 2016, *State-society relations and citizenship in situations of conflict and fragility: topic guide supplement*. Birmingham, UK: GSDRC, University of Birmingham.

Hardt, J. N. and Scheffran, J. 2019, 'Environmental peacebuilding and climate change: peace and conflict studies at the edge of transformation', *Policy Brief No. 68*: *Toda Peace Institute* (https://toda.org/assets/files/resources/policy-briefs/t-pb-68_hardt-and-scheffran_environmental-peacebuilding-and-climate-change.pdf).

Hirblinger. and Simons, 2015, 'The good, the bad, and the powerful: representations of the local in peacebuilding', *Security Dialogue*, pp. 1–18.

Huda, M. S. 2021, 'An ecological response to ethno-nationalistic populism: grassroots environmental peacebuilding in south Asia', *International Affairs*, 97 (1), pp. 119–138, https://doi.org/10.1093/ia/iiaa176.

Hughes, C., Öjendal, J., & Schierenbeck, I. (2015). The struggle versus the song – the local turn in peacebuilding: an introduction. *Third World Quarterly*, *36*(5), 817–824. https://doi.org/10.1080/01436597.2015.1029907

Hussein, K., Sumberg, J. and Seddon, D. 1999, 'Increasing violent conflict between Herders and Farmers in Africa: Claims and Evidence', *Development Policy Review*, 17, pp. 397–418.

Ide, T. and Tubi, A. 2019, 'Education and environmental peacebuilding: insights from three projects in Israel and Palestine', *Annals of the American Association of Geographers*, 110 (1), pp. 1–17.

Ide, T., Bruch, C., Carius, A., Conca, A., Dabelko, G. D., Matthew, R., and Weinthal, W. 2021a, 'The past and future(s) of environmental peacebuilding', *International Affairs*, 97 (1), pp. 1–16.

Ide, T., Palmer, L. R., & Barnett, J. 2021b, 'Environmental peacebuilding from below: customary approaches in Timor-Leste', *International Affairs*, 97 (1), pp. 103–117.

Kendrich, C. and Sanders, L. 2024, Don't call it Farmer-Herder conflict, The SAIS Review of International Affairs, 9 February, available at https://saisreview.sais.jhu.edu/dont-call-it-farmer-herder-conflict/.

Lemay-Hebert, N. and Toupin, S. 2011, 'Peacebuilding: a broad review of approaches, policies and practices', Peacebuilding, Ottawa, Canada. https://pure-oai.bham.ac.uk/ws/portalfiles/portal/4714879/LemayHebert_PeacebuildingApproaches.pdf.

Lemay-Hébert, N. 2013, 'Critical Debates on Liberal Peacebuilding', *Civil Wars*, 15 (2), pp. 242–252.

McKay, S. and Mazurana, D. 2007, 'Gendering peacebuilding', in Christie, D. J., Wagner, R. V., & Winter, D. A. Eds. (2001). *Peace, Conflict, and Violence: Peace Psychology for the 21st Century*. Englewood Cliffs, New Jersey: Prentice-Hall.

Medina, L., Ensor, M. O., Schapendonk, F., Sieber, S., Pacillo, G., Laderach, P., Hellin, J., & Bonatti, M. 2024, 'Community voices on climate, peace and security: a social learning approach to programming environmental peacebuilding', *Environment and Security*, 2 (1), pp. 75–104.https://doi.org/10.1177/27538796231207030

Moritz, M. and Mbacke, M. 2022, 'The danger of a single story about Fulani pastoralists', *Pastoralism* 12, 14, 1–10.

Neufeldt, R. C. 2024, 'Ethics of peacebuilding', *Oxford Research Encyclopedias*, https://doi.org/10.1093/acrefore/9780190846626.013.86.

Ogbaharya, D. G. 2008, '(Re-)building governance in post-conflict Africa: the role of the state and informal institutions', *Development in Practice*, 18 (3), pp. 395–402.

Olumba, E. E. 2024, 'The politics of eco-violence: why is conflict escalating in Nigeria's middle belt?' *Terrorism and Political Violence*, 36 (2), pp. 180–197.

Olumba, E. E., Nwosu, B. U., Okpaleke, F. N. and Okoli, R. C. 2022, 'Conceptualising eco-violence: moving beyond the multiple labelling of water and agricultural resource conflicts in the Sahel', *Third World Quarterly*, 43 (9), pp. 2075–2090.

Omotola, J. S. 2024a, 'Traditional institutions and the management of Herders-Farmers conflicts in Nasarawa State, Nigeria', in Ehrhardt, D, Umar, S. and Alao, D, Eds. *Traditional Authority and Security in Contemporary Nigeria*, London: Routledge, pp. 169–190.

Omotola, J. S. 2024b, 'SADC and peacebuilding in the Southern African Region', in Bereketeab, R. Ed. *Supranational Institutions and Peacebuilding in Africa: The African Union and Regional Economic Communities*, London: Routledge, pp. 171-186.

Oosterom, M., 2022, 'Youth and 'Everyday Peace' in the City of Jos, Nigeria', in *Youth and Non-Violence in Africa's Fragile Contexts,* Cham: Springer International Publishing, pp. 39–65.

Owonikoko, S.B., 2020, 'Beyond victimhood: women and resource conflict between Farming and Herding communities in Adamawa State', *Nigeria's Resource Wars. Series in World History*, pp. 134–154.

Paffenholz, T. 2015, 'Civil society and peacebuilding', *Development Dialogue, Part 3*, pp. 108–118. (http://www.daghammarskjold.se/wp-content/uploads/2016/01/DHF_DD63_p108-118.pdf).

Paffenholz, T. 2021, 'Perpetual peacebuilding: a new paradigm to move beyond the linearity of liberal peacebuilding', *Journal of Intervention and Statebuilding*, 15 (3), pp. 367–385. https://doi.org/10.1080/17502977.2021.1925423.

Rey, C. D. L. and McKay, S. 2006, 'Peacebuilding as a gendered process', *Journal of Social Issues*, 62 (1), pp. 141–153.

Smoljan, J. 2003, 'The relationship between peace building and development', *Conflict, Security & Development*, 3 (2), 233–250.

Stauffer, C. 2022, 'Development and peacebuilding: disparities, similarities, and overlapping spaces', in Charbonneau, B. and Ricard, M. Eds. *Routledge Handbook of African Peacebuilding*, London: Routledge.

Westerwinter, O. 2013, 'Formal and informal governance in the UN peacebuilding commission', in Jakobi, A. P., Wolf, K. D. Eds. *The Transnational Governance of Violence and Crime: Governance and Limited Statehood.* London: Palgrave Macmillan, pp. 61–83.

Wilén, N. 2022, 'Women, gender and peacebuilding in Africa', in Charbonneau, B. and Ricard, M. Eds. *Routledge Handbook of African Peacebuilding*, London: Routledge.

Yoshida, K. and Céspedes-Báez, L. M. 2021, The nature of Women, Peace and Security: a Colombian perspective, *International Affairs*, *97* (1), 17–34, https://doi.org/10.1093/ia/iiaa173

Zambakari, C. 2016, 'Challenges of liberal peace and statebuilding in divided societies', *Conflict Trends*, 4.

PART II

Case Studies

CHAPTER 3

Natural Resource Scarcity and its Implication for Farmer-Herder Conflicts in Burkina Faso

Tog-Noma Patricia Emma Bontogho

Introduction

Burkina Faso, a Sahelian country in West Africa, has more than 82% of its population involved in agriculture, contributing about 35% of the country's GDP (World Bank 2014). Animal rearing forms a significant part of this sector. In 2022, Burkina Faso's livestock included approximately 9,720,615 cattle, 11,129,114 sheep, 10,750,406 goats, 1,416,342 pigs, and 135,803,843 poultry. The livestock sub-sector accounts for 15% of GDP, 30% of export earnings, and 12% of added training value (Ministry of Animal Resources, MRA 2009). The contribution of the livestock sub-sector to the economy may have slightly declined over the years. Recent statistics indicate that while pastoralists represent 40% of the workforce, and still a formidable economic force to reckon with, with the Fulani as the dominant pastoralist group, the subsector represents 13.5% of the national GDP and 19% of export value (Bisson et al. 2021).

T.-N. P. E. Bontogho (✉)
High Institute of Sustainable Development, University Yembila Abdoulaye Toguyeni, Fada NGourma, Burkina Faso
e-mail: bontoghopatricia@yahoo.fr

J. S. Omotola (ed.), *Herder-Farmer Conflicts in Africa*,
https://doi.org/10.1007/978-3-031-80821-0_3

Despite its importance, the livestock sector remains under-exploited due to its dominance by traditional production systems. Pastoralists in Burkina Faso operate a hybrid system of nomadism and statutory systems, with nomads migrating to neighboring countries like Togo, Ghana, and Côte d'Ivoire during the rainy season (Belemsaga et al. 2005; Quaye et al. 2011; Babatunde et al. 2023). This migration is often driven by climate change, which negatively impacts crops and animal productivity (Sarr et al. 2015). The country faces prolonged droughts, increased dry spells, and high water evaporation (Ibrahim et al. 2014; Lèye et al. 2021), threatening agriculture, livestock production, food security, and human security.

In response, Burkina Faso implemented a National Action Plan (PNLCD) in 1985 to combat desertification. Despite these efforts, climate change continues to affect national security and development, notably escalating conflicts between farmers and herders. This chapter examines these conflicts' trends, causes, consequences, management strategies, and lessons for sustainable peacebuilding and development, focusing on natural resource availability and management. Understanding land uses/land cover (LULC) LULC dynamics is crucial for advancing debates on farmer-herder conflicts and finding sustainable solutions for food and human security.

As a coping strategy in response to the devastating impacts of climate change, Burkina Faso was one of the earliest West African countries to develop and implement a National Action Plan (see Ministry of Environment, Green Economy and Climate Change, 2021). This plan outlines a sequence of actions to combat desertification. Despite these and related state interventions, climate change has continued to significantly impact national security and development. One notable aspect of this issue is the escalation of conflicts between farmers and herders, which is the primary focus of this chapter.

The chapter examines the trends of herder-farmer conflicts in Burkina Faso, aiming to highlight their manifestations, causes, consequences, management strategies, and key lessons for sustainable peacebuilding and development. The chapter approaches these issues from the perspective of natural resource availability and management. This approach is beneficial because studies have established that decentralization and land tenure reform strongly impact natural resource management (Cabot 2017; Brockhaus et al. 2003). Understanding the dynamics of land use and land cover is essential for advancing the debates on farmer-herder conflicts, which can contribute to finding sustainable solutions to the problem, particularly concerning food and human security.

Study Areas, Data, and Methods

Study Areas

Burkina Faso is divided into three agro-climatic zones: the Sahel, the north-Sudanian, and the south-Sudanian zones. Climate change impacts vary across these zones, affecting rainfall, precipitation patterns, agricultural production, food security, grass availability, and natural resources. Analyzing farmer-herder conflicts at the agroecological scale can help understand the link between climate change and these conflicts. This study focuses on Pama (Sudano Sahelian zone), Manga (Sudanese zone), and Thiou (Sahelian zone) (Fig. 3.1). These areas have a tropical climate with a unimodal rainfall pattern, a short rainy season, and a long dry season lasting five to six months in Manga, seven to nine months in Ouahigouya, and three to four months in Pama.

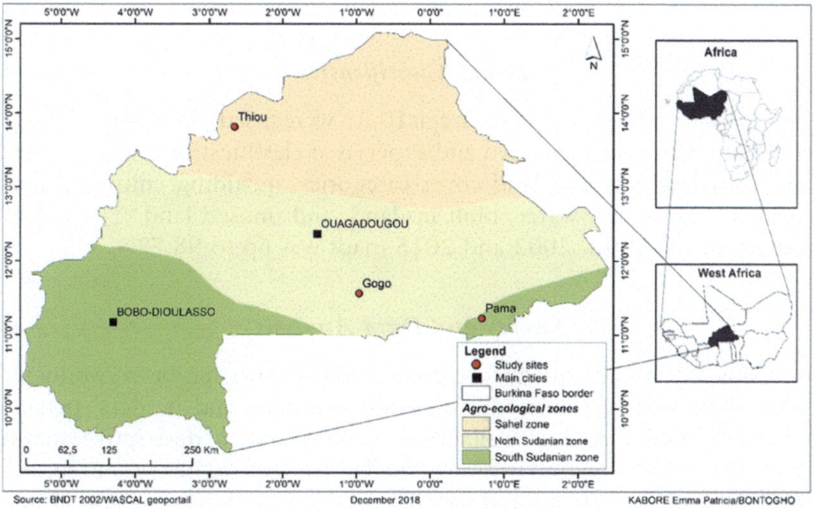

Fig. 3.1 Showing a map of the study areas

Table 3.1 Landsat images and resolution

Data	*Format*	*Resolution*	*Year*	*Source*
Administration	Sh	–	2012	IGB
Landsat TM 1990 image	Grid	30 m	1990	CNDD/ONDD
Landsat ETM image 2002	Grid	30 m	2002	CNDD/ONDD
Landsat OLI_TIRS 2015	Grid	30 m	2015	CNDD/ONDD

Data and Image Pre-processing

Multidate images including historical satellite imagery for 1990, 2002, and 2015 were retrieved from Landsat thematic Mapper (TM) and OLI-TIRS from the Global and Cover Facilities website to determine both landscape features and the spatial characteristics and the temporal dynamic of land-use and land-cover over the period 1990 to 2015. All images have a spatial resolution of 30 m (Table 3.1) and were geometrically rectified and registered to a common projection using Universal Transverse Mercator (UTM), Clarke 1880 Spheroid, and Adindan Zone 37 North datum.

Image Classification

Two software (Envi 4.7 and Arcgis10.3) were used for satellite image processing. Both unsupervised and supervised classifications were selected to identify land use and land cover categories, including cultivated land forestland, grassland, water, built-up land, and unused land. The overall accuracy of the 1990, 2002 and 2015 maps was up to 98.72%.

Survey and Data Analysis

Following the satellite image interpretation, fieldwork has been conducted within the scope of this study to identify farmers' and herders' perceptions of natural resource availability. To this end, a descriptive survey design using both quantitative and qualitative approaches was prepared, tested, refined, and structured for the interview. Indeed, In-depth Interviews (IDI) and Focus Group Discussions (FGDs) were applied to collect primary information. The sample included 200 participants farmers and herders: around 70 people were thus randomly selected in each location. Twenty (20) individual interviews were conducted among purposely selected community leaders (leader farmers, breeders). The time taken to interview a respondent was recorded and found to vary from 45 mn to 1 hour. Then two focus group discussions (FGDs) comprising of 5 to 8 persons were held among women and young in each locality, making a total of six FGDs. The statistical software SPSS (IBM SPSS Statistics for Windows, Version 20.0) was used for data analysis. Descriptive statistics including frequency distribution, mean, percentage, and standard deviation were used to examine farmers' perception of natural resource availability.

Results Presentation and Analysis

The Depth of the Problem

Burkina Faso has, over the past decade, emerged as one of the leading hotbeds of herder-farmer conflicts in Africa. Brottem (2021) argued, and quite correctly, that the surge in farmer-herder conflict in Africa has been concentrated in Nigeria, along the central Mali and northern Burkina Faso corridor. It further noted that such violence has increased in West and Central Africa over the past 10 years (2011–2020), with geographic concentrations in Nigeria, central Mali, and *northern Burkina Faso* (emphasis mine).

Over the past decade, herder-farmer conflicts in Burkina Faso have become recurrent, particularly in the northern region. High-risk areas for violent events between pastoralist and farming communities include Zoundweogo and Nahouri in the South-Central region, Gourma and Kompienga in the Eastern region, Sissili and Ziro in the Center-West region, and Poni and Noumbiel in the South-West region. Clashes intensified in the early 2000s, with the 2003 incident in Balere, where ten herders were killed and crops destroyed, marking a significant escalation. A 2010 report from the Ministry of Animal Resources recorded 55 deaths in 4000 clashes over four years. Some other studies claim that these conflicts have become rather endemic in recent times, accounting for more than 65% of all violence linked to competition for natural resources, with different sources reporting 'about 600 cases of farmer-pastoralist conflicts occurring annually in Burkina Faso' (UNECA, 2019).

But the problem predates this period. An old study on herder-farmer conflicts by Brockhaus et al. (2003: 3) revealed that 'over a period of three years, 111 conflicts were reported by 124 households. Out of these, 97 (87%) 'were typical farmer-herder conflicts about crop damages caused by livestock'. It is important to note that out of all these cases, '74 were reported by farmers, and 23 by the herders' (Brockhaus et al. 2003: 3). If this is already huge by all standards, recent statistics about the manifestations of these conflicts are much more worrisome. The Ministry of Animal Resources estimated that about '600 conflicts occur each year involving the death of pastoralists, farmers or government workers, the destruction of farms or houses and the injury or death of animals' in the country. In addition, Edithe Vokouma, Director of Pastoralist Affairs in the Ministry noted that some 55 people had been killed in 4000 recorded clashes over the past four years (2008–2012), with cases rising year on year (Reliefweb 2012). Another source, citing government records, revealed that from 2005–2011, there were 12,071 conflicts in Burkina Faso involving pastoralists, with 55 deaths (UNOWAS 2019: 27). In more recent times, precisely between 2019 and 2020, a comprehensive study on the subject across sub-Saharan Africa, using ACLED Data, documents that Burkina Faso recorded 580 incidents with 2231 fatalities during the period (Krätli and Toulmin, 2020: 24).

Herder-farmer conflicts in Burkina Faso are old, dating as far back to the 1970s and 1980s. However, relations between herders and farmers have not always been acrimonious. Before now, herder-farmer relations were cordial and built on reciprocal trust. Then, farmers used to entrust their cows to the pastoralists who would guard them for the farmers. Besides, pastoralists also 'sell manure for the agricultural sector, and their animal production fulfils the meat and dairy demands of an ever-increasing population in growing urban centres' of the country. However, these once symbiotic and mutually beneficial relationships have since given way, replaced by mutual distruct and suspicion, conflicts and associated consequences (see Bisson et al. 2021; Hussein et al. 1999: 419).

Causes and Consequences

Many factors account for the occurrence and worsening situation of hgerder-farmer conflicts in Burkina Faso. These factors incluenvironmemtal scarcity, climate change leading to desertification and loss of pasture land, blockage of transhumance routes and the political marginalization of pastoralists in decision-making (UNOWAS 2019: 22–30). Out of these factors, climate change has been accorded some priority (Abroulaye et al. 2015). Climate change has been held responsible for aggravating the vulnerability of both herders and farmers (Lèye, et al, 2021). This is because 'changes in climate patterns such as significant rainfall variability or the increase of temperatures leave them with less water, less pasture, crop failure, failure in livestock's productivity, and health issues leading to an increase of their vulnerability'. The study reveals that the more the vulnerability, the higher the level of exposure to food, economic, health and environmental insecurities. Again, higher insecurity at all levels contributes to conflicts.

Also of effect is the question of natural resource scarcity, which breeds migration and increased competition between farmers and herders. Natural resources such as land, pastures and water have always been in short supply. The shortage is also not unconnected to the effect of climate change. Brottem (2021) demonstrated this linkage very powerfully, with emphasis on growing land pressure. This pressure, according to him, is directly related to dramatic growth in the population of the region's rural areas, with the concomitant effect declining grazing lands for herders. This not only made grazing lands converted into cultivation, thereby making their livelihoods more challenging, but also forcing many of them to migrate in search of pasture for their animals. As the study reveals, 'over the past four decades, cropland has doubled in area reaching nearly 25% of the total land surface, a trend that scientists project to accelerate alongside population growth'. In responding, herders tend to move into otherwise 'protected areas, such as national parks and classified forests, and increases their dependence on nominally illicit practices such as tree branch lopping'. The chain of actions, including security responses, has all been implicated in these conflicts (see also West et al. 2008; Zampaligre et al. 2013).

Brottem (2021) also stressed the political instrumentalisation of existing fault lines as an excerbater of the conflicts. For him, the number of incidents and fatalities only tells one side of the story. For a broader appreciation of the problem, we must also pay attention to its amplification 'the emotionally potent issues of ethnicity, religion, culture, and land. This is important because, as Brottem (2021) argues, 'Militant Islamist groups in central Mali and northern Burkina Faso have instrumentalized such divisions to inflame grievances, thereby driving recruitment'.

Conflicts of interests and mistrust have also been identified as a major concern. This is critical because, as Brottem (2021) argues, once the peacebuilding process is tainted by the perception of mistrust, rumor, and suspicion among actors, 'aggrieved parties and their allies are often quick to assume that corruption played a role' and vice versa. Such a tendency can affect the credibility and legitimacy of post-conflict peacebuilding. These standoffs, according to Brottem (2021), have 'have historically involved traditional hunters' associations such as the Dozo in Mali and the Koglweogo in Burkina Faso', resulting into conflicts between the two groups, which have 'become more organized, protracted, and deadly contributing to self-perpetuating cycles of violence'. This is corroborated by Bisson et al. (2021) who 'finds a breakdown of intercommunal trust and social cohesion between pastoralists and farmers at the local level. This allows various extremist groups to spread their operational field and recruit local militants'.

Finally, Brottem (2021) highlighted the role of the problem in Mali in herder-farmer conflicts in Burkina Faso. The main issues here relates to the fact that 'most farmer-herder violence in central Mali is concentrated in the part of Mopti Region bordering northern Burkina Faso'. Increasing population density in the region has been contributing to heightened land tenure disputes, frustrating efforts to negate or redefine longstanding autochthon-migrant relationships … in certain localities'. The connection to land tenure is critical for obvious reasons. Notably, the question of land right has featured prominently in discourses about herder-farmer conflicts in the country. In fact, a study found that '48% of people in rural Burkina Faso feel insecure in their land and property rights' (Prindex 2020).

Other notable explanations that have been advanced for herder-farmer conflicts in Burkina Faso include historical factors, socio-economic issues bothering on marginalization and or/exclusion, growing extremist movements in the region, population growth, poor governance of natural resources (government policies and biased local governance systems, as well as structural change to the economic modes of production, and lack of Sectorial Policy Harmonization and laws enforcement (Garner 2022; Bisson et al. 2021; Abroulaye et al. 2015).

The conflicts have most often been counterproductive, with mostly negative consequences. Some of the most severe effects of these conflicts include deaths and injuries, destruction of infrastructures and properties, killing of livestock and destruction of farmlands and crops, resulting in loss of livelihood and revenues. The conflicts have also escalated mutual distrust and suspicion, leading to the formation of self-defence groups such as the Koglweogo, the development of criminal economies, strengthening to the foothold of terrorist groups, and the emergence of diverse actors with opposing platforms (Garner 2022). Other impacts of the conflicts include involuntary migration and psychological injuries or trauma that can hardly be quantified in monetary terms. Trauma reproduces stress, affects mental health and productivity in terrible ways. Taken together, these implications have threatened livestock and crop production, and undernined national, food and human security (Gaya 2018; UNOWAS 2019; Abroulaye et al. 2015; Reliefweb 2012).

Actors and Management of the Conflicts

Broadly speaking, two broad categories of actors are involved in these conflicts: state (official) and non-state (unofficial) actors. State actors are basically government institutions at various levels (national government, regional/departmental administration and local administration), while non-state actors are basically the main conflcting parties (pastoralists and farmers), NGOs and CSOs, criminal groups/networks, as well as private individuals connected to these conflicts one way or the other (Gaye 2018: 14–18; MRA, 2009).

Each of these actors has exhibited certain agency regarding herder-farmer conflicts, with differentiated and oftentimes overlapping roles. While pastoralists and farmers were identified as the main actors in the conflicts, often at each other's throat, the poor governance of natural resources, together with the ineffectiveness of peacebuilding initiatives, essentially by the government but not exclusively by it, has also been highlighted.

The national government, for example, has experimented with a number of responses in managing the conflicts. Depending on the level, state institutions are responsible for a number of activities directly or indirectly linked to the conflicts and their governance. These include the handling of land administration and land register, animal husbandry and justice system, including conflicts between farmers and herders. Be that as it may, the government has been responding to the challenges in diverse ways. For instance, confronted with rapid growth in livestock holding across the country, the government, particularly in the aftermath of the droughts in the 1970s, 'designated 185 pastoral zones, covering two million hectares' (UNECA 2019). The government also came up with the National Action Plan (PNLCD) in 1985, the primary objective of which was to combat desertification; the 1984 law, Réorganisation Agraire et Foncière, amended in 1991 and 1996; and the establishment of a national Commission du Conciliation Foncier, charged with regulating conflicts in pastoral zones (UNOWAS 2019: 30).

In recent times, however, the government would appear to have done more. The policy of decentralization vigorously pursued by the government the 2004 Decentralization Code, *the Code Général des Collectivités Territoriales*, 'which sought to give local bodies a larger role in land management', in addition to the establishment of 'village-level representative committees responsible for land management (Commissions Villageoises de Gestion des Terroirs, CVGTs), has also been helpful. These were in addition one of the most recent institutional responses - the establishment of legal frameworks that govern land and pastoralism, notably Burkina Faso's 2002 Pastoral Policy Act (UNOWAS 2019: 26–30).

Another helpful institutional intervention by the government is the creation of Village Development Councils (CVDs). These councils have been cited as 'playing the main role in conflict mediation and resolution and in addressing land tenure disputes' in the country. A good illustration of this is found in Firka village (Central-North Region), where the CVD was reportedly consists of 12 representatives, including traditional leaders, local administration, a women's leader, and representatives from traders, farmers and pastoralists. Invested my some level of trust and social capital, the CVD is credited with entertaining, and perhaps resolving most farmer-herder disputes that could not be handled between the parties themselves without formal mediation (UNOWAS 2019: 29). The government, theough the Ministry of Animal Resources, has also been holding a series of workshops for the two groups (pastoralists and farmers0, alongside other stakeholders such as community leaders, local governors and Mayors about various dimensions of the conflicts, including the need to eschew violence and embrace peace (Reliefweb 2012).

Non-state actors too, including traditional institutions/chiefs and community-based organisations, are gaining more traction in the field. Their roles, facilitated by increasing decentralization, these actors 'are increasingly involved in the management of powers transferred to local authorities and participate in the drawing up of local development plans'. This include designing and executing 'community projects in the areas of herding, agriculture and income-generating activities (IGAs) with support from political authorities, technical and financial partners (TFPs) and large ... NGOs' (Gaye 2018: 16). They also indulge in advocacy, canvasing for 'non-violence and intercommunity dialogue to resolve conflicts, either through traditional conflict-resolution mechanisms or modern mechanisms implemented by the government'. Yet, 'they act as relays between the communities and the State and play an important role in the pacification of the Delta and Soum Province communes affected by insecurity' (Gaye 2018: 16–17).

A good illustration about the positive effect of decentralisation on herder-farmer conflicts and peacebuilding is found in Dori, in the Sahel Region of northern Burkina. In this area, more informal types of mediation were said to be in use. It involves religious authorities (the local imam) and other local leaders—mainly men and unfortunately, excluding women who are rarely involved (UNOWAS 2019: 29).

Brottem (2021) also illustrated with case of eastern Burkina Faso, where the Pastoral Communication Network (Réseau de communication sur le pastoralisme, RECOPA) has been spearheading an initiative involving farmers and herders, communities, and the municipal government to overcome difficult land tenure obstacles and secure pastoral routes and grazing areas. Specifically, RECOPA is said to maintain basic land management infrastructure in the form of maps that are accessible to resource users and physical markers for land use boundaries through self-financing methods such as collecting small amounts from market receipts, which helps to 'sustain its activities and generate communal ownership of the organization'.

Despite progress made over the years, the effectiveness of these interventions in addressing the problem remains contentious. Some of the notable limitations associuated with these responses include failure to widely enforce extant laws and policies, as well as poor level of awareness of these legal frameworks, even among local authorities (UNOWAS 2019). Legitimate concerns about the persistence of most of the root causes of the conflicts, despite these interventions, and the poor level of women's representation and participation in these institutions also subsist.

Transhumance Trajectories

Three main transhumance trajectories were identified: a north-southern route crossing into Benin, Togo, and Ghana; a south-northern route;

and a northern route within Burkina Faso extending to Mali. These trajectories align with the geography of conflicts.

Sources of Conflict between Farmers and Herders

Table 3.2 presents results from the survey regarding sources of conflict. The responses were categorized into four levels, namely: institutional, leaders, farmers, and herders.

Figure 3.2 illustrates land use categories for Manga from 1990 to 2015. The main LULC changes during this period include forest galleries, housing areas, water bodies, tree savannah, bare soils, and cultivated areas.

Table 3.3 presents the land cover classification scheme within Manga. In 1990, the dominant LULC type in Manga district was Wooded Savannah (35, 57%) lands followed by cultivated areas. During the period 1990–2002, forest galleries have increased by a rate of 7%. Tree savannah decreased up to 3.1% between 1990–2002 and 2002–2015. Conversely, cultivated areas have expanded up to 6.92% and 10.87% respectively. Between 2002 and 2015, bare soils expanded by 13.3%. In addition, water bodies have slightly decreased by 0.08% during the same period.

Figure 3.3 illustrates the land use categories for Ouahigouya from 1990 to 2015. The main features of land use and land-cover change

Table 3.2 Main sources of farmer-herder conflict

Sources of conflict			
Institution level	*Leaders level*	*Farmers level*	*Herders level*
Poorimplementation of rules and regulations related to naturalresource allocation	Favoritism	Unwise identification of the author of cropdestruction	Unfair accessto water bodies' resources
Lake of early warning system	Unfair decisions	Decrease in soil fertility	Unfair access to land
Poor communication	Poor communication	Closing of corridor False report about cropdestruction	Feeling of marginalization
Weak representativity at the village level	Bad leadership style Lake of early warning system	Poor relations between herders and farmer's associations Poor tolerance	

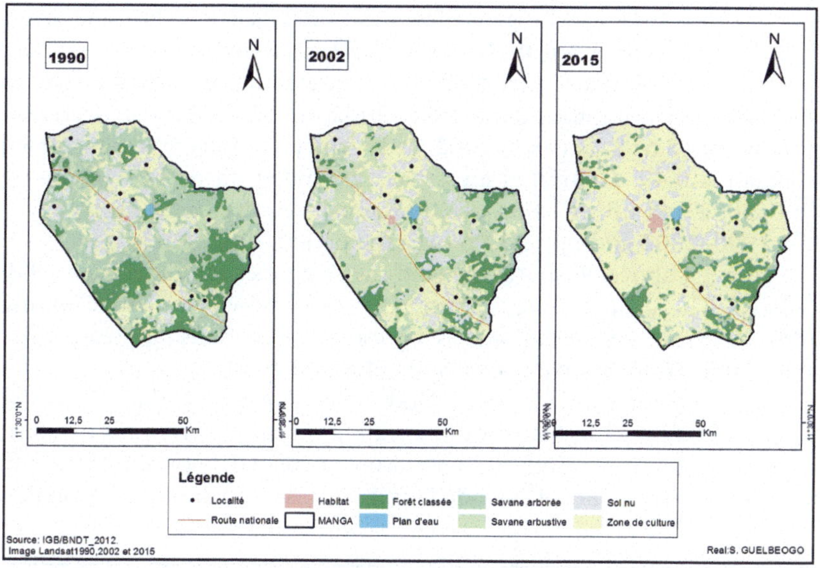

Fig. 3.2 Land use/land cover changes in Manga over the period 1990–2015

Table 3.3 Land cover classification scheme within Manga

MANGA	*1990*		*2002*		*2015*	
	Area		*Area*		*Area*	
	ha	*%*	*ha*	*%*	*ha*	*%*
Forest Gallery	4552.04	18.57	2836.92	11.57	2836.92	11.57
Housing Area	1.22	0.00	2.96	0.01	2.60	0.01
Water Bodies	59.85	0.24	90.01	0.37	71.97	0.29
Wooded Savannah	8721.40	35.57	1096.07	4.47	1096.07	4.47
Tree Savannah	3229.40	13.17	13003.63	53.04	7094.89	28.94
Bare Soils	3309.74	13.50	1147.28	4.68	4409.32	17.98
Cultivated Areas	4645.22	18.95	6341.99	25.87	9007.09	36.74
TOTAL	24518.87	100.00	24518.87	100.00	24518.87	100.00

during 1990–2015 can be generalized as Forest galleries, housing areas, water bodies, Tree savannah, bare soils, and cultivated areas.

Table 3.4 presents the land cover classification scheme within Ouahigouya. During the period 1990–2002, wooded savannah decreased by a rate of 13.61%. between 2002–2015, the rate of decrease of wooded savannah is 0.49. Cultivated areas have expanded up to 14.94% during 1990–2002 and up to 1.85%. Tree savannah has decreased up to 33.71 over 1990–2002 and up to 1.95 over the period 2002–2015.

Figure 3.4 above illustrates the land use categories for Pama from 1990 to 2015. The main features of land use and land-cover change during 1990–2015 can be generalized as Forest galleries, housing areas, water bodies, tree savannah, bare soils, and cultivated areas.

The results of the land use/ land cover dynamic within Pama are recorded in Table 3.5. Statistically, a significant upward trend is detected for agricultural areas. Indeed, agriculture increased between 1990 and 2015 in replacement of wooded and tree savannah areas. Conflicts

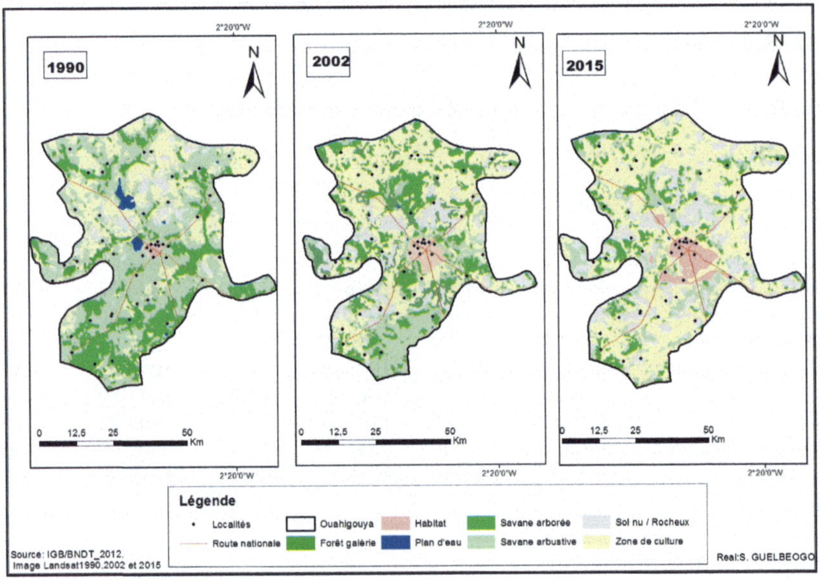

Fig. 3.3 Land use/land cover changes in Ouahigouya over the period 1990–2015

Table 3.4 Land cover classification scheme within Ouahigouya

OUAHIGOUYA	*1990*		*2002*		*2015*	
	Area		*Area*		*Area*	
	ha	*%*	*ha*	*%*	*ha*	*%*
Forest Gallery	883.72	1.79	8890.77	17.96	9001.77	18.19
Housing Area	290.57	0.59	1260.89	2.55	1374.89	2.78
Water Bodies	574.02	1.16	420.38	0.85	22.38	0.05
Wooded Savannah	9861.36	19.93	3125.56	6.32	2887.56	5.83
Tree Savannah	22837.07	46.14	6152.07	12.43	5188.07	10.48
Bare Soils	2652.93	5.36	9852.20	19.91	10312.20	20.84
Cultivated Areas	12390.86	25.04	19788.64	39.98	20703.64	41.83
TOTAL	49490.52	100.00	49490.52	100.00	49490.52	100.00

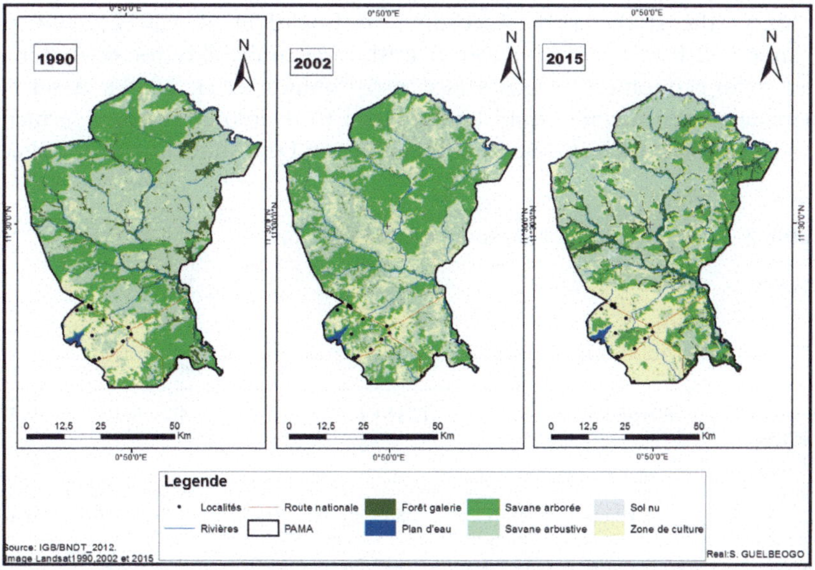

Fig. 3.4 Land use/land cover changes in Pama over the period 1990–2015

between farmers and herders have been linked to several drivers. A large majority of respondents attributed herders-farmers to poor management of natural resources (50%) and competition for resources within the study area. Indeed, competition for land through new land acquisition by climate-induced displaced farmers is also one of the conflict factors. Farming land expansion occurred over the three study areas.

Table 3.5 presents the land cover classification scheme within Pama. During the period 1990–2002, tree savannahs have decreased by a rate of 7%. Between 2002 and 2015, the rate of decrease of wooded savannah is 1.56. Cultivated areas have expanded up to 17.88% during 1990–2015.

The Land Use Land cover analysis of all sites shows a huge conversion of grazing areas into cultivated land. In addition, the water bodies are decreasing in the areas. These compound situations embed sustainable pastoralism and constitute a trigger to farmers-herders conflicts occurrence in the study areas. According to Bonsal et al. (2017), climate change will lead to a reduction in freshwater availability for ecosystems and socio-economics purposes (see also Ibrahim, et al, 2014). A set of management strategies could be deployed to overcome seasonal farmer-herder conflicts such as dysentery breeding, and transhumance in specified

Table 3.5 Land cover classification scheme for Pama

PAMA	*1990*		*2002*		*2015*	
	Area		*Area*		*Area*	
	ha	*%*	*ha*	*%*	*ha*	*%*
Forest Gallery	30865.94	6.17	12161.60	2.43	48805.40	9.76
Housing Area						
Water Bodies	1849.66	0.37	2389.50	0.48	2321.10	0.46
Wooded Savannah	163739.76	32.74	175415.28	35.08	94707.98	18.94
Tree Savannah	227359.74	45.46	191343.50	38.26	183534.81	36.70
Bare Soils	695.25	0.14	1628.01	0.33	5740.87	1.15
Cultivated Areas	75586.57	15.11	117159.03	23.43	164986.75	32.99
TOTAL	500096.92	100.00	500096.92	100.00	500096.92	100.00

protected areas. 57% of respondents state that poor relations between herders and farmer's associations and the poor regulatory frameworks for herding remain a main source of conflicts within the study area. They also highlighted the conversion of transhumance pathways to farms. In addition, competition for natural resources (water, natural vegetation, herbs, and browsing) is also indicated as one of the main factors raising conflicts between farmers and herders.

Conclusion and Lessons for Peacebuilding

This study investigated the implications of land use/Land cover dynamic on farmers and herders conflicts in Burkina Faso. For this purpose, satellite images for 1990, 2002, and 2015 were retrieved from Landsat Thematic Mapper (TM) and OLI-TIRS and analyzed. The study also engaged extant studies to gain understanding about the most salient factors responsible for the escalation of farmer-herder conflicts within Manga, Thiou, and Pama. It also examined the causes and consequences, as well as actors and management of the conflicts.

Since agriculture and breeding play a key role in Burkina Faso's economy, it is important to take some measures to ensure better control of this activity. Therefore, ranching could be initiated to mitigate considerably the breeding-related insecurity. In addition, the involvement of herders in decision-making related to land resources may help to overcome challenges related to farmer-herder conflicts. Government should elaborate a clear map of transhumance pathways, ensure the respect of texts related to corridors and grazing land, and declare a 'peacebuilding day'. In addition, there is a need to reinforce the social services in charge of reconciliation process facilitation at a local level. There is a need to install a framework for dialogue between Farmers and herders.

References

Abroulaye, S., Issa, S., Abalo, K., & Nouhoun, Z. 2015. 'Climate change: A driver of crop farmers-agro pastoralists conflicts in Burkina Faso', *International Journal of Applied Science and Technology*, 5 (3), pp. 92–104.

Babatunde, O. P., Adeigbe, O., Sobowale, O., Muyiwa, A., & Balogun, S. 2023. 'Cashew production and breeding in 5 West African countries', *Journal of Scientific Research and Reports*, 29 (5), pp. 28–39.

Belemsaga, D. M. A., Lombo, Y., Thevenon, S., & Sylla, S. 2005. Inventory analysis of West African cattle breeds. In Applications of gene-based technologies for improving animal production and health in developing countries (pp. 167–173). Dordrecht: Springer Netherlands.

Bisson, L., Cottyn, I., Bruijne, K., & Molenaar, F. 2021. *Between hope and despair Pastoralist adaptation in Burkina Faso,* The Hague, the Netherlands: Netherlands Institute of International Relations https://www.clingendael.org/sites/default/files/2021-02/between-hope-and-despair.pdf.

Bonsal, B. R., Cuell, C., Wheaton, E., Sauchyn, D. J., & Barrow, E. 2017. An assessment of historical and projected future hydro-climatic variability and extremes over southern watersheds in the Canadian Prairies. *International Journal of Climatology*, 37 (10), pp. 3934–3948.

Brockhaus, M., Rischkowsky, B., Nuppenau, E. A., & Steinbach, J. 2003. The role of the state in the management of farmer-herder conflicts in south west Burkina Faso. In Deutscher Tropentag.

Brottem, L. 2021. *The growing complexity of farmer–herder conflict in West and Central Africa.* Africa Security Brief 39. Washington: Africa Center for Strategic Studies.

Cabot, C., & Cabot, C. 2017. Case study: Farmer–herder conflicts in Burkina Faso, Côte d'Ivoire and Ghana. In Climate change, security risks and conflict reduction in Africa: A case study of farmer-herder conflicts over natural resources in Côte d'Ivoire, Ghana, and Burkina Faso 1960–2000 (pp. 113–155).

Garner, H. L. 2022. *Farmer-herder conflict in Burkina Faso between the Mossi and Fulani examined through agent-based modeling*, April, available at https://cdr.lib.unc.edu/concern/honors_theses/sf268f390?locale=en

Gaye, S. G. 2018. *Conflicts between farmers and herders against a backdrop of asymmetric threats in Mali and Burkina Faso,* Dakar-Fann: Senegal https://library.fes.de/pdf-files/bueros/fes-pscc/14174.pdf.

Hussein, K., Sumberg, J., & Seddon, D. 1999. 'Increasing violent conflict between herders and farmers in Africa: Claims and evidence', *Development Policy Review*, 17, pp. 397–418.

Ibrahim, B., Karambiri, H., Polcher, J., Yacouba, H., & Ribstein, P. 2014. 'Changes in rainfall regime over Burkina Faso under the climate change conditions simulated by 5 regional climate models', *Climate Dynamics*, 42, 1363–1381.

Krätli, S., and Toulmin, C. 2020. *Farmer-herder conflict in sub-Saharan Africa,* International Institute for Environment and Development (IIED), available at https://www.iied.org/sites/default/files/pdfs/2021-01/10208IIED.pdf

Lèye, B., Zouré, C. O., Yonaba, R., & Karambiri, H. 2021. Water resources in the Sahel and adaptation of agriculture to climate change: Burkina Faso.

In Climate change and water resources in Africa: Perspectives and solutions towards an imminent water crisis (pp. 309–331).

Ministry of Environment, Green Economy and Climate Change. 2021. *Evaluation of Burkina Faso's national climate change adaptation plan (NAP) 2015-2020: Final report*, available at https://napglobalnetwork.org/wp-content/uploads/2021/10/napgn-en-2021-evaluation-burkina-faso-nap-2015-2020.pdf

MRA. 2009. National survey on livestock numbers. Statistical directory of the livestock sector. Directorate of Animal Statistics of Burkina Faso.

Prindex, 2020. 'MEL study: Small farmer and pastoralist land rights in Burkina Faso', https://www.prindex.net/data/burkina-faso-deep-dive/

Quaye, W., Adofo, K., Buckman, E. S., Frempong, G., Jongerden, J., & Ruivenkamp, G. 2011. 'A socio-economic assessment of cowpea diversity on the Ghanaian market: Implications for breeding', *International Journal of Consumer Studies*, 35 (6), pp. 679–687.

Reliefweb, 2012. 'Preventing conflict between farmers and herders', https://reliefweb.int/report/burkina-faso/preventing-conflict-between-farmers-and-herders

Sarr, B., Atta, S., Ly, M., Slack, S., Ourback, T. E., Subsol, S. E., & George, D. A. 2015. 'Adapting to climate variability and change in smallholder farming communities: A case study from Burkina Faso, Chad and Niger', *Journal of Agricultural Extension and Rural Development*, 7 (1), pp. 16–27.

UNECA, 2019. 'Exploring farmer-herder conflicts in the West African Sahel: A multi-country study of Burkina Faso, Niger and Nigeria', https://archive.uneca.org/sites/default/files/uploaded-documents/CLPA/2019/Papers/Land-migration-and-regional-insecurity-nexus/herders_amp_farmers_conflict-edited_1.pdf

UNOWAS, 2019. *Pastoralism and security in West Africa and the Sahel: Towards peaceful coexistence*, Dakar: UNOWAS https://unowas.unmissions.org/sites/default/files/rapport_pastoralisme_eng-april_2019_-_online.pdf.

West, C. T., Roncoli, C., & Ouattara, F. 2008. 'Local perceptions and regional climate trends on the central plateau of Burkina', *Land Degradation and Development*,https://doi.org/10.1002/ldr.842.

World Bank, 2014. *Pastoralism and development in the Sahel: A road to stability?* Washington, D.C: Global Centre on Conflict, Security and Development.

Zampaligré, N., Dossa, L. H., & Schlecht, E. 2013 'Climate change and variability: Perception and adaptation strategies of pastoralists and agro-pastoralists across different zones of Burkina Faso', *Regional Environmental Change*, 13 (5), pp. 18–38.

CHAPTER 4

Managing Herder-Farmer Conflicts in Donga Mantung Division of the North West Region of Cameroon

Aloysius Nyuymengka Ngalim

Introduction

Sub-Saharan Africa faces various threats to peace and security partly due to conflicts arising from different circumstances and influences. Among other factors, the competition over scarce resources between pastoralist herders and farmers has resulted in recurrent and growing violence in terms of frequency, intensity, and geographic scope. This is especially the case in the North West of Cameroon, where the conflict has been complicated by ethnic, cultural, land, and natural resource issues. Most of the existing studies on farmer-herder conflicts have focused mainly on the causes and consequences of the problem and have given little attention to the role of non-state actors in managing the conflicts (Breuer, 2018; DeStefano and DeCanio, 2012; Little et al., 2004 and Homer-Dixon,

A. N. Ngalim (✉)
Department of History and African Civilizations, Faculty of Arts, University of Buea, Buea, Cameroon
e-mail: angalim2001@yahoo.co.uk; ngalim.aloysius@ubuea.cm

J. S. Omotola (ed.), *Herder-Farmer Conflicts in Africa*,
https://doi.org/10.1007/978-3-031-80821-0_4

1991). These studies all provide valuable insights into the causes and consequences of farmer-herder conflicts. However, their focus on state-centered approaches underscores the need for further research exploring the potential of non-state actors. This is because non-state actors are crucial for understanding the changing dynamics of the African farmer-herder conflicts. This study examines how farmer-herder conflicts are managed in Donga Mantung Division, one of the hotspots in the North West Region of Cameroon. The study explores how different stakeholders manage farmer-herder conflicts and what lessons can be drawn for sustainable peace. To do so, the study will first review the general characteristics and manifestations of the farmer-herder conflicts.

Study Area, Data and Methods

The study was conducted in Donga Mantung Division of the North West Region of Cameroon, focusing on communities from Binjeng, Nkfusang, Njema, Binka, Mbot, and Nwa, as well as Wat Sehn Wowo, Ntumbaw, Binshua, Nkambe, Mbipgo, Mbongon, Mbansang, and Kunchep. These communities were selected due to their status as major agro-pastoral production zones and conflict hotspots. The study involved major NGOs that participated in the peacebuilding process after the conflicts, including the Catholic NGO (Peace and Justice Commission), the Africa Institute for Economic and Social Development (INADE), the Netherlands Development Organization (SNV), the Mbororo Social and Cultural Development Association (MBOSCUDA), Heifer Project International (HPI) Cameroon, Community Human Rights and Advocacy Centre (CHRAC), Society for Initiatives in Rural Development and Environmental Protection (SIRDEP), Ecumenical Mission for Peace and Development Foundation (EMPED-Foundation), and Swiss Association for Development (HELVETAS) Cameroon.

The study employed a descriptive methodology, using both quantitative and qualitative approaches. Fieldwork was conducted between September 2018 and February 2019, involving the distribution of 130 questionnaires, with 100 validly returned and analyzed. Additionally, Key Informant Interviews (KIIs) and Life Histories (LHs) were conducted with 60 principal actors selected purposively and via snowball sampling techniques. These actors included herders, farmers, cattle owners, civil society organizations, traditional rulers, community leaders, security forces, government functionaries, politicians, and community members.

Six focus group discussions (FGDs) were also conducted with different stakeholder groups to elicit their views and experiences on the conflict and its management.

Data analysis utilized a triangulation of qualitative and quantitative methods, including the use of Statistical Package for Social Sciences (SPSS), version 20.0, for descriptive statistics such as frequencies and percentages, as well as the transcription, coding, and thematic analysis of FGDs and KII interview data from audio recordings.

Socio-demographic characteristics of the 100 respondents from Donga Mantung Division were as follows: 62% were male, with the majority aged between 35 and 54 (65%), and most had completed primary education (42%). The main occupations were farming (32%) and herding (27%). The distribution of respondents across various villages showed that Binka (12%), Nkambe (12%), and Mbongon (11%) were the most represented, while Mbot (1%), Nwa (2%), Sehn (2%), Wowo (2%), and Ntumbaw (2%) were the least represented. Furthermore, 88% of respondents had lived in their area for five years or more, suggesting a relatively stable residential population.

Presentation and Discussion of Findings

General Traits of Farmer-Herder Relations

This section briefly examines the general situation of farmer-herder relations in Donga Mantung Division. It was measured on a five-point Likert scale having items like Strongly Disagree (SD), Disagree (D), Undecided (U), Agree (A), and Strongly Agree (SA).

The study findings indicate a consensus among respondents regarding the significance of herder-farmer conflicts as a major security threat in Africa, with all respondents (100%) strongly agreeing with this notion. This aligns with existing literature that highlights the growing concern over the impact of such conflicts on regional stability and development (Adano, 2018; Idris, 2016). Additionally, most respondents (93%) acknowledged the emergence of new characteristics in recent conflicts, such as increased frequency, magnitude, intensity, and consequences. This finding resonates with studies that suggest a worsening trend in herder-farmer conflicts, attributed to factors like population growth, climate change, and resource scarcity (Verdier et al., 2020; Ogunrotifa, 2017). Furthermore, the study reveals a strong perception (72% of respondents) that these conflicts pose a significant threat to the peace and development of Donga Mantung Division. This perception is supported by scholarly works emphasizing the destabilizing impact of such conflicts on local communities and broader societal cohesion (Moritz, 2010). Additionally, the dominance of state actors in conflict management efforts was widely recognized by respondents (85%). This finding reflects a common critique in the literature, highlighting the need for more inclusive and participatory approaches involving non-state actors.

In summary, the study's findings underscore the gravity of herder-farmer conflicts in Donga Mantung Division, aligning with scholarly views on the complexity and multifaceted nature of these conflicts. The findings also point to the need for comprehensive and inclusive strategies that address the root causes of the conflicts and involve a diverse range of stakeholders in conflict management efforts.

The Overview and Manifestation of the Farmer Herder Crisis

This section analyzes the trends and patterns of farmer-herder conflicts in Donga Mantung Division. The competition over scarce grazing land and other resources has resulted in recurrent and escalating violent conflicts between farmers and herders in Donga Mantung Division of the North West Region of Cameroon. The conflicts have increased in frequency, intensity, and geographic scope over the years. Figure 4.1 shows an estimate of farmer-herder conflicts in Donga Mantung Division between 1995 and 2017. However, official statistics on the incidences of violence are scarce, and most of the information on the conflict dynamics was obtained from the local farmers and herders themselves.

Figure 4.1 shows the number of farmer-herder conflicts in Donga Mantung Division from 1995 to 2017, based on various sources (Nchinda et al., 2014: 20–21). The sources reported about 2081 conflicts in this period, but this may be an underestimate as many cases were not documented or reported thus no access to reliable data. The conflicts also involved Nigerian farmers and herders who crossed the border to Cameroon and competed with the locals for land and water resources. They sometimes caused damage, theft, and violence to the Cameroonian farmers and herders (Mbih, 2020: 10). Moreover, the Aku pastoralists from Nigeria who fled the Mambila Highlands due to the violent farmer-herder crisis settled in the Mbaw plains in the early 2000s. They often

Fig. 4.1 Estimates of Farmers-Grazier Conflicts in Donga Mantung Division, 1995–2017 (*Source* Ngwani Awudu. 2016. The Impact of Environmental Change on The Mbororo Ethnic Group of The Mbum Plateau, North West Region of Cameroon. M.Sc. Thesis, Department of Geography, University of Buea, Cameroon; Divisional and Sub-Divisional Officers of Nkambe and Ndu

clashed with the villagers over crop damage and encroachment into farmlands and transhumance zones, hampering agro-pastoral activities in the area (Mbih, 2020: 10–11).

The above information shows that farmer-grazier conflicts have a long history between the two communities. However, the conflict worsened as from 2018 due to the ongoing Anglophone crisis or the Ambazonian War of Independence, which started in 2016 (see Kindzeka, 2022; Foute, 2020: 1; Hazbun, 2020; Wanchia, (n.d.) The conflict escalated in severity, with the crisis reaching a peak in 2017. However, due to underestimation by sources, the true extent of the conflicts remains unclear, as many cases were not documented or reported, resulting in a lack of access to reliable data. The secessionist militia accused the Mbororo Fulani of being allies of the Cameroonian army and attacked them. The Mbororo Fulani fought back and launched several raids against the local farmers. In February 2020, they attacked the Ngarbuh community in Nwa, Donga-Mantung Division, and killed over 21 people, including pregnant women and children, and destroyed property. The government exploited the local conflicts and labeled the native communities as pro-separatists. The government also promised the Mbororo Fulani land rights and status improvement if they helped fight the secessionists. Armed with megaphones, machetes, and other weapons, the Fulani herders carried out over a dozen raids against the Nwa villages in 2019. The Fulani raids on the Nwa natives were allegedly retaliation for the separatist attacks on the Fulani and their cattle. The Fulani fled to Nigeria and the Adamawa region in North Cameroon and recruited their kin to fight back. The Nwa community faced attacks from three directions: Nigeria, Adamawa, and Nwa Central Town (Mbih, 2020: 10).

Fulani herders launched a series of raids on Nwa Sub-division villages in early 2021. On January 31, 2021, Fulani herders launched a violent attack on Ngung village, resulting in the murder of an elderly man. Additionally, one villager was shot, and his wife was sexually assaulted. The attackers also singled out a Baptist Church, expelling worshippers and setting the structure ablaze. Similar assaults were carried out on churches in Rom, Ngang, and Mbak Mfe. On February 18, 2020, in Mfe village, an 88-year-old woman and her daughter were ambushed by Fulani herders. The daughter sustained stab wounds while attempting to defend her mother, who tragically succumbed to her injuries. On February 22, 2021, Nyang and Ntong villages were besieged by Fulani herders who set homes ablaze and killed two elderly men. Between February 22 and 27, 2021, the region experienced significant displacement and casualties. Approximately 4,200 individuals were uprooted from various villages in Nwa Subdivision. Many sought refuge in neighboring areas within the region, while others crossed into Nigeria. The exact number of refugees in Nigeria remains unknown. By February 27, 2021, three churches and around 100 houses had been destroyed and looted. However, the actual extent of the destruction is likely greater, as many villages are deserted, and comprehensive assessments are still ongoing. The number of injuries sustained during displacement has not yet been documented (Centre for Human Rights and Democracy in Africa, n.d). Many people fled to nearby villages in Nwa and Nkambe sub-divisions or to Nigeria. In Mamba Kungi, only non-Mbororo Fulani graziers were allowed to graze cattle. In 2001, a Bessa corpse was found at the river Kinken bordering the Misaje and Ako sub-divisions (Pelican, 2017:123). According to Jabiru Mohammadou Adamou, a Fulani elite, the conflict has a long history since the British colonial era (See Njeuma & Awasom, 1990; Nchinda et al., 2014; Ngalim, 2015a, Ngalim, 2015b; Foute, 2020, Tem, 2021). This section has shown the events and impacts of farmer-herder conflicts in Donga Mantung Division. The next section will explore the causes of the conflicts.

The Causes of Herder-Farmer Conflicts

This section examines the various factors that contribute to the emergence and escalation of farmer-herder conflicts in the North West of Cameroon. Farmer-herder relations in the North West of Cameroon have been marked by conflicts, especially after independence, due to changes in modes of production, environmental conditions, and demographic pressures. These factors have been exacerbated by security threats, displacement and relocation, increased deaths, destruction of farmland, deaths of cattle, and reduced co-existence between herders and sedentary pastoralists. Donga Mantung Division has witnessed violent clashes between local farmers and Mbororo Fulani herders, like those reported in other parts of the Region, Central Africa, West Africa, and the Sahel (Sulieman, 2018; Mercy Corps, 2015; Tonah, 2008; Tonah, 2005; Wilson, 1984). The causes of these conflicts are complex and multifaceted, and often include: incessant encroachment into farmland and destruction of crops by Fulani cattle; invasion of pastoral land; lack of resource demarcation; cattle rustling; competition over natural resources, land-use rights, and access; land grab by the elite; ethnic cleavages; contamination of water bodies; chemical weeding; poor regulatory frameworks; lack of appropriate institutions; inverted governance of resources and the conflicts; and corrupt state mediators, judiciary and security forces (Brottem, 2021; Bukari, 2017: 26; International Crisis Group, 2017; Ngwoh, 2014; Cordes, 2013; Blench, 1994; Moritz, 2010; Shettima & Tar, 2008; Ngalim, 2006; Tonah, 2000: 557; Spencer, 2000: 19–22; Harshbarger, 1995: 63; Homer-Dixon, 1994).

Fieldwork conducted in Donga Mantung paints a stark picture of the factors fueling farmer-herder conflicts in the region. A staggering 98% of respondents identified environmental scarcity as a major culprit, alongside competition for dwindling resources. This scarcity is further exacerbated by poor land management practices, as evidenced by the strong agreement (84%) on this issue as a driver of conflict. The data reveals a complex web of contributing factors. A lack of clear regulations regarding land use (69% strongly agreed) creates a breeding ground for disputes. The relationship between farmers and herders themselves is also identified as a critical factor, with a unanimous recognition of this tension. Interestingly, the encroachment on grazing routes by farmers, often cited as a source of conflict, received only moderate support (69%). This suggests a deeper layer to the issue, where competition for resources takes center stage.

Additionally, the abuse of social media and the spread of misinformation were not perceived as major triggers (24% agreed).

These findings resonate with wider research on farmer-herder conflicts across the Sahel region. Climate change, deforestation, and unsustainable land use practices are identified by scholars like Burkari (2022) and De Haan et al. (2016) as key contributors to resource scarcity, ultimately leading to violent clashes. This situation is further complicated by the lack of enforcement or ineffective implementation of existing pastoral laws. Benjaminsen et al. (2012) and Ba & Benjaminsen (2009) highlight the link between weak regulatory frameworks and increased communal violence. While countries like Cameroon have established legal codes, their application remains patchy across the Sahel (De Haan et al., 2016). The qualitative data, gleaned from focus group discussions with local communities, sheds further light on the specific triggers in Donga Mantung. Here, competition for space – grazing versus crop cultivation – emerges as a central theme. The movement of pastoralists during dry seasons, population growth leading to land use changes, and uncontrolled grazing by young herders all contribute to tensions. Furthermore, participants highlighted the corrosive impact of a compromised justice system, with accusations of delayed and corrupt practices among judiciary and security personnel. Incidents like cattle deaths from poisoned pastures and herd encroachment causing crop damage further escalate tensions. This aligns with observations made by Benjaminsen et al. (2012), Schilling et al. (2010), and Gaye (2018) regarding the Sahel region.

In summary, the data paints a concerning picture of a "perfect storm" brewing in Donga Mantung. Multiple variables, from environmental degradation to social dynamics, contribute to a hostile environment between farmers and herders. These factors have intensified conflicts with tragic consequences, including fatalities and stunted rural development. The next section delves into the existing mechanisms for managing these conflicts and assesses their effectiveness in mitigating these tensions.

Management of Herder-Farmer Conflicts

In the management of herder-farmer conflicts in Donga Mantung Division, various actors play distinct roles, facing several constraints. Traditional chiefs, community elders, cattle owners, opinion leaders, and farmer associations, as local actors, are crucial in conflict resolution. They provide insights into local dynamics and traditional conflict resolution mechanisms. However, their effectiveness is hindered by limited resources and capacity, especially in handling complex, escalated conflicts. Government officials, including the police, assembly members, and agricultural officials, are also involved. The government's performance in conflict management has been deemed unsatisfactory by 92.0% of respondents due to poor responses to early warning signals (39.0% strongly agreed, 60.0% agreed) and the failure to arrest and prosecute offenders (25.0% strongly agreed, 65.0% agreed). Additionally, 45.0% strongly agreed and 55.0% agreed that poor regulatory frameworks hindered conflict resolution efforts. The politicization and ethnicization of conflicts further complicate management efforts, with 30.0% strongly agreeing and 63.0% agreeing that these factors make conflict management difficult.

Secondary sources and interviews highlight the involvement of both state and non-state actors in managing conflicts. The government, through the Agro-Pastoral Commission, is officially responsible for conflict mitigation. However, its top-down approach has been criticized for its ineffectiveness, with increasing unresolved conflicts causing economic and social challenges. Local communities distrust the government due to perceived political support for cattle owners and Fulani herders, eroding trust in the state's mediation role (Kinsam, 2021: 137; Ngalim, 2006: 122). They are suspicious of the government because of perceived political support for cattle owners and Fulani herders. Elfversson (2013: 4) argues that the state is not often trusted as a mediator or third party because of favouritism towards either party. In Tanzania's Morogoro region, research by Rweyemamu (2019) highlights a paradox. Agropastoralists, despite being a minority, possess a greater capacity to bribe officials due to their livestock wealth. This advantage is strategically used to compensate for their lack of political influence. These findings are corroborated by Benjaminsen et al. (2009: 423–445) and Mwamfupe (2015: 2), who similarly report widespread corruption among officials in Morogoro regarding land acquisition. Olaniyan et al. (2015)provide a compelling example from Ghana's Agogo state. There, an expulsion policy targeting Fulani herders failed due to their ability to bribe local chiefs for permission to occupy village lands. Brottem (2021) emphasizes the corrosive impact of such practices. When accusations of corruption taint state institutions tasked with conflict mitigation, trust in the entire process evaporates.

Non-state actors, such as CSOs, CBOs, and NGOs, have stepped in to facilitate peacebuilding. For example, CHRAC organized workshops in Nwa sub-division to foster a culture of peace and mutual dependence between farmers and herders. Joshua Kwai, the CHRAC project coordinator, said that peace, collaboration, and cohabitation were essential for prosperity, as farming and herding complement each other. He added that this required trust and respect among the communities (Yufenyu, 2010). In Binshua, Nkambe Central Sub-Division, and Misaje Sub-Division, the SNV helped create dialogue platforms where graziers, crop farmers, and traditional rulers could peacefully resolve conflicts and plan for an integrated crop-livestock system (Kinsam, 2021). The ISCG project trained MBOSCUDA to promote Mbororo rights and community-based organizations to provide paralegal services to the communities. Ballotiral conducted seminars on farmer-herder conflict awareness and transformation in Nkambe in 2001 (Pelican, 2017: 123). Village Aid projects set up Dialogue Platforms (DPs) to prevent violent conflict between crop farming and cattle grazing communities by encouraging them to discuss issues such as cattle grazing, crops, or water supplies before they worsen (Village Aid, 2015).

Our focus group discussions highlighted shifting dynamics and the influence of environmental changes, urban expansion, and population growth on conflicts. Participants noted that community-led dialogues, agricultural partnerships, and dialogue platforms (DPs) have played a role in mitigating conflicts and fostering collaboration between farmers and herders. During these intimate sessions, we explored the experiences of women, men, and young people, revealing a multifaceted landscape of aspirations, challenges, and dreams. Participants expressed that:

> The hostility between farmers and herders can be reduced through community-driven dialogue. The main institutions here were Village Management Committees (VMCs), composed of elected community members representing the main user groups interested in farmer-herder relationships. To support collaborative management, villages were grouped into clusters. Cluster Platforms (CPs) were formed to enhance community participation and facilitate information exchange for a dialogue. We used to live like relatives, and we want to do so again. Farming alliances have recently reduced land conflicts and their intensity. Trust and confidence are growing between farmers and pastoralists. This cooperation allows us to access fertile lands and livestock feed peacefully. Another beneficial innovation is the DPs, which have saved us money that would have been spent

> on litigation and other costs. This capital accumulation has encouraged us to improve our pastures and invest in other socio-economic activities, spreading risk. Many local communities have established DPs in their areas, and MBOSCUDA has trained them in mediation and conflict resolution techniques. This compassionate approach enables exchange visits between the communities, where they share experiences that can foster positive peace and development.

However, challenges persist, such as corruption within the police and Gendarmerie, which encourages bad behavior among herdsmen who believe they can bribe their way out of offenses. The judicial system is also seen as ineffective, expensive, and corrupt, contributing to the escalation of conflicts. In the face of corrupt civil servants and powerful graziers who swayed the courts with bribes (Harshbarger, 1995: 63; Ngalim, 2006: 122), farmers found themselves at a disadvantage in state courts. Litigation was a highly undesirable option for resolving conflict: expensive, riddled with corruption, slow, and ultimately ineffective (Ngalim, 2006: 122). As Bukari (2017: 234) argues, courts were incompatible with the bottom-up approach that fostered peace and consensus between farmers and herders. Fieldwork also highlights the bias inherent in state actors. Bassett's (1988: 453–472) observations on the Farmer-Grazier Commission in Cameroon exemplify this. Residents, particularly farmers, perceived the state as favouring the Mbororo Fulani graziers (Bassett, 1988: 453–472). Furthermore, state intervention was reactionary, occurring only after conflicts erupted. This, as Nader & Todd (1978: 22–23) point out, constitutes "slow access is no access." Consequently, from the farmers' and herders' perspectives, state failure manifested as a lack of clear legislation governing cattle rearing and the absence of effective measures to prevent and resolve violent conflicts. Traditional institutions' diminishing powers, especially over the Mbororo Fulani, further complicate conflict resolution efforts. Thus Brockhaus (2005) concluded that there was much evidence of the institutional failure of traditional authorities across West Africa regarding herder-farmer conflict.

In managing herder-farmer conflicts, a multifaceted endeavor involving numerous actors, significant hurdles persist. These challenges include shortcomings in government performance, a lack of sufficient resources, and the ever-present issue of corruption. Despite commendable efforts by non-state actors, achieving lasting peace and sustainable development in these regions necessitates sustained support and a spirit of cooperation from all stakeholders. The next section will explore lessons learned from West African countries' experiences in dealing with herder-farmer conflicts. By examining these experiences, we can inform and inspire more inclusive, sustainable, and context-specific peacebuilding approaches across the continent.

The Lessons for Peacebuilding

Herder–farmer conflicts in the North West of Cameroon, especially in Donga Mantung Division, and other parts of Africa, are complex and multifaceted. They demand a critical review of the factors that have hampered previous peace efforts, and a reorientation of the peacebuilding approaches that can tackle the root causes of the conflicts and foster a lasting and positive peace. This is essential because peacebuilding missions have the dual task of stopping violence and preserving peace once it is achieved. Effective peacebuilding missions can create opportunities for post-conflict reconstruction that can prevent the recurrence of violence, by addressing the underlying issues that fuel conflict and building a resilient and harmonious society. The findings of the study reveal some key lessons for peacebuilding.

Results from fieldwork data show the opinions of respondents on various aspects of conflict management and peacebuilding in Donga Mantung. Most respondents (99%) agreed or strongly agreed that delays in responding to early warning signs should be avoided, while only one respondent (1%) disagreed. Similarly, most respondents (99%) agreed or strongly agreed that a clear and focused regulatory framework was needed, while only one respondent (1%) disagreed. None of the respondents chose the neutral option for these two questions. Moreover, almost all respondents (95%) supported the involvement of more non-state actors in the handling of farmer-herder relations, and more than half of them (61%) called for an effective regulation of social media space to prevent the spread of fake news that could undermine the peacebuilding process between the farmers and herdsmen. Finally, most respondents (97%) favored the synergy between state and non-state actors in the management of herder-farmer relations, while only two respondents (2%) disagreed, and one respondent (1%) was undecided.

In addition to the survey results, the interviews and FGDs revealed other important lessons for peacebuilding, especially regarding grazing arrangements. The participants suggested that the state actors, from the national to the sub-district level, should collaborate with the traditional authorities to survey, demarcate, and officially document the existing grazing reserves that have not been encroached on by human settlements and infrastructure. They also recommended that the MINEPIA should establish new grazing reserves in all the Divisions and Sub-Divisions of the North West Region, following the model of the International Fund for Agricultural Development (IFAD), which has funded three or more reserves in Sokoto state of Nigeria. Furthermore, they proposed that alternative modes of grazing, such as ranching and zero grazing, should be adopted instead of uncontrolled open grazing, which has increased the conflict between farmers and herdsmen, given the continuous growth of human and livestock populations.

Price (2020: 2) argued that interventions to address farmer-herder conflicts should be based on a sound understanding of pastoralism and should challenge the negative stereotypes of pastoralists as insecure and backward. Both farmers and herders expressed the need for local platforms that could investigate, negotiate, and resolve conflicts without bias or prejudice. They also emphasized the role of traditional organizations that could collaborate with the government, especially where there is legitimacy, fairness, and respect for the rule of law. However, they also urged the traditional rulers to avoid partisan politics and partiality in dispensing justice. Moreover, they appealed to all stakeholders to communicate through non-state organizations (CSOs, CBOs, NGOs) and their traditional rulers to harmonize and prioritize community needs in conducive environments. For example, in the Misaje sub-division in Donga Mantung Division, the traditional council is the main mechanism for conflict resolution, while only cases of mass crop damages are referred to the crop farmer grazier commission. Similarly, in Nigeria, Mercy Corps (2015) advocated for civil societies to support local mechanisms for conflict management and resolution, recognizing the influence and importance of traditional and community leaders in establishing peace, security, and stability across communities. Therefore, there is a need to foster community dialogue and strengthen traditional conflict prevention mechanisms to resolve herder-farmer disputes. In addition, best practices that promote peaceful coexistence and cooperation between farmers and graziers should be encouraged and replicated. These include alliance farming, dialogue platforms, night paddocking, and pasture improvement programs. Exchange visits could be organized to facilitate the learning and sharing of these practices among different communities.

The Donga Mantung Division of Cameroon faces complex challenges in managing conflicts between farmers and herders. Here's a roadmap for sustainable peacebuilding.

Proactive Measures

- Early Warning, Early Action: Delays in responding to early warning signs should be avoided, as they can escalate tensions. Establishing effective mechanisms for early detection and response can prevent conflicts from worsening. Swift responses are vital. Train community members to identify early warning signs and report them promptly.
- Clear Rules, Shared Understanding: Develop a transparent and well-defined legal framework for managing interactions between farmers and herders. This framework should outline clear regulations on land use, grazing rights, and dispute resolution procedures. Ensure all stakeholders understand their rights and responsibilities.
- Broadening the Tent: Integrate a wider range of actors into conflict management. Involve NGOs, civil society organizations, and traditional authorities alongside government agencies. Community-driven initiatives like Village Management Committees (VMCs) and Cluster Platforms (CPs) foster dialogue, build trust, and offer inclusive solutions.
- Combating Misinformation: Curb the spread of fake news on social media platforms. Misinformation can rapidly inflame tensions and derail peacebuilding efforts. Advocate for responsible social media use and explore options, as suggested in the field research (61% support), for regulating social media to prevent the spread of inflammatory content.

Collaboration for Peace

- State and Non-State Synergy: Foster strong collaboration between state and non-state actors. This allows for the pooling of resources, expertise, and networks. Combined efforts lead to more comprehensive and sustainable solutions for conflict prevention and resolution.

- Community Ownership: Establish inclusive and participatory forums for honest dialogue and conflict management at the community level. Empower local leaders to take ownership of peacebuilding efforts. These platforms should enable them to reach agreements on resource sharing, define grazing routes and plowing areas, and develop localized dispute resolution mechanisms in partnership with local authorities.

Addressing Root Causes

- Security and Stability: Ensure timely and adequate deployment of well-equipped security agents in conflict zones. Security forces should be impartial, responsive, and motivated to prevent violence and resolve conflicts effectively. A careful and gradual withdrawal strategy is crucial to avoid a security vacuum.
- Depoliticization: Promote sincere cooperation among all stakeholders to reduce the politicization of conflicts. Focus on local forms of dispute resolution and reconciliation to foster a climate of community recognition and understanding.
- Resource Management: Address underlying resource scarcity issues. Provide access to clean and safe drinking water points for both humans and livestock. Review land tenure policies to guarantee the security of land tenure for all parties involved.

Building a Sustainable Future

- Empowering Women: Recognize the crucial role women play in peacebuilding. Empower women and actively involve them in peacebuilding initiatives.
- Education for Peace: Introduce curriculum on conflict resolution, particularly farmer-herder conflicts, at all educational levels. Promote nomadic education where applicable to equip future generations with the skills and knowledge for peaceful coexistence.

By implementing this multi-faceted approach, Donga Mantung Division can move towards a future where collaboration and understanding replace conflict. This framework addresses the root causes of tension, fosters inclusive participation, and promotes peaceful solutions for a thriving future for all.

Conclusion

In conclusion, this paper has examined the causes, consequences, and responses to farmer-herder conflict in the Donga Mantung Division of the North West Region of Cameroon. It has shown that the conflict is complex and multifaceted, involving historical, socio-economic, political, environmental, and cultural factors. It has also shown that the conflict has negative impacts on the livelihoods, security, and social cohesion of both farmers and herders, as well as the development and stability of the region. The paper has highlighted the various efforts made by state and non-state actors to manage and resolve the conflict, such as dialogue platforms, alliance farming units, agro-pastoral commissions, early warning, and response systems, etc. However, it has also identified some of the challenges and gaps that hinder the effectiveness of these responses, such as lack of adequate resources, coordination, participation, accountability, enforcement, etc. The paper has argued that there is a need to assess the effectiveness of these responses within the broader context of the state's responsibility to protect its citizens, as well as the ability of communities to build or strengthen their management of local conflicts. The paper has also suggested some lessons for peacebuilding between farmers and herders in Donga Mantung Division, such as providing access to clean and safe water points for humans and livestock, reviewing and updating land policy and legislation to ensure security of land tenure for all, aligning land and livestock policies and bylaws to avoid more conflicts, controlling the local manufacture/fabrication and civilian possession of arms in line with the Convention on Small Arms and Light Weapons, strengthening and supporting the Regional and National Early Warning and Response System and indicators on Transhumance and Conflicts, reinforcing the role and contribution of women in peacebuilding and development, introducing curriculum on conflicts at all levels of education (Nursery to University), creating and reinforcing nomadic education where necessary, etc. The paper has concluded that despite the protracted nature and character of the conflicts between farmers and herders in Donga Mantung Division, there is a desire between the Mbororo Fulani and farmers to reclaim their symbiotic past. This desire can be harnessed by providing full support to state and non-state actors who are working to prevent violence between farmers and herders in Donga Mantung Division and elsewhere in the North West Region of Cameroon.

This paper serves to consolidate the responses to farmer-herder conflict in the Donga Mantung Division of the North West Region of Cameroon. Despite the protracted nature and character of the conflicts between farmers and herders in Donga Mantung Division, efforts have been made to address the rising tensions. Despite these efforts, challenges remain. From this review, there is a clear need to assess the effectiveness of these responses within the broader context of the state's responsibility to protect its citizens, as well as the ability of communities to build or strengthen their management of local conflicts. In Donga Mantung Division, farmers and herders have had relationships that were synergetic, reciprocal, and mutually beneficial for large periods in the history of the Region. The collapse of social, economic, and political relations between the two groups in recent times especially within the Anglophone crisis has made conflicts between the herders and farmers more violent and dangerous. Despite the violence, fieldwork interviews and discussions reveal that there is a desire between the Mbororo Fulani and farmers to reclaim the symbiotic past. This is epitomized in the soaring numbers of dialogue platforms and alliance farming units in the Donga Mantung division and elsewhere in the North West Region of Cameroon. Views sampled from the various stakeholders suggested that with the full support of state and non-state actors, violence between farmers and herders can be prevented.

Acknowledgement This study was made possible by support from the Social Sciences Research Council's African Peacebuilding Network research grant with funds provided by the Carnegie Corporation of New York.

References

Adano, W. R. 2018. Herders-farmers Conflicts in East Africa: A Review of the Literature. *African Security Studies*, 27 (2), 45–62.

Bassett, Thomas. 1988. The Political Ecology of Peasant-Herder Conflicts in the Northern Ivory Coast. *Annals of the Association of American Geographers*, 78 (3), 453–472.

Benjaminsen, Tor. A & Ba, Boubacar. 2009. "Farmer–herder Conflicts, Pastoral Marginalisation and Corruption: A Case Study from the Inland Niger Delta of Mali." *The Geographical* Journal, 175 (1), 71–81.

Benjaminsen, Tor, Maganga, Faustin, and Abdallah, Jumanne Moshi. 2009. The Kilosa Killings: Political Ecology of a Farmer–Herder Conflict in Tanzania. *Development and Change*, 40 (3): 423–445. https://doi.org/10.1111/j.1467-7660.2009. 01558.x.

Benjaminsen Tor, Alinon Koffi, Buhaug Halvard., and Buseth Jill Tove. 2012. Does Climate Change Drive Land-use Conflicts in the Sahel? *Journal of Peace Research*, 49(1), 97–111. https://doi.org/10.1177/0022343311427343.

Blench, Roger. 1994. "The Expansion and Adaptation of Fulbe Pastoralism to Subhumid and Humid Conditions in Nigeria." *Cahiers d'Études Africaines*, 133–135, XXXIV (1–3), 197–212.

Breuer, Anita. 2018. "Climate Change and Conflict: Evidence from Bossaso, Somalia." *Journal of Peace Research*, 55 (3), 347–362.

Brockhaus, M. (2005). Potentials and Obstacles in the Arena of Conflict and Natural Resource Management: A Case Study on Conflicts, *Institutions and Policy Networks in Burkina Faso.* Cuvillier Verlag.

Brottem, Leif. 2021. "The Growing Complexity of Farmer Herder Conflict in West and Central Africa." *Africa Security Brief*. No. 39.

Bukari, K. N. 2017. Farmer-Herder Relations in Ghana: Interplay of Environmental Change, Conflict, Cooperation and Social Networks. PhD Dissertation, George-August University of Gottingen.

Bukari, Kaderi Noagah. 2022. "Violent Farmer–herder Conflicts in Ghana: Constellation of Actors, Citizenship Contestations, Land Access and Politics." *Canadian Journal of African Studies.* https://doi.org/10.1080/00083968.2022.2031235.

Centre for Human Rights and Democracy in Africa (CHRDA). The Fulani Problem in the North West Region of Cameroon. https://www.chrda.org/wp-content/uploads/2021/04/THE-FULANI-PROBLEM-IN-THE-NWR-AS-2-Beri-1.pdf.

Cordes, Kaitlin. 2013. "Cameroon Pastoralists Fight for their Way of Life." *Think Africa Press*. https://ccsi.columbia.edu/sites/default/files/content/docs/publications/CORDES_cameroon.pdf.

De Haan, Cees, Etienne Dubern, Bernard Garancher, and Catalina Quintero. 2016. Pastoralism Development in the Sahel: A Road to Stability? (Washington, DC: World Bank, 2016). http://documents.worldbank.org/curated/en/586291468193771160/Pastoralism-development-in-the-Sa-hel-a-road-to-stability.

DeStefano, Anthony L., and Stephen J. DeCanio. 2012. "The Economic Geography of Conflict: Agriculture and Livestock in the Sahel." *Journal of Development Studies*, 48 (2), 295–314.

Elfversson, Emma. 2013. "Third Parties, the State, and Communal Conflict Resolution: A Comparative Study of Evidence from Kenya." Paper Presented at the Thomas Ohlson Memorial Conference, Uppsala, April 18–20.

Foute, Frank. 2020. "Cameroon: The Tense Relationship between Fulani and Anglophones." *The Africa Report*. https://www.theafricareport.com/34308/cameroon-the-tense-relationship-between-fulani-and-anglophones/.

Gaye, Serigne Bamba. 2018. *Conflicts Between Farmers and Herders Against a Backdrop of Asymmetric Threats in Mali and Burkina Faso*. Dakar: Friedrich-Ebert-Stiftung.

Harshbarger, Camilla Lyn. 1995. "Farmer-Herder Conflict and State Legitimacy in Cameroon." DPhil thesis, University of Florida. 63

Hazbun, Claire. 2020. "Cameroon's NWSW Crisis Ignites New Fault Line of Conflict." https://www.refugeesinternational.org/reports/2020/4/6/cameroons-nwsw-crisis-ignites-new-fault-line-of-conflict.

Homer-Dixon, Thomas. 1994. "Environmental Scarcities and Violent Conflict: Evidence from Cases." *International Security*, 19 (1), 5–40.

Homer-Dixon, Thomas F. 1991. "Environmental Scarcity and Violent Conflict: Evidence from Chiapas, Mexico." *International Security*, 16 (1), 76–108.

Idris, A. B. 2016. Conflict Management Strategies in Herders-farmers Conflicts: A Case Study of Nigeria. *Journal of Peace and Conflict Studies*, 14(3), 112–129.

International Crisis Group. 2017. "Herders Against Farmers: Nigeria's Expanding Deadly Conflict." *Africa Report* No. 252, Brussels, Belgium.

Kindzeka, Moki Emmanuel. 2022. "Cameroon Says Separatists Attack Border Mbororo Ethnic Community." *VOA*. https://www.voanews.com/a/cameroon-says-separatists-attack-border-mbororo-ethnic-community/6522238.html.

Kinsam, James et at., 2021. "Farmer-grazier Conflict Resolution Methods and Mitigation Mechanisms in Bui-Donga Mantung Divisions, North West Cameroon." *International Journal of Research and Innovation in Social Science (IJRISS)*, V (II), February 2021. ISSN 2454-6186.

Little, Peter D., Paul de Sherbinin, Arnold S. Kugelman, and Peter P. Hobbs. 2004. "On the Edge: Combining Demographic and Environmental Risks for Food Security and Conflict." *Annals of the Association of American Geographers*, 94 (1), 130–152.

Mbih, Richard Achia. 2020. The politics of Farmer–herder Conflicts and Alternative Conflict Management in Northwest Cameroon. *African Geographical Review*. https://doi.org/10.1080/19376812.2020.1720755

Mercy Corps. (2015). "The Economic Costs of Conflict and the Benefits of Peace: Effects of Farmers-Pastoralist Conflict in Nigeria's Middle Belt on State, Sector, and National Economies." Retrieved from https://www.mercycorps.org/sites/default/files/Mercy%20Corps%20Nigeria%20State%20Costs%20of%20Conflict%20Policy%20Brief%20July%202015.pdf.

Moritz, Mark. 2010. "Understanding Herder-farmer Conflicts in West Africa: Outline of a Processual Approach." *Human Organization*, (69), 2, 138–148.

Mwamfupe, Davis. 2015. "Persistence of Farmer-Herder Conflicts in Tanzania." *International Journal of Science and Research Publications*, 5(2), 2.

Nader, Laura. & Todd, Harry (eds.). 1978. *Legal Procedures: The Disputing Process: Law in Ten Societies*. New York: Columbia University Press, 22–23.

Nchinda, Valentine, Che, Marcellus, Ijang, Tata Precilia, Abubakar, Shidiki, and Chi, Napoleon. 2014. "In Search of Common Ground" for Farmer-grazer Conficts in the Northwest Region of Cameroon." https://doi.org/10.13140/2.1.1912.4163.

Ngalim, Aloysius Nyuymengka. 2006. "The Cattle Industry in the North West Province of Cameroon, 1972–2003." Ph.D Thesis, Department of History, University of Nigeria, Nsukka.

Ngalim, Aloysius Nyuymengka. 2015a. "Cattle Rearing Systems in the North-west Region of Cameroon. Historical Trends on Changing Techniques and Strategies." *Journal of Educational Policy and Entrepreneurial Research*, 2 (5), 180–182.

Ngalim, Aloysius Nyuymengka. 2015b. "Cultural Boundary Dynamics: The Aghem and Fulani of Menchum, North West Region of Cameroon, 1950–2013." *International Journal of Information Research and Review*, 2, (05), 705.

Ngwoh, Venantius Kum. (2014). "The Dynamics of Farmer-Herder Conflicts Across the Bamenda Grassfields, 1947–2006." Ph.D. Thesis, University of Buea.

Njeuma, Martin and Nicodemus Awasom. 1990. "The Fulani and the Political Economy of the Bamenda Grasslands: Opportunity and Conflict, 1940–1960." *Paideuma*, 36, 217–233.

Ogunrotifa, A. F. (2017). Climate Change and Herders-farmers Conflicts in Nigeria: A Quantitative Analysis. *Environmental Security*, 21(3), 311–328.

Olaniyan, Azeez, Michael Francis, and Ufo Okeke Uzodike. 2015. "The Cattle Are 'Ghanaians' but the Herders are Strangers: Farmer–Herder Conflict, Expulsion Policy, and Pastoralist Question in Agogo, Ghana." *African Studies Quarterly* 15 (2): 53–67.

Pelican, Michaela. 2017. "A Shift to Economic Competition? Farmer–Herder Conflict and Cattle Theft in the Misaje Area." In *Masks and Staffs: Identity Politics in the Cameroon Grassfields*. Berghahn Books, 123.

Price, Roz. 2020. "Lessons Learned in Promoting Accountability and Resolution of Natural Resource-based Conflicts in Africa." K4D Helpdesk Report 782. Brighton: Institute of Development Studies. https://opendocs.ids.ac.uk/opendocs/bitstream/handle/20.500.12413/15816/921_Promoting_accountability_and_resolution_of_natural_resource_based_conflict_in_Africa.pdf?sequence=1&isAllowed=y.

Rweyemamu, Dennis. 2019. "Understanding the Factors Leading to Conflicts among Agropastoralist and Farming Communities in Morogoro Region, Tanzania, and their Implications for Wellbeing". Unpublished PhD Thesis, Lincoln University. 75–76.

Schilling, Janpeter, Scheffran, Jürgen, and Link, Michael. 2010. "Climate Change and Land Use Conflicts in Northern Africa." *Nova Acta Leopoldina*, 112 (384), 173–182

Shettima, Abba Gana., and Tar, USman. A. 2008. "Farmer-pastoralist Conflict in West Africa: Exploring the Causes and Consequences." *Information, Society and Justice*, 1 (2), 163–184. https://doi.org/10.3734/isj.2008.1205.

Spencer, Paul. 2000. "Pastoralism and the Growth of Civilization in the Sahel: Islam, Evolution, or the Tragedy of the Commons?" In H. Sørensen et al. (eds), Natural Resources and the Muslim Traditional Culture in the Sahel-Sudan Region, 17–29. Copenhagen: University of Copenhagen (North/South Priority Research Area).

Sulieman, Hussein. 2018. Exploring the Spatio-temporal Process of Communal Rangeland Grabbing in Sudan. *Pastor. Res. Policy Pract*, 8 (14). https://doi.org/10.1186/s13570-018-0117-5.

Tem, Protus Mbeum. 2021. "Changing Legislation and Neglect of Local Government's Role in the Management of Farmer-Grazier Conflicts as Rational for the Degeneration of Crises in the Bamenda Grasslands of Cameroon." *International Journal of Research and Innovation in Social Science* (IJRISS), V (I).

Tonah, Steve. 2000. "State Policies, Local Prejudices and Cattle Rustling along the Ghana-Burkina Faso Border." *Africa* 70 (4), 551–567. https://doi.org/10.3366/afr.2000.70.4.

Tonah, Steve. 2005. "The Unholy Alliance between Chiefs and Fulani Herdsmen in the Middle Volta Basin." *Ghana Social Science Journal*, 2(1&2), 71–93.

Tonah, Steve. 2008. Migration, Resource Use Conflicts and Stakeholders in the Middle Volta Basin. In C. M. Amoah, G. S. K. Adiku, and E. O. Owusu (eds), *New Developments of Health, Agricultural Resources and Socio-economic Activities in the Volta Basin, Ghana*, 136–154. Legon Accra: Volta Basin Research Project University of Ghana.

Verdier, P., Smith, J., and Ahmed, M. (2020). Understanding the Dynamics of Herders-farmers Conflicts in Africa. *Journal of Conflict Resolution*, 36(4), 567–584.

Village Aid. 2015." Dialogue Platforms: Reducing Conflict Between Herders and Crop Farmers in North West Cameroon." *Cameroon, Programme News*. https://www.villageaid.org/dialogue-platforms-reducing-conflict-and-improving-relationship-between-herders-and-crop-farmers-in-north-west-cameroon/.

Wanchia, Cynthia (n.d.). "How Social Media Has Influenced Attacks on the Mbororo Community within the Context of the Anglophone Crisis." https://affcameroon.defyhatenow.org/how-social-media-has-influenced-attacks-on-the-mbororo-community-within-the-context-of-the-anglophone-crisis/.

Wilson, Wendy. 1984. "Resource Management in a Stratified Fulani Community." Ph.D Dissertation, Howard University, Washington, D. C.

Yufenyu, Jeff Ngawe. 2010. "Nwa Identified as Farmer/Grazier Conflict Zone." *Cameroon Postline*. https://cameroonpostline.com/nwa-identified-as-farmer grazier-conflict-zone/%E2%80%8Bp.1.

CHAPTER 5

Incidents of Farmer-Herder Conflicts in Benue State, Nigeria

Akachi Odoemene

Introduction

The so-called "farmer-herder" violent conflicts—particularly over their livelihoods which are critically dependent on reliable access to land and water—are a sub-Saharan Africa-wide phenomenon. They have not only been very pervasive in the continent, but have also become a major source of instability in the Western Sudan regions (Kwaja and Smith, 2020: 8). Within this context, however, the Nigerian case and experience have been the most virulent and deadly in the continent. In this respect, these conflicts truly represent not just "an ongoing grassroots war …between Fulani herdsmen[1] and farming communities" (Okeke, 2014: 66), but also an episodic, low-intensity conflicts particularly in the north-central and southern zones of Nigeria (Odoemene, 2017). Escalating in

[1] In this paper, "herders", "herdsmen" and "pastoralists" are used somewhat interchangeably to mean the same.

A. Odoemene (✉)
Department of History and International Studies, Federal University Otuoke, Otuoke, Bayelsa, Nigeria
e-mail: akachioo@fuotuoke.edu.ng

J. S. Omotola (ed.), *Herder-Farmer Conflicts in Africa*,
https://doi.org/10.1007/978-3-031-80821-0_5

the last decade and assuming a deadly dimension over the past five years, these conflicts easily constitute one of the greatest security risks in Nigeria (Abati, 2016; Okeke, 2014). The farmer-herder conflicts in Nigeria have become so threatening to national integration (Awotokun et al., 2020) as the country often degenerates to a carnage level leading to the wanton loss of thousands of lives and property worth millions of dollars (ICG, 2018, 2017). As Abati (2016) clearly captures the state of affairs:

> From Benue, to the Plateau, Nasarawa, to the South West, the Delta, and the Eastern parts of the country, there have been very disturbing reports of nomadic pastoralists killing at will, raping women, and sacking communities, and escaping with their impunity, unchecked, as the security agencies either look the other way or prove incapable of enforcing the law.

While these conflicts have inadvertently occurred across different parts of Nigeria, Benue state is undeniably one of the most endemic (Vanger, 2018; Omokhoa and Okuchukwu, 2018). Such incidents in the state represent some of the most vicious examples of, as well as demonstrate nuanced dimensions to the conflicts.

As with so many other places around the country, the farmer-herder crises in Benue State of Nigeria are an old age problem which has only intensified in modern times due to diverse circumstances. Its evolving violent nature has been "against the backdrop of social differences, resource scarcity, increase in the population of resource users, lack of adequate grazing reserves and poor state of the existing ones, unequal resource distribution and the consequent failure of patrimonial states" (Oladotun and Awosusi, 2019: 615–616). These erstwhile relations between farmers and herders since the pre-colonial times were noted as being largely peaceful, cordial, symbiotic, and void of unhealthy competition over scarce resources (Odoemene, 2017; Abati, 2016). However, the prevailing conflicts have thwarted the hitherto largely peaceful relationship. Thus, violent contestations, ferocious communal attacks and vicious reprisals have been rife and a prominent feature of such conflicts in Benue State since the turn of the twenty-first century (ICG, 2018, 2017). Furthermore, since the last five years or more, these conflicts have assumed very dangerous dimensions in Benue State, with the related violence increasing exponentially, both in terms of frequency, intensity and scope (FGD III, 2019; Yaro and Tobias, 2019; Li, 2018; Leme, 2017).

For a proper understanding of the nature and contexts of these conflicts, there would be need, prior to delving into the essay proper, for a dissection and interrogation of the riding notion—"farmer-herder conflicts"—which have been widely used to define the conflicts' key binary characters and actors. The idea often given off is that the conflicts are between "farmers" and "herders". While the latter label is thought to be appropriate and refers strictly to nomadic herdsmen of Fulani ethnicity—though this fact is often suppressed in some literature for some seemingly 'ethical' reasons and considerations (see Odoemene, 2017)—the former label ("farmers") is thought to be grossly erroneous, simplistic in description, and thus, a misnomer. While a good number—maybe a majority—of these supposed "farmers" were horticultural farmers, some in those communities were not 'farmers'. They rather engaged in many other corporate, public service or 'white-collar' occupations, including civil service, school teaching, medical services, and the likes (FGD V, 2019). A good number of them were also private business men/women or skilled artisans, thus, involved in a variety of service and product delivery across the country. Indeed, some are also into cattle ranching and herding, much like the Fulani.

In other words, attacks by Fulani herdsmen were often against whole 'heterogeneous communities', few members of whom were farmers (FGD III, 2019; Odoemene, 2017). Therefore, it needs to be made clear that the oft-used notion of "farmer-herder conflicts" is conceptually erroneous. Despite this identified conceptual flaw in the proper identification of a major party to the conflict, this essay would tag along the same usage, as the issues of such erroneous conceptualization is beyond the mandate of this present essay. It would, however, be appropriately dealt with later and elsewhere. The task of this paper is to interrogate, better understand and properly articulate the incidents—causes, dynamics, consequences and effects of the farmer-herder conflicts in Benue State. As well, it would explore the various management strategies that have been utilized to contain and/or resolve the conflicts and finally abstract key lessons for peacebuilding.

Methodology of the Study

Fieldwork activities involving both quantitative and qualitative techniques took place in four key locations. These are Gwer West, Agatu, Guma and Logo Local Government Areas (LGAs) which are located in the norther fringes of Benue State. These locations were purposely chosen for the study due to their record of very high incidents of farmer-herder conflicts. Research subjects were selected for the study from Naka, Obagaji, Gbajimba, and Ugba communities in the respective LGAs, which lie within the transition belt between the equatorial main belt of the southern Nigeria and semi-arid areas of northern Nigeria (Ogebe et al., 2019). The inhabitants were of Tiv and Idoma *ethnies* whose primary occupation was horticultural farming (growing yam, rice, millet, maize and some other Nigerian staples). Equally, some were white-collar work employees. The ethnic Fulani also exists there, and were primarily herdsmen—tending, pasturing and trading their cattle. Kwaja and Smith (2020: 8) instructively observed that the "farmers" tended to be sedentary, while the "herders" (pastoralists) were traditional nomadic and semi-nomadic moving (with their cattle) in line with seasonal migrations and search for pasture and water to sustain their herds.

Fieldwork activities took place between 21 January and 15 February, 2019 and were conducted with the help of experienced field assistants who were affiliated with Benue State University (BSU), Makurdi. A total of 270 structured questionnaires were randomly administered out of which 255 were retrieved and analyzed for the purposes of the study. These were in addition to nine (9) Focus Group Discussions (FGDs) and twenty-four (24) in-depth interviews using simple random and purposive sampling techniques, some of which were also conducted in the second phase of the fieldwork (which held between 19 and 27 August 2019). This later fieldwork was essentially a 'follow-up' based on the feedback from the "Dissemination Workshop" in July 2019. Secondary sources were also explored to enrich the study's data quality. These included a collection of extant works in print (published and unpublished), such as books, journal articles, newspapers and magazine articles, online literature and sources, as well as scholarly dissertations.

Though scientific research has produced substantial social benefits, it has, however, also posed some troubling ethical problems, particularly in respect to the abuse of, and threats to human participants and/or their rights in social research. Thus, in consonance with ethical standards in research, the research participants for this study had the right to remain anonymous, especially due to the nature of this study. In this regard, therefore, in order to enhance confidentiality of informants due to the possible security risks of this paper, pseudonyms have been used in place of real names of informants and their occupation or means of livelihood sometimes excluded herein, so as to effectively protect them from any possible danger.

Historical Trajectory

Contact between Fulani herdsmen and the local populations in what is today Benue State has been long and dates back to the pre-colonial times. Indeed, such contact and interactions had continued since the nineteenth century Fulani Jihad (1804–1804), which was successfully resisted by local populations of the Middle Belt area (including the Tiv and Idoma groups), thus halting the further capture of territories down south, beyond the present-day Lafia (Suleiman, 2012; Idrees and Ochefu, 2002; Dabup, 1999). Despite the exigencies of the Jihad, this was recorded as a period when the groups (Fulani herdsmen and the local populations) witnessed sustained harmonious co-existence with respect to their respective agricultural practices, built relations of reciprocity, product exchange, and support (Akerjiir, 2018; Odoemene, 2017). According to Vanger (2018: 38):

> ...the traditional farming practices in Tivland characterised the mutual rights to factors of production, extensive land use evidenced in shifting cultivation and fallowing, subsistence production and semi intensive livestock management practices. The herder practices ... featured extensive land use; herders owned the herd and the herd size was small. They also bargained entry into Tivland and observed the conditions of entry. The herders lived in allocated habitations, duration of residency was seasonal, and pastoralism was exclusive and nomadic.

In other words, during this period noted above, the conflicts between herdsmen and local farming communities were easily managed (Odoemene, 2017). The colonial contact, however, significantly altered these traditional farmer-herder practices and relations (Vanger, 2018: 38). Further exacerbation of the situation was witnessed in the post-independence era with government agricultural interventions of the 1960s. For these vast areas, often next to rivers, were appropriated and converted by law into grazing routes and reserves exclusively used by nomadic Fulani herders for their cattle (Odoemene, 2017). These helped in mitigating the dysfunctional conflicts between herders and farmers. Thus, interactions between herders and farmers had very limited violence, and their conflicts were often swiftly settled by the leaders of the different groups. Payment of compensation was often the resolution mechanism when a case of infringement was proven by any party. For instance, herdsmen who went outside designated grazing reserves were arrested and fined, and the money was used to compensate farmers for damaged crops, while any farmer who was ascertained to have acted untowardly towards herders and their cattle was equally arrested and made to pay compensation for any established damages he or she may have caused (Odoemene, 2017; Abati, 2016). These twentieth century contacts between these groups have been with the rural populations and were largely seasonal—the herdsmen often came with their cattle during the dry season and departed when the rains came (Ortserga, 2012).

The twenty-first century witnessed changing context and dynamics in the herder-farmer relations. As Vanger (2018: 38) argues, such context "conspired with population dynamics, climate surges and modernization and institutional arrangements to moderate the traditional agricultural practices ...and the conflicts thereof". Since the last decade and half the situation further deteriorated, becoming even more dramatic and virulent. The conflicts witnessed particularly the launching of coordinated deadly attacks by the herdsmen from about 2011, with widespread killings and displacement of populations (Vanger, 2018). Without a doubt, the sedentary societies of Benue state equally engaged in violent reprisals and/or other provocative acts which often engendered violent conflicts between the bitterly competing groups (FGD I & V, 2019; ICG, 2018). The conflicts began to peak from about 2014 when they began to be located on the outskirts of Makurdi, the state capital, and reached a crescendo in 2017, with the passage of the contentious Open Grazing Prohibition and Ranches Establishment (BOGPRE) Act. This law prohibited the movement and grazing of herds of cattle by nomadic herdsmen within Benue State. In contradistinction, the settled ranching practice for the cattle was encouraged by the bill (Sule, 2020; Akuul, 2020; Gever, 2019). As we shall see later, this law has remained a source of further bitter conflicts between the feuding parties.

Causes of the Conflicts

The farmer-herder conflicts in Benue state, like elsewhere in Central Nigeria, were triggered and sustained by multi-causal factors which could be divided into remote and immediate causes. These factors would be discussed in some detail.

Remote Causes

(a) ***Climate change and deteriorating environmental conditions***

Underpinning the escalation in frequency of these conflicts is a confluence of environmental and demographic forces. For instance, desert encroachment (desertification) of the Sahel region, which is caused by climate change, is one of the underlying factors of the conflicts. This change in climate condition has led to draught and desertification, as well as other deteriorating environmental conditions. These have ultimately affected the lives and livelihood of herdsmen and led to the trans-human movement from north to the south of these Fulani nomads in search of available space and land from where they can get green(er) and richer pasture and fresh waters for their herds. As Chukwuemeka et al. (2018: 3) and Ibekwe and Onyewuchi (2020: 1) contended, "the Fulani pastoralists have traditionally pastured or grazed their animals in the northern Sahel Region of the country but changing climatic conditions and desertification have imposed on them a southward migration to where the grass is much greener". The resulting consequence became the unhealthy competition over land access and use between the two interest groups.

(b) ***Population growth and explosion***

The natural rapid increase in the human population of farming communities as well as livestock population (but with no corresponding increase in land mass) was equally identified as one of the remote causes of the prevailing conflicts. This natural human increase led to deforestation, urbanization and expansion of agricultural activities which necessitated the need for more farmlands by the farmers. Such increase in livestock population also meant more grazing areas for the cattle of the herders. The pressure put on lands by these increases meant more acquisition and usage of hitherto fallow lands and migration into wetlands where the herders normally bring their cattle for succor in the dry season.

Thus, the Fulani herdsmen, having been denied access to their usual dry season resources in the south/middle-belt, were soon moving into the rain forests of the central and southern states where high population growth over the last four decades has heightened pressure on farmland (Ibekwe and Onyewuchi, 2020). This also meant getting into frequent competition, disputes and deadly conflicts with pastoralists over scarce land resources. These resulted in subsequent generation of associated conflicts over crop damage, water pollution and cattle theft.

(c) ***Extinction of grazing routes***

The gradual extinction of previously delineated government-approved cattle routes and grazing reserves—which helped mitigate dysfunctional conflicts between farmers and herders –

accentuated the conflictual situation. Unfortunately, these routes and reserves were under a neglected agricultural sector, and thus received very little or no attention from succeeding administrations (Vanger, 2018; Odoemene, 2017). As Vanger (2018: 46) further reports, some of such cattle grazing routes "fall on lands that form the home-domain of (Tiv) farmers and any attempt by the herders to lay claim to such lands especially without negotiated entry is met with stiff resistance". Thus, when these routes began to be interrupted, encroached on, interfered with and eventually extinguished due to human activities, the herders moved to other locations further down south where they began to put more pressure on the available landed resources in such areas. This led to conflicts and clashes with host communities (Odoemene, 2017). Undeniably, one of the points which came out clear in the study was pastoralists' complaints of encroachment on their traditional transhumance routes and reserves.

Immediate causes

In respect of the proximate causes of the farmer-herder conflicts, seven key factors are clearly identified. These include:

(a) ***Land rights: ownership, use and grabbing tendencies***

Gross inadequacies in land resource governance was identified as a major contributor to and cause of the conflicts in focus (Omokhoa and Okuchukwu, 2018). Land in Nigeria, nay Africa, has always been an important natural resource, which importance cannot be overemphasized, as most human activities ranging from shelter, food, industrial activities and movement are greatly dependent on land and its resources (Odoemene, 2021; Omokhoa and Okuchukwu, 2018; Opafunso, Bruno-Imokhai and Akinbosade, 2015: 1). Because of its great importance in human society, the inadequacies and insufficiency of relevant laws that govern the acquisition and use of land became instrumental to the nurturing of the deadly farmer-herder conflicts (FGD VII, 2019; Omokhoa and Okuchukwu, 2018: 105). Land is very crucial to both parties to the conflict as it lies at the heart of their economic, social, cultural and political lives. It remains a major factor in their well-being because of the crucial cultural and social recognition and status it confers. Contestations over land by the two groups in the Benue crisis, like all other such cases across the country, is directly hinged on the indigene/settler question (Maiangwa, 2017; Adebanwi, 2009), as well as citizenship rights which have times without number thrown up ethnic, religious and political sentiment (Adebanwi, 2009).

The indigenous ethnic groups in Benue state lay claim to ownership of the lands which they have farmed and used over the past centuries. They insisted that the herdsmen were mere "settlers" who now constituted 'nuisance' to the land owners, because they challenged the *status quo* in respect of land ownership and use (FGD I, 2019; Stephen Aondona, 2019: Personal Communication; Moses Edache, 2019: Personal Communication). The seasonal Fulani herders, however, invoke the constitution and sub-regional statutes in laying claims to their settlement on lands and their usage of them thereof (FGD III, 2019; Ahmed Jauro, 2019: Personal Communication; Sule Umar, 2019: Personal Communication). Another important aspect to the land-related conflicts were the allusions made, particularly by the native ethnic groups, to land grabbing. In this respect, the herdsmen's acts of forcefully annexing and occupying locals' arable lands at the expense of the natives was of great concern to many (FGD IX, 2019; Moses Edache, 2019: Personal Communication). This development was referred to as 'land grabbing' by the indigenes of the host communities, especially their farmers, and was said to have occurred often and with impunity (FGD V, 2019). Often times when efforts were made by the indigenes of the host communities—without state support—to recover such 'grabbed lands' always resulted in violence and painful loss of lives (FGD IX, 2019; Moses Edache, 2019: Personal Communication).

In Africa, and particularly in Nigeria, land is not just a factor of production—as many are wont to see it—but a major determinant of the people's livelihoods, beliefs and a sense of belonging (Vanger, 2018: 40). Indeed, land is very crucial in Nigeria, nay Africa, as it lies at the heart of the people's economic, social, cultural and political life. It remains a major factor in the well-being of the vast majority of the people. This is not only because of the economic values of land but also because of the crucial cultural recognition and social status it confers on its owner(s), whether persons, families or communities (Odoemene, 2021; Sall, 2011). Indeed, as Africa's most important resource, land remains the 'crown jewel' of any African society (Odoemene, 2021: 811). Thus, if relinquished, it means that the affected society has put itself at the mercy of others (Moyo and Tsikata, 2015), especially the new acquirers of such land. As Odoemene (2021: 811) argues:

> the dispossessing of whole communities and generations of their 'ancestral lands' amounts to exposing them to the untold dire socio-cultural challenges and consequences of landlessness in a culture-continent where land is, to say the least, 'all that matters'. This is particularly so as land is often the only source of both wealth and survival for so many persons on the African continent.

A spokesman of the Benue State chapter of the Miyetti Allah Cattle Breeders' Association of Nigeria (MACBAN, popularly known as "Miyetti Allah"), the umbrella body for cattle headers across Nigeria herders' union, Sule Umar (2019: Personal Communication), chided the notion of 'land ownership' as claimed by indigenous communities in the state. He noted that only personal belongings can be claimed, but never the free gifts of nature, such as lands, rivers, and the likes.

(b) ***Threats to livelihoods (and lives)***

There were diverse angles to this factor. Not only were the conflicts between farmers and herdsmen clearly reinforced by the farmers' extension of the boundary of their farms into previously delineated livestock routes, but also the wandering of herds of cattle belonging to herdsmen into the natives' farms to eat and/or destroy farm crops (FGD II, 2019; David Akuma 2019: Personal Communication). There were several reports of cattle entering farms to feed on the foliage of crops, even in the presence of herdsmen who were said to pretend not to notice such destruction by their cattle (FGD VI, 2019; David Akuma 2019: Personal Communication; Aneh Atama 2019: Personal Communication). To be sure, the negligence on the part of the government to have good policies that govern cattle rearing in Nigeria was also an issue in this respect (Omokhoa and Okuchukwu, 2018). In addition to this, another contentious issue was over-grazing which occurred because the nomadic herdsmen normally allowed such. While most farmers regarded this as a main source of conflict, the herdsmen did not consider it as that (FGDs III & IX, 2019). The farmers further argued such a practice caused erosion on arable lands, which rendered them infertile and uncultivatable (FGD V, 2019; Stephen Aondona, 2019: Personal Communication).

A Tiv farmer, Fanen Kator (2019, Personal Communication), considered bush burning, which causes destruction to crops, a major source of the conflicts between farmers and herders. As grasses and forage dried up in the dry season, nomads believed that if the dried vegetation is burnt, fresh pasture would regenerate quickly soon. However, it was noted that in the process of the bush burning—mostly by herdsmen—the fire (inadvertently or even as planned) spread into adjourning farms destroying planted crops on the field (FGD IV, 2019; Fanen Kator, 2019: Personal Communication). Another issue was the contamination of the local streams by loose herds of cattle. Enayi Akum (2019: Personal Communication) argued that these local streams were essential sources of domestic water supply for most of the host Benue communities whose members believed such contaminations led to the outbreak of epidemics and diseases. Indeed, there had been incidents of such water-borne diseases as cholera, typhoid fever and liver fluke, in many of the rural communities of Benue state. These were readily attributed to the activities of the herdsmen (FGD IV, 2019).

Cattle-rustling by local host populations was a major underlying cause of the conflicts. To be sure, miscreants existed in every community. Thus, frequent theft and slaughter of stray cattle belonging to the nomadic herders occurred. Such acts were not really unthinkable, given that the local hosts have had their planted crops on their farms destroyed by cattle, and without real concerns or compensation from the herdsmen (FGD VII, 2019; Moses Edache, 2019: Personal Communication). In other words, as Moses Edache (2019: Personal Communication) opined, cattle rustling was often perpetrated as a reactionary response or reprisals by host communities in Benue. Instructively, due to the attachment of the

Fulani herdsmen to their cattle, such rustling acts sometimes led to the killing of the culprits—an extreme action which often further enraged the local populations and heightened the tensions in the communal relations of the affected groups (FGD V, 2019).

Also important to note were incidences of prevention (or refusal) of the herders' cattle from grazing by some locals. What came out clear in this respect was that many of the locals preferred preventing the cattle from entering nearby bushes to graze lest they strayed into farms and damage valuable crops (FGD III, 2019; Imotan Sedoo, 2019: Personal Communication). This was because not only did herders always refuse to compensate farmers for destroyed crops by straying cattle, but herders often showed no remorse for such destructions (Enayi Akum, 2019: Personal Communication). However, the prevention of cattle from grazing was not an acceptable practice to the herders. They did not consider the reasons behind such an act as cogent and reasonable enough to warrant the disruption of the feeding of their cattle (FGD III, 2019; Moh Yahya, 2019: Personal Communication; Ibrahim Chuto, 2019: Personal Communication). This was often contentious, often leading to palpable tension in the communities, and sometimes escalated into violence.

These diverse but dire incidences—destruction of farms, contamination of streams, prevention of cattle from grazing, as well as cattle rustling—were strongly argued by both the host communities and the nomadic herdsmen as threatening to their respective livelihoods, and as such to their survival. It should be noted that all these incidents were clearly within the control of the conflictual groups respectively. In other words, as each of these incidences negatively impacted the livelihood and well-being of each of the groups, their refusal or negligence in handling them were directly responsible for the conflicts witnessed between the feuding groups.

(c) ***Issues of cultural intolerance***

Many research participants within the indigenous communities indicated that the disrespect of and disregard for their cultures and traditional authorities by the visiting Fulani herdsmen were a significant cause of bitter conflicts between the herders and their hosts (indigenes) in Benue state. Paul Torkwase, a civil servant, surmised this opinion:

> The Fulani herdsmen behave like lords in our land; they do not accord due respects to our kings, or institutions, or to other aspects of our cultures in general. Like any other group, even amongst the Fulani themselves, these our cultures are our ways of life, and are very dear to us. We resent watching these Fulani visitors to our communities, whom we often welcome with open hearts, treat our revered institutions and traditions with contempt and utter disrespect. This does not go down well with our people. It has to stop. (2019: Personal Communication).

Also under the cloak of such cultural intolerance could be added the issues of the 'seemingly incessant' sexual harassment of indigenous hosts' females by Fulani herders. Indeed, several cases of such assaults and rapes were noted in this respect. Attacks on such females often took place in the bushes where they go to farm, and where they were often confronted and/or waylaid by their assailants (FGD I, 2019; Paul Torkwase, 2019: Personal Communication; Ichekani Idoko, 2019: Personal Communication; Yaro and Tobias, 2019). Indisputably, rape and other forms of sexual harassment remain taboos, even in African societies and among the indigenous communities of Benue State. Thus, issues in such lines were not taken lightly by the host communities. While it is pertinent to note that the Fulani respondents for this study unambiguously denied such allegations, labelling them as 'spurious, unfounded and ungodly' (FGDs III & VIII, 2019; Ahmadu Fula, 2019: Personal Communication; Ibrahim Chuto, 2019: Personal Communication), it is instructive to point out that there have been several similar incidents of sexual harassments and rape by Fulani herders in many other parts of the country (Ajibefun, 2018; ICG, 2018; Falino, 2015). Ofuoku and Isife (2010) also reported these (rape and/or sexual harassment) as major sources of conflict between herders and their hosts. Thus, such accusations are difficult to discountenance in the face of similar proven cases elsewhere. In addition to these, however, the Fulani herdsmen equally highlighted the harassment of nomadic herders by the youth of host communities (Ahmadu Fula, 2019: Personal Communication).

(d) ***Mutual suspicion and competing victimhood***

As noted earlier, interactions between Fulani herdsmen and the ethnic groups around the north-central axis existed prior to the nineteenth century Fulani *Jihad*. That religious movement swept across the entire northern regions (Nigeria) and was heading southwards, but was effectively challenged and its wild expansion completely halted by a coalition of diverse indigenous groups in the north-central region (Yuwa Dooshima, 2019: Personal Communication). While the key factors in the *jihad* were the purification of Islam (where it hitherto existed) and its spread into areas where it never existed, the north-central region where the indigenous groups in what eventually became Benue State remained largely and mostly Christians (UK Home Office, 2020; Vanger, 2018). Therefore, the incursions of Fulani herders into Benue farmlands and territories—even when with cattle which presupposes that the intention was for the pasturing of their flock—was often interpreted and considered by the hosts as a decoy by the Fulani to continue the halted *jihadist* expansion across their territories. These indigenous groups bitterly resented this possibility and idea (Paul Torkwase, 2019: Personal Communication; Yuwa Dooshima, 2019: Personal Communication). In another vein, the herdsmen also suspected almost every move of the hosts as targeted at them and endangering their lives and livelihood (Hassan Kabiru, 2019: Personal Communication). It is noteworthy that in these prevailing circumstances, each of the parties believed and presented members of their groups as the conflicts' real victims (FGDs III & VIII , 2019).

New Dimensions to the Conflict

Since the turn of the twenty-first century, the farmer-herder conflicts in Benue State took some new dimensions which were hitherto unknown in the crisis. Indeed, such 'new' trends in the conflicts have helped in amplifying the conflicts as well as intensifying the virulence and intractability associated with the crisis. Two of such new trends would be discussed.

President Muhammadu Buhari came to power in May 2015 and has been the present till date. Clearly, this period witnessed a peak in the farmer-herder conflicts. Interestingly, Buhari is not only an ethnic Fulani, and a cattle herd owner, breeder and major dealer who employed itinerant herders to herd his cattle (Olugbenga, 2017), but also the grand patron of the cattle headers' umbrella union in Nigeria, "*Miyetti Allah*" (Ibekwe and Onyewuchi, 2020; Fasan, 2018; Ezukanma, 2018). Despite the several adverse reports about the activities of Fulani herdsmen and their violence and killings across the country, the government of President Buhari seems to be docile about such factual and dangerous reports (Fasan, 2018; Ezukanma, 2018; Olugbenga, 2017). Indeed, it is enlightening that till date no single Fulani killer-herdsman has been arrested, docked and/or convicted for the many widespread killings both in Benue state and elsewhere across the country. Peter Wesotee, a Tiv merchant, aptly captures the associated frustrations thus: "Since Buhari came to power, these herdsmen just behave like 'untouchables'; they wreak havoc and mayhem anywhere they went to, and did so with crass impunity. Even the security operatives are afraid of them" (2019: Personal Communication).

This largely unserious approach towards the criminality of killer-herdsmen in the country has been attributed to their ethnic alliance with President Buhari (Olugbenga, 2017). The emotional ethnicization of the crisis is a dangerous, particularly due to the problems of dysfunctional ethnicity in Nigeria (Egwu, 2015; Omotola and Hassan, 2015). Lending credence to this belief of an ethnicization angle to the conflicts, Abati (2016) aptly opines:

> ...the nomadic pastoralist has been overtaken by a certain sense of unbridled arrogance arising from that notorious *na-my-brother-dey-power*[2] mentality and the assumption that "the Fulani cattle" must drink water, by all means, from the Atlantic ocean.

Importantly too, majority of the heads of the security outfits of the State—the army, navy, air force, police, secret police, national security organization, immigration, customs, and so on—in the Buhari administration were mostly of Muslim Fulani ethnic stock (Oketola et al., 2016). In contrast, the Benue communities were mostly Christians of diverse ethnicities, as have been noted earlier. In other words, the later felt uncomfortable with what they perceived as 'Fulani domination' (Peter Wesotee, 2019: Personal Communication). In the context of the crisis between farmers and herders, this perception did not inspire confidence amongst a majority of Benue indigenes; they felt threatened and disconcerted (FGD II, 2019; Francis Oche, 2019: Personal Communication). Such feeling of consternation was further heightened with the news of Buhari government's unilateral gifting of some One Hundred Billion Naira ($276 million USD) to *Miyetti Allah* in 2019

[2] Roughly translated as 'it is my brother who is in power'.

for unspecified reasons. Though this 'gift allegation' news was strenuously denied by the government (Ailemen, 2019), skeptics doubted such denials (Nwachukwu, 2019).

In other words, the fact of President Buhari's emergence as the leader of the country, as well as his administration's posture (and 'body language') towards the activities of his kinsmen—the Fulani herdsmen—gave an ethnic colouration and perception to the conflicts, and at the same time helped embolden the herdsmen in their acts.

The proliferation and infiltration of small arms and light weapons into Nigeria—a situation which is on the increase and easily attributable to the country's very porous borders (Fyanka, 2018; Ayuba and Okafor, 2015)—is another new dynamic which has affected the farmer-herder conflicts in Nigeria generally. Due to the influx of such arms and ammunition into the country, it was possible usually easy for killer-herdsmen to acquire them from across the borders, thus upsetting the country's security architecture (Abati, 2016). The influx of such deadly weapons into the country (Nigeria) in recent times were traceable from the unstable Sahel region, due to the exigencies of Muammar Gaddafi of Libya, the civil unrests and insurgency in Mali and Central African Republic, as well as the exigencies of the *Boko Haram* networks (Odoemene, 2017; Abati, 2016). Indeed, even President Buhari also alluded to this during his audience with President Donald Trump of America in 2019. The fact of this dimension raised the suspicion of many that the herdsmen had contacts with international terrorist networks who availed the herdsmen illegally trafficked weapons (Odoemene, 2017; Abati, 2016). Of course, the frequent use of such weapons by the herders gave room for other interpretation of the sources of and purpose for such weapons. For instance, many have also argued that the patrons/sponsors of the herders were also directly responsible for arming them with such dangerous weapons, which they freely carried without let or hindrance, and causing breach of the peace (FGD VI, 2019; Yuwa Dooshima, 2019: Personal Communication; Onma Ujah, 2019: Personal Communication).

Consequences and effects of the Conflicts

As with almost all resource-based conflicts across the Nigerian landscape and elsewhere, the farmer-herder conflicts in Benue state has impacted on both individuals and society in diverse ways. There were several violent attacks, mainly by the herdsmen, though there are a few cases of attacks by farmer-communities—mostly reprisals (Ngoundu Tiza, 2019: Personal Communication; Philip Ngbede, 2019: Personal Communication). Such a situation created security tension in the state where residents felt unsafe and were always 'on their toes' (FGD I, 2019; Aminu Daura, 2019: Personal Communication; Moses Edache, 2019: Personal Communication). This kind of state of affairs did not create a conducive atmosphere for genuine development and the resolution of the now-seeming intractable farmer-herder conflicts. Regrettably, these conflicts have led to the death of thousands of persons, the maiming of another tens of thousands of people, the destruction of property worth billions of Naira, and the displacement of thousands of people who were located in internally displaced persons (IDPs) camps within the state (FGD IV, 2019; Vanger, 2018; ICG, 2017, 2018). As usual, women and children have been the most victims of this situation.

These incessant conflicts and the resultant losses recorded thus far have adversely affected socio-economic activities, particularly farming and pasturing, in the affected communities (Vanger, 2018; ICG, 2017, 2018), and engendered new security arrangements which feed on the mutual suspicions of the parties (FGD II, 2019; ICG, 2017, 2018). For instance, it was noted that these conflicts often resulted in the destruction of food systems of many key communities, and therefore have inadvertently led to the drastic reduction in both farm and animal (meat) outputs. It should be pointed out that both the farmers and the herders are key food producers in Benue State, which has, "Food Basket of the Nation" as its *alias* (FGD II, 2019; Francis Oche, 2019: Personal Communication). Indeed, for most farmers affected by the crisis, farming is no longer a business as usual; very credible reports suggest several local farmers who were displaced and dispossessed of their farms due to the conflicts have abandoned farming altogether and fleeing for safer territories, for fear of being attacked and killed by the herdsmen (Vanger, 2018; ICG, 2017, 2018). Furthermore, for fear of their own lives too, herdsmen's pasturing activities drastically reduced, particularly during the tense periods (FGD III, 2019; Ahmed Jauro, 2019: Personal Communication). These developments have adversely affected agricultural production, continued to threaten the state's quest to boost food security (and sufficiency), and often heightened the fear of hunger and starvation in not only the affected communities, but throughout Benue State (FGD VII, 2019).

An important consequence of the conflicts was the enactment of the Benue State Open Grazing Prohibition and Ranches Establishment

(BOGPRE) Act. This Act, which became very controversial as soon as it was being crafted, was passed by the Benue State House of Assembly on 04 May 2017 and signed into law on 22 May 2017, while its implementation commenced on 01 November 2017. (Sule, 2020; Gever, 2019; Vanger, 2018; Atelhe and Ogayi, 2018). As government officials clearly explained, this was a policy move to help not only end hostilities but also allow both feuding parties to peacefully coexist (Yahimba Gowon, 2019: Personal Communication). Whether this novel state-wide law was able to achieve such a lofty objective was another case altogether, as we shall see later.

Management of the Conflicts

Despite the myriads of criticisms heaped on the Federal Government over the farmer-herder conflicts in Benue State, it would be fair to say that the central government has done quite a bit to mediate, contain, manage and/or resolve the conflicts. Some of these efforts include: the creation of Grazing Reserves in 1965, as was noted earlier, which was meant to keep the herders away from farmlands, thus reduce the incidents of conflicts. The other was the establishment of the National Commission for Nomadic Education (NCNE) in 1989, with the goal of integrating the pastoralists into the society and national life through mobile basic education and skill acquisition training (Atelhe and Ogayi, 2018; Alabi, 2015; Olaniran, 2013). In one's estimation, the idea for the establishment of NCNE was to bring the nomadic Fulani to be better informed about the vagaries of their trade, thus making them less susceptible to be conflicts with their hosts.

The federal government equally utilized the Nigerian security forces to curb internal insecurity such as could have been engendered by the farmer-herder violent clashes. For instance, the Special Task Force as the 'Operation Safe Haven' (STF-OSH), as well as the deployment of and the a 1000-man Special Intervention Force of the Nigeria Air Force (NAF) to Makurdi to degrade bandits and criminals in Benue and Nasarawa states were direct products of this (Odigbo, 2019). Similarly, as the *Vanguard Newspaper* (2018) had reported on this issue, "The Police have deployed additional Five Units of Police Mobile Force, Police Special Forces, Police Aerial Surveillance Helicopters and Special Police Joint Intelligence and Investigation Team to Benue State" (Atelhe and Ogayi, 2018). In trying to tackle one of the primary sources of the conflicts, the Federal Government also set up the Great Green Wall Agency in 2013, with a mandate to combat the desertification process in the Northern parts of the country (Atelhe and Ogayi, 2018; Fulani, 2017). If achieved, this venture would help keep the Fulani nomads within their traditional northern 'homeland', thus limiting the possibilities of their coming in contact with farmers and farming communities located southwards (FGD IX, 2019).

There have also been recent proposals by the federal government towards addressing the herdsmen-farmer conflicts. The first of these was the establishment of the National Grazing Reserve Bill (2016) which was sponsored in the National Assembly but was defeated due to opposition from different stakeholders due to a lack of confidence in it (Egbuta, 2018: 45). Another proposal was the Cattle Ranching System (2018) through which a 10-year National Livestock Plan at a cost of about ₦179 billion Naira was approved. It was designed to culminate in the establishment of 94 ranches in 10 pilot states in the country (Ibid, 46). However, this proposal died like the former due to state governments' (especially in the Southern and North Central areas) rejection of the proposal due to the provisions of the Land Use Act (1978). The state governments argued that they did not have enough lands in their respective states for such projects. Lastly, the Rural Grazing Area (RUGA) policy was equally introduced by the Federal government in 2019. Through RUGA, the federal government sought to create reserved communities where herders will live, grow and tend their cattle, as well as undertake other activities without having to move around in search of grazing land for their cows (Yahimba Gowon, 2019: Personal Communication). It is instructive that the Federal Government provided relief items to affected populations in IDP camps within Benue State. Generally, however, there was a strong perception by the indigenes that the federal government failed in the handling of the conflicts (FGDs I & V, 2019).

On its part, the Benue State government continued to aid in the provision of relief to affected populations and persons (Vanger, 2018), though the dominant opinion amongst the indigenes was that the state government, like the federal (central) government, equally failed to adequately protect them or act in their interest (UK Home Office, 2020; FGD II, 2019; Ngoundu Tiza, 2019: Personal Communication). Likewise, as noted earlier, the state also enacted and enforced BOGPRE Act which it put in place so as to mitigate and contain the conflicts, and enshrine peaceful co-existence in the state. However, as this state law seemed to 'favour' one party to the conflict (the farmers) over the other (the herders)—the later was effectively prohibited from conducting their 'traditional' open grazing in the state—BOGPRE Act became not only controversial but also notorious and potentially perilous (Sule, 2020; Gever, 2019; Vanger, 2018). It, thus, was yet another veritable source of conflict between the feuding parties (FGD I & VI, 2019; Sule Umar, PC: 2019; Sule, 2020; Gever, 2019). Particularly, the herders strongly rejected and resisted it in its totality. A spokesman of the Fulani herders contended thus:

> As far as we [the herders] are concerned, no one can restrict us from moving around in any part of this country. As you know, the constitution guarantees that. Not so? And come to think of it, no one restricts the movements of their [Benue] people in the northern parts of the country; they come when they want, move around freely as they like, and do their businesses without any problems from or harassment by our people over there. So, why can't we enjoy same treatment here in Benue State? ...I don't think such a law is right. It will not stand (Sule Umar, 2019: Personal Communication).

Beyond the state, traditional leaders and institutions in Benue State, particularly its first class chiefs (like the *Tor Tiv*, *Ochi Idoma*, etc.), tried using the traditional methods of conflict management in their respective societies to handle the crisis. However, not much was achieved in that sphere (FGD V & VIII, 2019; Yuwa Dooshima, 2019: Personal Communication; Yahimba Gowon, 2019: Personal Communication). Interestingly though, many indigenes rather often saw them as 'compromised' (Onma Ujah, 2019: Personal Communication), as diverse reports existed which often presented them as taking bribes from the Fulani, and/or being huge investors in the herders' cattle business (FGD I, 2019). Reports further indicated that religious leaders and institutions were usually agents for the provision of relief to displaced persons, particularly their adherents. At another level, many of the Non-Governmental Organizations (NGOs) and Community Based Organizations (CBO) were involved in the mediation of the conflicts, as well as in the provision of relief to affected populations in the IDP camps. Some were also directly involved in the management of the IDP camp (FGD, IV 2019).

The media, which have been highlighted as key players—often for peaceful purposes—in diverse conflicts across Nigeria and the world, were, on the other hand, perceived as being utterly negative in the farmer-herder conflicts in Benue State (Gever, 2019). For instance, it was argued that the reportage on these conflicts (within the media) was largely negative, and generally carried on in a manner that favoured some parochial interests (FGD IX, 2019; Gever, 2019). Similarly, media practitioners were equally accused of partaking in the "fake news" syndrome in respect of these conflicts, which often encouraged violence and heated up the system (FGD VI, 2019). Oftentimes, skewed media accounts, particularly in the social media, tended to favour farmers and local indigenous communities the more, while they often criminalized the Fulani herdsmen (FGD I, 2019; Sule Umar, 2019: Personal Communication; Ahmed Jauro, 2019: Personal Communication).

Lesson for Peacebuilding

The farmers-herders' conflicts in Benue State, which are age-long but have only escalated within the last two decades and assumed very deadly dimensions, are loaded with significant historical trajectories, the proper understanding of which leaves one with diverse instructive lessons. This is particularly so in respect of 'the way forward' for peacebuilding prospects. For the purposes of this present study, the following ten (10) key lessons are clearly and evidently perceptible:

1. There is some urgency to these conflicts, particularly due to their devastating nature. The death toll, physical destructions, emotional trauma, threats and severe tensions, as well as dislocations which these conflicts have left communities with are shocking and overwhelming (FGD IV, 2019). These call for urgent action both by governments (federal, state, and local) and the international community towards arresting these ugly trends in human society.
2. These conflicts are culture-based and fundamentally 'ethnic' in nature. In other words, they equally demand culture-specific management strategies for their handling or containment (Paul Torkwase, 2019: Personal Communication). This is important as the often extraneous 'one-size-fit-all' prescriptions of conflict management and peacebuilding approaches—often 'imported' from other climes and imposed on these uniquely different conflicts (FGD II, 2019)—seem to lack the required potency and robustness to contain the needful demands of these conflicts.

3. The intractable nature of the conflicts readily points to the fact that there is need for a return to the previously abandoned indigenous/traditional conflict resolution/management and peacebuilding mechanisms. Indeed, these traditional models—both of the Fulani and the other affected ethnic groups of the Benue, namely: Tiv, and Idoma)—were 'tried out' (but not well utilized) during the diverse processes of managing the conflicts, but they failed. Evidence from the field clearly indicate that the failures were not necessarily due to the ineffectiveness of the models, but in their half-hearted application to the situations. In consequence, these traditional methods were not well and properly utilized towards the adequate management of the conflicts (FGD I, 2019).
4. There seem to be a lack of synergy between the Federal and State governments on the issue of the feud, particularly in the present times. This is certainly not surprising. For instance, the earlier clearly seem to be protecting the interests of the Fulani for reasons which have been discussed earlier in the paper, while the later protects the interest of the indigenous locals of Benue State. These claims of support for different sides to the conflicts, which clearly make for intractability, were severally made during the course of this research (FGD II, 2019; Yuwa Dooshima, 2019: Personal Communication). Indeed, the nature and execution of some of the containment strategies also point in that direction.
5. The non-containment of the free flow of small arms and light weapons into the country constitutes a danger to peace, sustainable development and meaningful progress. The ever-presence and widespread use of these weapons have helped in exacerbating the conflicts. Furthermore, the non-reaction or laxity of government agencies in arresting those who parade these weapons with impunity serves as further threat to the situation. In this respect, it should be noted that there seem to operate two sets of rules for these government security agencies: Fulani herdsmen with weapons are not treated as offenders, but carefully avoided—never arrested—while the diametrically opposite was often the fate of indigenous persons of Benue State (FGD IX, 2019; Paul Torkwase, 2019: Personal Communication; Moses Edache, 2019: Personal Communication). Such disparities in treatment will have to change.

6. As dialogue is critical in conflict situations, there is need for the promotion of constructive and sustained dialogue between the parties to the conflicts. A prime objective of such dialogue should be for the groups to carefully LISTEN to UNDERSTAND each other—the other's needs, intensions and motives, fears, aspirations, and so on—and not to merely hear them out and respond with a view to tackling each of the raised points, as has often been the case with previous interactions (FGD III, 2019; Aneh Atama 2019: Personal Communication; David Akuma, 2019: Personal Communication). Understanding and empathy are key in this respect.
7. For the above, there is need for more critical roles for non-partisan, non-state actors in the mediation of the farmer-herder relationships and interactions. Though this may have been a feature in the mediation processes in these conflicts, the non-state actors involved have often been quite partisan—like religious leaders and groups, traditional institutions and indigenous Community Based Organizations (Yuwa Dooshima, 2019: Personal Communication; Peter Wesotee, 2019: Personal Communication)—and thus, usually carry 'baggage of untrustworthiness' before the parties to the conflict.
8. The need for adequate training of both traditional and religious leaders and institutions on conflict management/resolution and peacebuilding modes is noted and highly recommended. This will help build their capacities for utilization at the very rural levels where these conflicts emanate. In this respect, therefore, such previously neglected (or abandoned) indigenous Early Warning Systems (EWS) and Early Warning Response (EWR) mechanisms must also be re-activated and put into good use to mitigate these conflicts. Thus, such training would be for enhancing the abilities of direct key players on both sides towards positively impacting the farmer-herder conflicts at the very early stages and rural levels, before they escalate and become deadly.
9. As was made clear earlier, government failures, at all levels, were felt across the Benue communities where this study was carried out. This calls for not only credible intervention by the government, but also greater collaboration between the various levels of government and non-state actors in the management of the conflicts. This has become pertinent particularly due to the very inimical posture of the conflicts for national security and development.

10. Better ways of life and occupation for the parties should be promoted. It is the informed belief of the present researcher that some of these better ways of doing their businesses would certainly encourage peaceful co-existence between the groups. For instance, ranching, as against nomadic life-style, is significantly beneficial to both the cattle, their products (meat/beef, milk, etc.) and the pastoralists/herdsmen. Therefore, this line of thinking should be promoted and encouraged as a reasonable, more viable and lasting alternative to the presently preferred nomadic style of cattle herding, which also ensures peaceful and symbiotic co-existence.

Conclusion

The conflicts between farmers and herders remian an enduring feature of social life in almost all the six geo-political zones of Nigeria. This study afforded the researcher the remarkable opportunity to interrogate the dynamics and exigencies of this very instructive communal crises, particularly as it affects Benue State of Nigeria. The farmer-herder conflicts are still very latent and pervasive in Benue state. The increased struggles of these groups have often led to violent confrontations which clearly portended grave dangers and had dire consequences for both human security and true development in the affected areas. They not only led to deaths, forced displacement and destruction of agriculture and livestock, but also have very disintegrative effect on the social relations in the affected communities. These have affected various aspects of human life and survival systems and were inimical to unity, peace and development, in addition to exposing humanity—particularly women and children—to situations of terror and horror. More remarkably, the entire farmers-herders conflicts often brought to the fore the indigene/settler question, as well as fed into the land ownership and citizenship rights debates which often threw up ethnic, religious and political sentiments in the country.

Undeniably, the farmer-herder skirmish constitutes one of the biggest challenges threatening the corporate existence of Nigeria today and has been a major factor of instability in the rural areas of the country, particularly in the central (middle belt) region (Odoemene, 2017). This situation calls for urgent action and concerted efforts by all concerned stakeholders towards the effective management and containment of the conflicts.

However, from all indications and with what is presently on ground—seemingly complicit governments, determined actors unwilling to make compromises, very 'weak' non-state stakeholder actors, dangerous new dimensions to the conflicts, and the proliferation of small arms and light weapons in the country—it is safe and quite reasonable to suggest, or even conclude that there would continue to be an intensification of violent exchanges between farmers and herders in Benue State in the near future. Any possible shift from this trend would only emerge from a spirited and thorough adherence to a combination of the listed peacebuilding lessons/ propositions.

Interviews (Personal Communication)

1. Akum, Enayi. Interviewed Friday, February 15, 2019; Ugba (Logo LGA).
2. Akuma, David. Interviewed Wednesday, August 21, 2019; Obagaji (Agatu LGA).
3. Aondona, Stephen. Interviewed Friday, February 8, 2019; Gbajimba (Guma LGA).
4. Atama, Aneh. Interviewed Friday, February 15, 2019; Ugba (Logo LGA).
5. Chuto, Ibrahim. Interviewed Saturday, August 24, 2019; Gbajimba (Guma LGA).
6. Daura, Aminu. Interviewed Friday, January 25, 2019; Naka (Gwer West LGA).
7. Dooshima, Yuwa. Interviewed Tuesday, February 12, 2019; Gbajimba (Guma LGA).
8. Edache, Moses. Interviewed Wednesday, February 6, 2019; Obagaji (Agatu LGA).
9. Fula, Ahmadu. Interviewed Thursday, February 14, 2019; Gbajimba (Guma LGA).
10. Gowon, Yahimba. Interviewed Wednesday, February 13, 2019; Ugba (Logo LGA).
11. Idoko, Ichekani. Interviewed Saturday, February 2, 2019; Obagaji (Agatu LGA).
12. Jauro, Ahmed. Interviewed Tuesday, February 12, 2019; Gbajimba (Guma LGA).
13. Kabiru, Hassan. Interviewed Wednesday, February 13, 2019; Ugba (Logo LGA).
14. Kator, Fanen. Interviewed Friday, January 25, 2019; Naka (Gwer West LGA).
15. Ngbede, Philip. Interviewed Wednesday, February 6, 2019; Obagaji (Agatu LGA).

16. Oche, Francis. Interviewed Friday, February 8, 2019; Gbajimba (Guma LGA).
17. Onma, Ujah. Interviewed Sunday, January 27, 2019; Naka (Gwer West LGA).
18. Tiza, Ngoundu. Interviewed Tuesday, January 29, 2019; Naka (Gwer West LGA).
19. Torkwase, Paul. Interviewed Tuesday, August 27, 2019; Ugba (Logo LGA).
20. Umar, Sule. Interviewed Thursday, February 14, 2019; Gbajimba (Guma LGA).
21. Wesotee, Peter. Interviewed Sunday, January 27, 2019; Naka (Gwer West LGA).
22. Yahya, Mohammed. Interviewed Saturday, February 2, 2019; Obagaji (Agatu LGA).

Focus Group Discussions (FGDs)

FGD I: Thursday, January 24, 2019; Naka (Gwer West LGA).
FGD II: Saturday, January 26, 2019; Naka (Gwer West LGA).
FGD III: Monday, February 4, 2019; Obagaji (Agatu LGA).
FGD IV; Saturday, February 9, 2019; Obagaji (Agatu LGA).
FGD V: Friday, February 15, 2019; Gbajimba (Guma LGA).
FGD VI: Friday, February 15, 2019; Gbajimba (Guma LGA).
FGD VII: Tuesday, August 20, 2019; Obagaji (Agatu LGA).
FGD VIII: Wednesday, August 21, 2019; Ugba (Logo LGA).
FGD IX: Tuesday, August 27, 2019; Ugba (Logo LGA).

Reference

Abati, Reuben. 2016. "Fulani herdsmen as the new Boko Haram?", (29 April); http://africanspotlight.com/2016/04/29/fulani-herdsmen-as-the-new-boko-haram-by-reuben-abati/ (accessed 18 June 2016).

Adebanwi, Wale. 2009. "Terror, Territoriality and the Struggle for Indigeneity and Citizenship in Northern Nigeria." *Citizenship Studies*, Vol. 13(4), 349–363.

Ailemen, Tony. 2019. "FG Never Gave N100b to Miyetti Allah—Presidency", *Business Day Newspaper* Online (10 May); https://businessday.ng/uncategorized/article/fg-never-gave-n100b-to-miyetti-allah-presidency/ (accessed 02 October 2020).

Ajibefun, M.B. 2018. "Social and Economic Effects of the Menace of Fulani Herdsmen Crises in Nigeria", *Journal of Educational and Social Research*, Vol. 8(2) (May), 133–139.

Akerjiir, Anastasia Sandra. 2018. "Increasing Farmer-Herder Conflict in Nigeria: An Assessment of the Clashes between the Fulani Herdsmen and Indigenous Farmers in Ukpabi-Nimbo Community, Enugu State", Master's dissertation, Wageningen University and Research, The Netherlands.

Akuul, Timbee. 2020. "Efficacy of Benue State Open Grazing Prohibition and Ranches Establishment Law 2017 and Farmers-Herders Conflict Resolution", *Fudma Journal of Politics and International Affairs*, Vol. 2(2), 105–115.

Alabi, T.C. (2015). Nigeria: "Poor Funding, Insecurity Challenge to Nomadic Education"; www.allafrica.com/stories/201507161190.html (accessed 15 August 2019).

Atelhe, George A. and Ogayi, Cornelius O. 2018. "The Nigerian State and the Management of Farmer-Herder Conflict: An Evaluation", *International Journal of Peace and Conflict Studies* (*IJPCS*), Vol. 5(2), 8–20.

Awotokun, Kunle, Nwozor, Agaptus and Olanrewaju, John Shola. 2020. "Conflicts and the Retrogression of Sustainable Development: The Political Economy of Herders-Farmers' Conflicts in Nigeria", *Humanities and Social Sciences Reviews*, Vol. 8(1), 624–633.

Ayuba, Caleb and Okafor, Gerald. 2015. "The Role of Small Arms and Light Weapons Proliferation in African Conflicts", *African Journal of Political Science and International Relations*, Vol. 9(3), (March), 76–85.

Chukwuemeka, E.E.O., Aduma, A. and Eneh, M.I. 2018. "The Logic of Open Grazing in Nigeria: Interrogating The Effect on Sustainable Development", *International Journal of Family Business and Management Studies*, Vol. 2(1), 1–17.

Dabup, P.L. 1999, "The Political Economy of Resistance in the Cultural Middle Belt." In Bagudu, N. and Dakas, C.J. (eds.), *The Right to be Different: Perspectives on Minority Rights, the Cultural Middle Belt Constitutionalism in Nigeria* (Jos: League for Human Rights).

Egbuta, Ugwumba. 2018. "Understanding the Herder-Farmer Conflict in Nigeria", *Conflict Trends*, Issue 3; The African Centre for the Constructive Resolution of Disputes (ACCORD), 40–48.

Egwu, Samuel G. 2015, "The Political Economy of Rural Banditry in Contemporary Nigeria". In Kuna, M.J. and Ibrahim, J. (eds.), *Rural Banditry and Conflict in Northern Nigeria* (Abuja: Centre for Democracy and Development [CDD]), 14–68.

Ezukanma, Tochukwu. 2018. "The Ominous Silence of Fulani Herdsmen", *Guardian Newspaper* Online (27 December); https://guardian.ng/opinion/the-ominous-silence-of-fulani-herdsmen/ (accessed 15 June 2019).

Falino, B. 2015. "Nigeria: Farm Invasion, Sexual Harassment by Fulani Herdsmen"; http://falinoworld.blogspot.com.ng/2015/02/nigeria-farm-invasion-sexualharassment.html (accessed 18 June 2019).

Fasan, Rotimi. 2018. "Miyetti Allah, Muhammadu Buhari and the Rest of Us", *Vanguard Newspaper* Online (10 January); https://www.vanguardngr.com/2018/01/miyetti-allah-muhammadu-buhari-rest-us/ (accessed 15 June 2019).

Fulani, I.D. 2017. "Poor Funding Affecting Nigeria's Great Green Wall Project", *Premium Times* Online (17 July).

Fyanka, Bernard B. 2018. *International Patterns of Arms Proliferation: An Evolutionary Assessment and the Imperative for Strategic Control* (Mauritius: Scholar's Press).

Gever, C.V. 2019. "When Solution Triggers More Conflicts: Frames and Tones of Media Coverage of the Anti-Grazing Law of Benue State, Nigeria", *Media, War and Conflict*, Vol. 12(4), 468–482.

Ibekwe, Chineze Sophia and Onyewuchi, Nkemjika Anthony. 2020. "A Legal Evaluation of the RUGA Settlement Scheme as Response to Herder-Farmer Conflicts, Food Scarcity and Unemployment in Nigeria", *Nnamdi Azikiwe University Journal of Commercial and Property Law*, Vol. 7(1), 14–26.

Idrees, Aliyu A. and Ochefu, Yakubu A. 2002. *Studies in the History of the Central Nigeria Area* (Vol. 1) (Lagos: CSS Limited).

International Crisis Group (ICG). 2018. "Stopping Nigeria's Spiralling Farmer-Herder Violence", *Africa Report* N°262 (26 July), Brussels: International Crisis Group.

International Crisis Group (ICG). 2017. "Herders Against Farmers: Nigeria's Expanding Deadly Conflict", *Africa Report* N° 252 (19 September), Brussels: International Crisis Group.

Kwaja, Chris M.A. and Smith, Katie. 2020. "Transnational Dimensions of Conflict between Farmers and Herders in the Western Sahel and Lake Chad Basin", Policy Brief (April); Forum on Farmer and Herder Relations in Nigeria (FFARN) and Search for Common Ground.

Leme, Abdulrahman U. 2017. *Understanding Farmers-Herdsmen Conflict and the Way Forward*; https://www.thecable.ng/understanding-farmers-herdsmen-conflict-way-forward (accessed 15 February 2018).

Li, Ningxin. 2018. "Nigeria's Fulani Herdsmen-Farmers Conflict and Peace Building", *Global Journal of Agricultural Research*, Vol. 6(5), (December), 1–15.

Maiangwa, B. 2017, "Conflicting Indigeneity" and Farmer–Herder Conflicts in Postcolonial Africa, *Peace Review*, Vol. 29(3), 282–288.

Moyo, Sam and Tsikata, Dzodzi. (eds.) 2015. *Land in the Struggles for Citizenship in Africa* (Dakar: CODESRIA).

Muhammed, I., Ismaila, A.B. and Bibi, U.M. 2015. "An Assessment of Farmer-Pastoralist Conflict in Nigeria Using GIS", *International Journal of Engineering Science Invention*, Vol. 4(7), 23–33.

Nwachukwu, John O. 2019. "Zamfara killings: President Buhari Under Fire for Offering Fulani Militia, Bandits N100bn", *Daily Post Newspaper* Online (5 May); https://dailypost.ng/2019/05/05/zamfara-killings-president-buhari-fire-offering-fulani-militia-bandits-n100bn/ (accessed 08 July 2020).

Odigbo, Jude Okwudili. 2019. "Grazing Conundrum: Herdsmen-Farmers Conflict and Internal Security Crisis in Nigeria", In Oshita, O., Alumona, I., Onuoha, F. (eds.) *Internal Security Management in Nigeria* (Singapore: Palgrave Macmillan), 99-121.

Odoemene, Akachi. 2017. "Whither Peacebuilding Initiatives? The Escalation of Herder-Farmer Conflicts in Nigeria", *Kujenga Amani* (April 7); www.kujenga-amani.ssrc.org/2017/04/07/whither-peacebuilding-initiatives-the-escalation-of-herder-farmer-conflictsin-nigeria (accessed: 08 April 2017).

Odoemene, Akachi. 2021. "The 'Global Land Grab': Why Africa Is and May Remain a Critical Target," In Osakwe, Chukwuma C.C. and Odeh, Lemuel E. (eds.) *History and The Niger Delta: Oil, Politics and Culture* (Festschrift in Honour of Professor Samuel Ovuete Aghalino), (Kaduna: Nigeria Defence Academy Publishers).

Ofuoku, A.U. and Isife, B.I. 2010. "Causes, Effects and Resolution of Farmers-nomadic Cattle Herders Conflict in Delta State, Nigeria", *Agricultura Tropica et Subtropica*, Vol. 43(1), 31–41.

Ogebe, F.O, Daniel Abah and Ligom, L.S. 2019. "Land Use Conflict between Farmers and Herdsmen in Gwer West Local Government Area of Benue State, Nigeria", *IOSR Journal of Agriculture and Veterinary Science (IOSR-JAVS)*, Vol. 12(1), Ser. III (January), 23–31.

Okeke, Okechukwu E. 2014. "Conflicts between Fulani Herders and Farmers in Central and Southern Nigeria: Discourse on Proposed Establishment of Grazing Routes and Reserves", *AFRREV IJAH: An International Journal of Arts and Humanities*, Vol. 3(1), 66–84.

Oladotun, Olagbaju O. and Awosusi, Oladotun Emmanuel. 2019. "Herders-Farmers' Communal Conflict in Nigeria: An Indigenised Language as an Alternative Resolution Mechanism", *International Journal of Multidisciplinary and Current Research*, Vol. 7 (Sept/Oct issue), 615–623.

Olaniran, Sunday Olawale. 2013. "Education for Including the Excluded: Case Study of *Almajiri* Education in Nigeria", proceedings of the 2013 International Pre-Conference of the Commission for International Adult Education (CIAE) of the American Association for Adult and Continuing Education (AAACE); November 3–5, Lexington, Kentucky, USA, 180–189.

Olugbenga, E.O. 2017. "Peace by Pieces: The Politics of Herdsmen's Attacks, Grazing Policy and the Ekiti State Grazing Regulation Law, 2016", *Advances in Social Sciences Research Journal*, Vol. 4(5), 72–89.

Omokhoa, Imongan Ernest and Okuchukwu, Chukwuemeka Egberase. 2018. "Land Resource Governance and Farmers-Herders Conflict in Nigeria", *International Journal of Law*, Vol. 4(3) (May), 104–112.

Omotola, J.S. and Hassan, I. 2015, 'Herders' and Farmers' Associations and Social Conflicts in Northern Nigeria', In Kuna, M.J. and Ibrahim, J. (eds.) *Rural Banditry and Conflict in Northern Nigeria*, Abuja: Centre for Democracy and Development (CDD), 217–256.

Opafunso, Z.O.; Bruno-Imokhai, J.O. and Akinbosade, B.A. 2015. "Effects of the 1978 Land Use Act on Sustainable Mining and Petroleum Industries in Nigeria", *Arts and Social Science Journal*, Vol. 6(2), 1–5.

Ortserga, D.S. (2012). Towards a Model Explaining Change in Agricultural Land Use Patterns in Ute Districts of Vandeikya Local Government Area, Benue State, Nigeria", *International Journal of Humanities and Social Science*, Vol. 2(4), 251–264.

Sule, Peter E. 2020. "Open Grazing Prohibition and the Politics of Exclusivist Identity in Nigeria", *African Review*, 1–17.

Suleiman, S. 2012. "Exhuming Passions: Religion and the Emergence of the Middle Belt Struggle in Nigeria", *Annual Review of Islam* Vol. 11, 18–24.

UK Home Office. 2020. "Country Background Note: Nigeria" (Version 2.0) (January); Nigeria-Background-CPIN-_v2.0__january_2020_ Gov.uk.pdf (accessed 08 November 2020).

Vanger, Emmanuel Terngu. 2018. "Conflicts, Peace-Building and the Sustainability of Farmer-Herder Practices in Tivland of Benue State, Nigeria", Unpublished Doctoral Thesis, University of Nigeria, Enugu Campus, Enugu, Nigeria.

Vanguard Newspaper Online. 2018. "We've Taken Steps to End Herdsmen, Farmers' Clash—FG" (18 May).

Yaro, Suaka D. and Tobias, T. 2019. "Exploring the State of Human Insecurity in Nigeria: The Root Causes of the Farmers-Herdsmen Conflict in Benue State and Its Manifestation on the Livelihood of Rural Farmers and Pastoralists", *ADRRI Journal of Arts and Social Sciences*, Vol. 16(6) (4), 60–98.

CHAPTER 6

Understanding Herder-farmer conflicts in Nasarawa State, Nigeria

J. Shola Omotola

Introduction

The primary objective of this chapter is to contribute to a holistic understanding of herder-farmer conflicts in Nasarawa state, Nigeria. In doing this, we focus on a number of critical issues: historical trajectories and manifestations, actors, causes, consequences and critical lessons for security, development and peacebuilding.

Such a focus is important for many reasons. Once built on mutual trust and interdependence, the relationships between herders and farmers in most parts of Africa have taken a different turn, characterized by fierce competition for space, power and resources, with attendant threats to and/or violations of each other's means of livelihoods, thus creating a relationship fueled by fear and mutual suspicion. The results have not been palatable: national and human insecurity, wanton killings, destruction of property worth billions of dollars, humanitarian emergencies such

J. S. Omotola (✉)
Department of Political Science, Federal University OyeEkiti, Oye-Ekiti, Ekiti, Nigeria
e-mail: sholaomotola@yahoo.com; shoal.omotola@fuoye.edu.ng

J. S. Omotola (ed.), *Herder-Farmer Conflicts in Africa*,
https://doi.org/10.1007/978-3-031-80821-0_6

as refugees and internal displacement of persons and rising tensions. These have had negative implications for social cohesion and nation building, as well as the overall security and development of affected countries (Olumba, 2024; Olumba, et al, 2022; Sabo, 2022; Tade and Yikwab, 2020; Nwankwo, 2024).

What are the underlying causes and consequences of herder-farmer conflicts in the state? How effective have been state and non-state's responses to the problem? What lessons can be learnt from these conflicts and their management sustainable peacebuilding? This chapter engages these questions with a view to deepening knowledge and understanding of the subject-matter. For empirical validation and in-depth analysis, the chapter study focuses on Nasarawa state, one of the middle Belt states, or better still, what is today known as North Central geopolitical zone of Nigeria. As will be shown shortly, the North Central in general and Nasarawa state in particular has been the epicenter of herder-farmer conflicts in Nigeria in recent times (Omotola, 2024a; Nwankwo, 2024; Amnesty International, 2018; International Crisis Group, 2018).

The chapter is organized into sections and subsections. After this introduction, the first substantive section addresses issues in data and methods. The second is devoted to the presentation and analysis of data. This is further divided into eight (8) subsections. These are socio-demographics of respondents, characteristics of herder-farmer conflicts in the state, trends and manifestations, actors and their roles, cause, consequences, management and lessons for peacebuilding. The concluding section basically recaps the key findings and submissions of the chapter.

Study Area,[1] Data and Methods

Popularly referred to as the 'Home of Solid Minerals', Nasarawa state is located in North Central Nigeria. The state was created out of neighbouring Plateau state on 1 October 1996. It is bordered to the West by the Federal Capital Territory, the North by Kaduna, the South by Benue and Kogi, and to the East by Plateau and Taraba states. The state has an area of 27,117 square kilometers, and an estimated population of 2,532,395 million in 2016. Administratively, the state has thirteen Local Government Areas and sixteen Development Areas.

[1] The information in this section was reproduced almost verbatim from my previous work on Nasarawa state (Omotola, 2024a: 172–173).

Like most other states in the region, Nasarawa state is home to many minority ethnic groups, many of which fall into the category of what Omotola (2007, 2008) calls 'sub-ethnic identities', notably the Koro and Yeskwa in the far northwest; the Kofyar in the far north-east; the Eggon, Gwandara, M ada, Ninzo, and Nungu in the north; the Alago, Goemai, and Megili in the east; Eloyi in the south; the Tiv in the southeast; the Idoma in the southwest; and the Gade and Gbagyi in the west while the Hausa and Fulani live throughout the state. The state is also multi-religious, with about a 60%Muslim population, a 30%Christian population, and the remaining 10% are comprised of traditional ethnic religions (Liman and Wakawa, 2012).

Largely agrarian, the economy of the state is predominantly based on agriculture, notably crop farming such as maize, yam, groundnut, millet, soybeans. Animal farming is also practiced, including livestock herding and ranching: cattle, goat and sheep. Though historical, the state has in recent times witnessed the escalation of diverse forms of conflicts, including ethnic and religious conflicts, cattle rustling and rural banditry, herder-farmer conflicts and so on. The ethnic composition of the state, together with the agrarian nature of its economy that not only engenders poverty and inequality, but also compels the cohabitation of farming and cattle herding, has been one of the main triggers and drivers of herder-farmer conflicts in the state (Omotola, 2021a; Aderinto and Achem, 2019).

The study adopts the descriptive research design—qualitatively and quantitatively. Data were collected from both primary and secondary sources. Primary data were collected through surveys using structured questionnaire, Focus Group Discussions (FGDs) and Key Informant Interviews (KII) administered on purposefully selected participants and stakeholders in the selected communities.

Specifically, the fieldwork[2] covered four local government areas (LGAs) in the state, namely Awe, Doma, Lafia and Obi. These were the most affected areas of the state as at the time of the field work in 2019 and later 2021. Lafia, the state capital was included for several reasons. Not only did it host most of the Non-Governmental Organisations (NGOs) involved in post-conflict peacebuilding, it also hosts the head office of Miyetti Allah, the flagship association of Fulani herders in the state. Notable NGOs in Lafia include the Catholic NGO, the Justice Development and Peace Commission (JDPC), whose state Coordinator, Rev. Fr. Mathew Ofoku, was interviewed; Centre for Women, Youth and Community Action (CWYCA), whose Programme Officer in charge of Youth Unit, Mrs Ozioma Ihuoma, also interviewed; and the Shelter Life Environmental Initiative (SLEI), whose Executive Director, Mr. Dan J. Embaga, was also interviewed. I also conducted KII with the leader (King/Paramount ruler) of Miyetti Allah in the state. Again, Lafia hosted the highest number of refugees/displaced persons as a result of the conflicts. The specific communities covered include Ihuman, Imon, Agbashi, Lafia, Migilli, and Agon, among others. Keana, another deeply affected LGA was excluded to accommodate Lafia for the aforementioned reasons.

Overall, 240 copies of the questionnaire (60 per LGA) were administered on purposively selected respondents from which 207 were retrieved and analysed. This was in addition to five (5) FGDs and 17 KIIs. Secondary data were collected from books, journals and reliable online sources. The Armed Conflict Locations and Event Data Project (ACLED) was particularly helpful for the comprehensiveness and currency of

[2] The fieldwork was facilitated by Dr. Chukwuma Okoli of the Department of Political Science, Federal University Lafia (FULAFIA), who is without any doubt one of the most published scholars on the subject in Nigeria. Not only did he bring to bear his wealth of knowledge on the fieldwork, but also assisted in the recruitment of field assistants. A total of six research assistants led by Mr. Michael Chukwu Egwu, then an M.Sc. student in the department, were deployed for the administration of questionnaire in December 2018. It is important to note that Mr. Egwu had been educated in Lafia from Primary up to postgraduate school. He speaks Hausa and other local languages very fluently. The interviews and FGDs were conducted in January/February 2019, with Mr. Egwu and Mr. Jacob S. Abigi, a native of Imon in Awe LGA and a graduate of political science at FULAFIA and other assistants in securing appointments, access and interpretation, where necessary. We lost Mr. Egwu to the cold hands of death in 2022. May his soul continue to rest in peace.

its data. Data analysis was done qualitatively and quantitatively, using frequency distribution, percentage analysis and chats.

Presentation and Discussion of Findings

I. Socio-Demographics of Respondents

In this section, we present the socio-demographics of the respondents, notably sex, age, education, occupation and residency. As noted in the methodology section, a total of 240 copies of the questionnaire were distributed, out of which 207 was retrieved and analyses, indicating 82.8% response rate. Data from the social-demographics shows that 134 (64.7%) of the respondents were male, while 73 (35.3%) were female. A total of 84 (40.6%)) of the respondents fell within the age group of (35–44). This is not surprising being about the productive age group. In addition, 53 (25.6%), 40 (19.3%) and 30 (14.5%) of the respondents represent age groups of 15–24, 25–34 and 45–54 respectively.

In terms of occupation, 81 (39.1%) of the respondents were farmers, 45 (21.7%), herders, 22 (10.6%) civil service and 7 (3.4%) students. Moreover, 17 (8.2%) and 3 (1.4%) were in the NGOs/CSOs and lecturers in higher institutions respectively. The remaining 32 (15.5%) were into trading and business. This occupational distribution of respondents bodes well for the study as slightly above average (50.8%) of them were into farming and herders, suggesting that they have adequate knowledge of the problem under investigation.

In terms of education, 104 (50.2%) had primary education, while 43 (20.8%), 13 (6.3%), and 47(22.7%) possessed secondary, tertiary and informal education respectively. The length of residency of the respondents, which is helpful to certify the validity of their responses, shows that a reasonable number of them (86%) have lived in the state for five years and above; while 5 (2.4%) and 24 (11.6%) had lived in the state between 1- 2 years and 3 -4 years respectively.

II. **Characteristics of Herder-farmer conflicts**

The form and character of herder-farmer conflicts in the state, including its history and changing dynamics were considered Majority

(93.2%) of the respondents believed that herder-farmer conflicts represent one of the greatest sources of security threats in the state. Again, while 84.6% acknowledged a history of such conflicts in the state, 82.6% of the respondents highlighted some of the recent characteristics herder-farmer conflicts in the state, notably higher frequency, intensity and consequences. This suggests that the conflicts are not new in the state. It is longstanding, as in most other parts of the country and Africa. Data sourced from ACLED presented in Figs. 6.1 and 6.2 and other sources support this position (Atelhe and Okoli, 2014; Eke, 2020; Omotola, 2024a).

Majority of the respondents also agreed that herder-farmer conflicts constitute threats to the peace, stability and development of the state. This is not surprising because the state is basically agrarian, with large proportion of the population engaged in farming as full or part-time occupation. The economy of the area thus relies to a great extent on agriculture, which has been the dominant means of economic power for a vast majority of the people of the state. The dislocation to farming communities as a result of these conflicts has really disrupted the local economy with concomitant effect on human security (Ejiofor, 2022; Adigun, 2019; Akov, 2017).

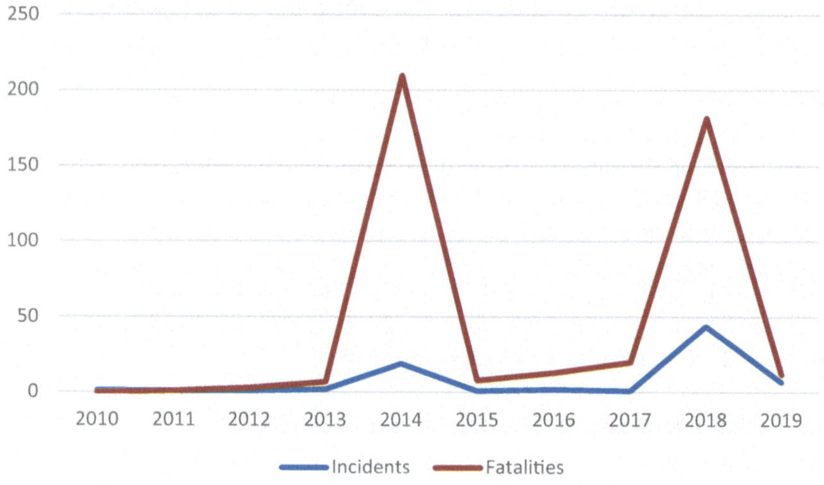

Fig. 6.1 Trend of incidents and fatalities of pastoralist conflicts in Nasarawa (*Source* Data extracted from ACLED)

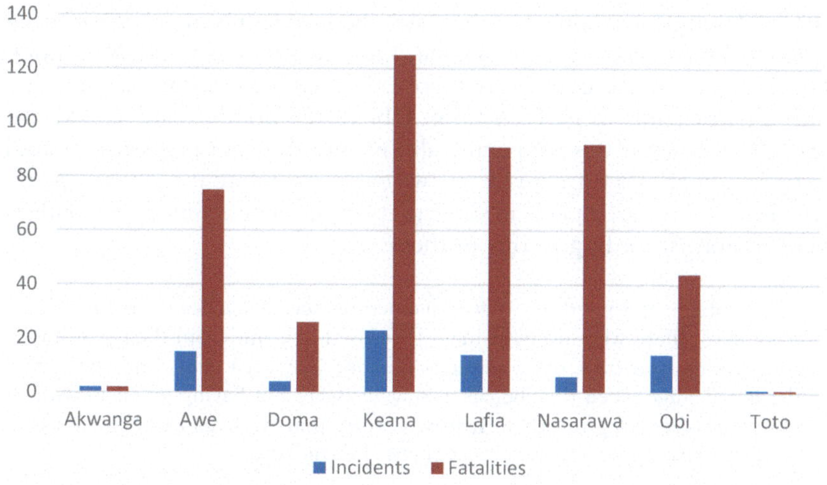

Fig. 6.2 Spatial Distribution of pastoralist conflict in Nasarawa by LGAs (*Source* Data extracted from ACLED)

Additionally, 73.9% of respondents noted that efforts aimed at managing herder-farmer conflicts in the state have been dominated by state actors. This is not to say that non-state actors have been totally excluded. However, 55.5% of the respondents attested to their marginalisation in the handling of herder-farmer conflicts in the state. Moreover, 78.3% of respondents felt that both state and non-state actors have not lived up to expectations in the management of herder-farmer conflicts. Some of the reasons adduced for this include the marginalization of non-state actors and the lack of mutually reinforcing synergy between the state and non-state actors (Madu and Nwankwo, 2021; Omotola, et al., 2019).

III. **Manifestations of Herder-farmer conflicts in Nasarawa State**

Herder-farmer conflicts in the state were not new, with some participants claiming that it had been in existence for over 50 years in the area. The difference, according to them, lies in their changing form and character epitomized by higher manifestations, intensity, casualties, and other wider implications, including the proliferation of small arms and light weapons (Okunade and Kohon, 2023; Yikwab and Tade, 2022; Blench,

2010). Though widespread in the state, the problem is more pronounced in some LGAs, namely Awe, Doma, Obi, Keana, Lafia and Nassarawa. The frequency of the conflicts in these LGAs has increased in recent times, with a participants in FGD at Imon Obi village noting that: 'Unlike last year, 2018 when it was happening almost monthly, but previously it used to be in sometimes once a year or twice a years before it reoccurs again'. However, a few participants in some parts of the state claimed the conflicts were recent. According to one of them:

> The problem is something that is happening recently, because before we were here, there were no herdsmen, they used to come from their pastoral activities and go back. As time goes on they began to come and stay. At the initial stage when they began to stay, we were not having problem with that, we were living in peace. It was recently that we began to experience conflict between we (farmers) and them (herdsmen).

While it is a settled matter that these conflicts have existed for some time in the area, the absence of official records made it difficult to know the accurate number of cases and fatalities. The few available sources based their accounts on selected newspaper reports that are hardly exhaustive. For example, Okoli and Atelhe (2014: 9) reported only 10 incidents between 2010 and 2012. In another study, Okoli and Ogayi (2018) listed 18 attacks, which resulted into 259 deaths nationwide in 2015. None of these cases was attributed to Nasarawa state. They also reported 37 attacks and 752 deaths nationwide between January and April 2016. Only one of these attacks was credited to Nasarawa state, claiming 12 lives. Similarly, Akov (2017: 296) documented 25 cases of herder-farmer conflicts in North Central Nigeria between February 2011 and June 2016. Only four (4) of these occurred in Nasarawa state.

Similarly, Amnesty International (2018: 5) reported 196 deaths as a result of herder-farmer conflicts in the state between January 2016 and October 2018, but nothing was said about the number of incidents. The International Crisis Group (ICG, 2018: 2) reported that the state recorded 260 deaths between January and June 2018 in the southern zone of the state covering Doma, Awe, Obi and Keana. The contradictions in these statistical data provided by various sources are glaring. While Amnesty International reported 196 deaths over a period of three years,

ICG reported 260 over a period of six months (half a year). These uncoordinated figures point to the challenge of documentation and accurate data on the problem.

ACLED provides a much more reliable source of data on the conflicts. It documented 15,610 incidents of armed conflicts in Nigeria between 1997 and 2019. Out of these, 1,473 (9.4%) of the total incidents involved pastoralists, out of which 79 incidents (5.4%) occurred in Nasarawa State. The details are presented in Fig. 6.1.

Figure 6.1 reveals that a total of 79 pastoralist conflicts were documented in Nassarawa state between 2010 and 2019. The first was recorded in 2010 without any fatality. The years 2011 and 2012 also recorded only one incident each and two in 2013. By 2014, the incidents jumped to 19, but declined again to one, two and one in 2015, 2016 and 2017 respectively. There was another sudden increase in the number of cases to 44 in 2018, before it dropped again to seven (7) in 2019. The rise of the incidents beginning from 2010 upward is not totally surprising. As studies have shown, the state experienced 'the appearance of "new" pastoralists since 2011, when the Boko Haram insurgency began to hit the Borno communities' (Blench, 2010: 7).

The sudden quantum leap in the number of incidents and fatalities from one (1) and (0) respectively in 2010 to 44 and 182 in the same order in 2018 deserves some comments. The first and the most basic thing that comes to mind relates to the fact that 2018 preceded the 2019 general elections. As the elections drew closer, the country witnessed the escalation of herder-farmer conflicts. The rise in attacks fueled speculations about the political undertones of most of those conflicts, the same way it reinforced the claim about the politicization of the conflict. As the ICG (2018: 31) puts it, 'today's agrarian-pastoralist conflict in Nigeria is grounded in environmental and political transformations long in the making'.

In terms of fatalities, the 79 incidents produced a total of 456 deaths between 2010 and 2019. Although, on the surface the data suggest the likelihood of the fact that the higher the number of incidents, the higher the number of fatalities. After all 19 incidents produced 210 fatalities in 2014; the same way 44 incidents produced 182 deaths in 2018. A critical examination, however, suggests the need for caution. On the average, one incident in 2014 produced 11 fatalities, compared to 4.1 in 2018. Moreover, one incident produced an average of 1, 3, 3.5, 8 and 6.5 in

2011, 2012, 2013, 2015 and 2016 respectively. The highest fatality of 20 deaths was produced by a single incident in 2017 (Omotola, 2024a).

What the foregoing suggests is that the relationships between incidents and fatalities deserve a close examination. Beyond the number of incidents, much may depend on many other factors, including the actors involved in each incident, the types of weapons deployed and the nature of response(s) to the incident in terms of their timeliness and effectiveness.

Figure 6.2 speaks to the spatial distribution of the conflicts by LGAs across the state. The 79 incidents occurred in eight out of the 13 LGAs in the state. Keana LGA recorded the highest number of 23 incidents and 125 fatalities. This was followed by Awe LGA with 15 incidents and 75 fatalities. Lafia LGA had 14 incidents and 91 fatalities; followed by Obi LGA with 14 incidents and 44 fatalities, and Nassarawa LGA with six (6) incidents and 92 fatalities. Doma LGA had four (4) incidents and 26 fatalities; followed by Akwanga LGA with two (2) incidents and two (2) fatalities; and finally Toto LGA with one (1) incident and one (1) fatality.

Again, the data in Fig. 6.2 corroborate our earlier position that fatalities are not always directly related to the number of incidents. In Keana with the highest number of 23 incident and highest number of fatalities (125), for example, an incident caused an average of 5.4 deaths. The average death per incident is far lower than that of Nasarawa LGA with a total of 6 incident and 92 fatalities. This amounts to an average of 15.3 deaths per incident.

IV. **Actors in Herder-farmer conflicts in Nassarawa State**

For some of the FGD participants, there are two major actors involved in the conflicts, namely herders and farmers. For some others, especially majority of those interviewed, several other actors abound. These include governments at various levels (federal, state and local), security agents (formal and informal), civil society organisations (CSOs), traditional institutions, religious organizations, the media, etc.

Specifically, herders and farmers were recognized as the leading actors in the conflicts by 76.8% and 73.9% of the respondents respectively. Others in the order of their rating are the youths (70%), traditional institutions (68.6%), security agents (67.1%), religious associations and insurgents (both at 66.6%), pan-ethnic associations (65.7%), vigilante groups (64.2%), women and community associations (both by 63.8%), the media (63.7%), and CSOs/NGOs (43.0%).

The roles of these actors have been documented in the literature (see Nwankwo, 2021; Tade and Yikwabs, 2020; Blench, 2010, Kwaja and Ademola-Adelehin, 2017). But for the FGD participants, what herders and farmers tend to complicate the problem through 'exaggeration, by telling others what did not happen'.

These findings are in tandem with the qualitative data generated from FGDs and KIIs. One specific area of interest is the dual but conflicting roles ascribed to traditional rulers (Omotola, 2024a. For the people of Imon Obi village, traditional institutions and rulers were parts of the problem. As they content:

> When they (herdsmen) started staying here, indigenous rulers, the emirs and politicians- began to sell to them our land. When you go there to farm you find it difficult to farm- that is the major problem. They sold people's farms to them; they built their houses there now. By so doing they deny the people access to their ancestral land for farming.

The people also complained about the allocation of their lands for grazing routes, which they objected. In response, they mounted a lot of pressure, including protests, on their traditional rules to no avail. The failure to heed their demands by the traditional rules further contributed to the conflicts. According to one of the FGD participants at Imon Obi village:

> There have being series of protests. They wanted to divide our land to create grazing route, which was cut across many farms without our consent. This action was done between the Fulani Herders and the Traditional rulers, so we stood against it that it couldn't work.

The role of the media in the conflict also received mixed assessment. While they were credited with reporting the conflicts, some accused them of bias (see Eke, 2020). As an interviewee noted:

> They were biased because the accurate result of their coverage was not what was really happening especially the state media. The report is not comprehensive enough. Sometimes you discovered they put it on air that two people were killed, but in real sense ten people would have been killed. And sometimes they may say it is unknown people that carried out

> the attack when they knew the perpetrators and what was happening, that the herdsmen carried out the attacks. So the media are biased.

Security agents were also recognized as one of the important actors in the process, whose main roles are to enforce and keep peace in the areas. Although they were credited to have always responded to distress calls for help by communities under attacks, there were also criticisms against their professionalism and overall performance (Kwaja and Ademola-Adelehin, 2018a, 2018b). Some of the allegations against them include failure to work proactively based on early warning signals, late deployment of personnel, corruption and extortions, early withdrawal or reduction in the number of personnel, and in some instances, violation of human rights of the locals. At times, 'order from above' or the nature of the mandate given to them for the mission by the deploying authorities may have encumbered them. A participant at the FGD in Imon village noted that during 'certain periods when such invasions are witnessed beyond the premises of the town and the security men especially the MOPOL are notified, they are reluctant or quickly pull back saying they were not permitted to go beyond the town to settle dispute'. Additionally, security personnel were also accused of failing to arrest any of the perpetrators, let alone prosecuting them. This failure, some alleged, contributed to the protracted nature of the conflicts. As one FGD participants at Imon Obi village lamented:

> We never witnessed any arrest from the attackers. They have always done it and gone free. They are always reported as unknown gunmen. None of them has even been arrested not to talk of prosecuting them.

V. **Causes of Farmer-Herder Conflicts**

Many explanations have been offered for herder-farmer conflicts in Nigeria generally and Nasarawa state in particular (Okunade and Kohon, 2023; Adigun, 2019; Ndubusi, 2018; Okoli and Ogayi, 2018; Shettima and Tar, 2008). These include environmental factors such as drought, scarcity and migration, all leading to migration and competition for resources; self preservation, each defending their source of livelihood; local peculiarities/dynamics, including the role/influence of politicians and traditional rulers; encroachment/destruction and/or occupation of farmlands by herders –some respondents called it 'illegal' cattle rearing; the impact of fake news, misinformation, disinformation; indigeneity and identity crisis; influence of the availability and use of hard drugs; proliferation of small arms and light weapons; a feeling of deprivation of rights by herders occasioned by blockage/farming on grazing routes; and poor management of the problem by the government.

For elaboration, one of the major drivers of the conflicts is their poor management, including failure to arrest and prosecute offenders—86% of the respondents shared this view. Again, 67.1% of respondents also considered security agencies as threats to stable herder-farmer relation in the area. Lack of professionalism by security agents was identified by 69.5% of the respondents as a key challenge. Poor herder-farmer relations (82.6%) were also fingered. This is not surprising because herders and farmers association were noted to be influential factors for a stable herders and farmers relation (see Omotola and Hassan, 2015). Other causes of the conflicts highlighted by respondents include poor regulatory framework (81.6%); the proliferation and use of small arms and light (76.3%), ethnicization and politicization of tensions (75.9%), environmental scarcity (75.4%), abuse of social media (70.5%), fake news (66.2%), publication of hate speeches (64.3%), encroachment on grazing routes by farmers (59.9%), competition for resources (58.5%), and poor management of resources (58.4%).

The defence of source of livelihood by both herders and farmers was also highlighted as one of the causes of the conflict. As gathered from one FGD in Awe LGA, 'herders are defending the cattle; farmers are defending the farms'. This tension is not unconnected to what some participants called 'illegal' cattle rearing; illegal because 'anywhere they like, even in somebody's farm, they rear their cattle'. Dan Embega, Executive Director of Shelter Life Environmental Initiative, a leading NGO in Lafia, narrated to me in a KII how one Musa Sadam was returning from office in Lafia only form him to be greeted with an ugly incident that bothered on impunity. According to him:

> Muwa was returning from office one day and saw some Fulani returning from their house coming and when he got home his sister told him that you see those Fulani men; they harvested their father's rice, brought it home and put the cow on the farm to graze. Supposing their father was to harvest 100 bags of rice and they brought 20 or even lesser, what happens?

A woman (secondary school teacher) who participated in the FGD also narrated her personal experience thus:

> Our problem with these herdsmen, like me, there was a time I was inside my farm so I saw many of them coming into my farm to eat up what I planted. When I was talking the Fulani boys said it is their wish to allow me to work in there, if they do not allow me to work there I will not work there so I should not talk to them. When I was angry they just put the cattle inside my farm to eat it up. When I was running to come, so the boy now removed his cutlass and threatened to attack me. What am I to do? I was afraid because of my life and I ran away and left them with the farm and they have eaten it all. It is one of my fellow teachers here that I carried him to go and witness how the Fulani ate up my farm. So I say OK if that is the case, let me just pack my seed and go away but the teacher said I should not pack that there would be solution for it. Since that time up till today, there is no solution. That is our problem with these herdsmen. When you talk they will just remove the cutlass then because of your farm you will sell your life to the Fulani, you run away. That is why you see us, we are moving helter-skelter now.

Another one noted that the problem goes beyond destruction of farms to actual occupation of farm lands by herdsmen. According to him, destruction of farm land by herders and the killings of farmers whenever they see that their farm crops cannot be destroyed are common. The occupation of the farmland also happen once conflicts erupted. When probed further, he revealed that such occupations could last for as long as nine (9) months in some cases. During such periods of occupation, the farmers allegedly survive on handouts from local government authorities. According to one of those interviewed at Imon, during such periods:

> There will be nothing for them to feed on and they couldn't farm but the authorities given them money that is why you meet them at home now for your study when they are supposed to be in the farm. They are farmers they should be preparing their land for the next farming seasons. But there is nowhere to go to because the farmlands have been occupied by herdsmen.

Another major cause of the conflict relates to the passage of the Anti-Grazing Law in neighbouring Benue state. Studies have documented how the anti-open grazing law contributed to the escalation of the problem in Nasarawa state. Although the state does not have such a law of its own, the passage of the law in neighbouring Benue state led to the migration and massive influx of herdsmen and cattle from Benue into the state (Tade and Yakwabs, 2020; Kwaja and Ademola, 2017).

The 'forced' migration was justified by the migrants on a number of reasons. One, the law was so sudden and enforcement almost immediate without room for preparation and adjustment. Two, those enforcing the laws, including livestock guards, allegedly resorted to extortions of herdsmen through livestock seizure and imposition of heavy fines before the animals are released. Three, bandits and rustlers also took advantage of the situation to seize 'cattle arbitrarily under the pretext of enforcing the law'. Four, bearing the costs of ranching, including the 'production and supply of feed and buying grass, rice chaff and water for their cattle, costs they had never borne before, meant the loss or lack of profits (ICG, 2018).

Different figures have been bandied for the number of herders and cattle that migrated from Benue state as a result of the anti-grazing law. With respect to Nasarawa state, 'MACBAN leader Alhaji Musa Muahhed-Mati in a KII session with me asserted that 'two million cows from Benue state had crossed into Awe local government area as of 3 November 2017'. This contradicts the official position of the state, which claimed through the Benue state governor's special assistant on herders' matters, Alhaji Shehu Tambaya that 'about 3,600 of the 6,000 herders had left, along with some 10,000 of the 16,000 cattle owned by Fulani in the state'. In his own account, the Benue MACBAN leader said that 'about 3,000 herdsmen have moved to neighbouring states in Nasarawa and Taraba'. The key point, as the rightly argued, is the fact that irrespective of the different figures, the migration of herders and their cattle from Benue to Nasarawa contributed to the conflict. As the ICG poignantly puts it:

> Regardless of these discrepancies, the sudden influx of thousands of cattle into Nasarawa state created new tensions between the predominantly Fulani herders and the mostly Tiv farmers. In spite of the state government's efforts, the mistrust soon degenerated into deadly violence (ICG, 2018: 11).

Although environmental scarcity and attendant competition for resources have been one of the dominant explanations in the literature, our fieldwork in Imon Obi village suggested the need to be careful not to overgeneralize those factors. As one of the FGD participants pointed out:

> There are no farms during the dry season. Our water here do not dry up during the dry season. Farms are destroyed mostly in the raining season when there is no scarcity of grasses and water. Another thing is that if there are no grasses during the dry season, they will be plucking people's mangoes and destroying economic trees. And when you ask them, they will say, it is very important for their animals to eat.

VI. **Consequences of Herder-farmer conflicts in Nasarawa State**

Herder-farmer conflicts have had diverse consequences for the state and beyond as attested by the findings of this study. This aligns with the mainstream literature on the subject (Sabo, 2022; Nwanko, 2021; Mohammed, et al, 2021; Yikwab and Tade, 2022). Findings reveal that the conflicts constitute threats to the peace, stability and development of the state. Specifically, some of the most notable negative impacts of the conflicts include loss of lives and properties as supported by 87.4% of the respondents, internal displacement (85.5%), destruction of farm lands (82.2%), food scarcity or insecurity (80.7%), unemployment (79.7%), loss of revenue (76.46%), huge cost of rehabilitation (69.5%) and challenges associated with returning and reintegration (75.4%). Other negative effects include their psychological and traumatic effect (75.4%) and impact on women and children (67.6%).

One major effect of the conflicts relates to huge destruction of lives and properties in the state. With respect to deaths, we have already shown in Figs. 6.1 and 6.2 how the conflicts claimed 456 lives in 79 incidents across eight LGAs of the state between 2010 and 2019. The bulk of these deaths were recorded in 2014 and 2018, years preceding the 2015 and 2019 elections respectively. At the risk of repetition, 19 incidents claimed 210 lives in 2014, while 44 incidents claimed 182 lives in 2018. This trend tends to support the allegations about the politicization of the herder-farmer conflicts (see Figs. 6.1 and 6.2).

There have also been socioeconomic consequences of the conflicts. In terms of destruction of properties, houses, churches, farms and cattle would appear to be the greatest victims. An interviewee noted: 'When they eat up the yams in the farm, the attack the community and in the process they also cause displacement of their settlement. The people are displaced from their homes, killings of human life and setting ablaze of their shelters, their houses.' Another participant at FGD at Imon Obi village captures it more aptly:

> The inhabitants of this place are typical farmers, and they depend entirely on farming as their life. When farms are destroyed then your hope is shattered...Giving you a typical example of what has happened few months ago, the herdsmen walked into farms where yam seedlings were preserved for the next planting seasons and they set fire on it. This happened in this very area, just a few metres from where we are sitting. The farmers when they discovered and met some herdsmen with their ammunition, they (herdsmen) set fire on the farm and ran away.

The humanitarian effects of the conflicts have also been well documented. These include forced migration and internal displacements of persons (IDPs). Again, the ICG (2018: 12) documents that between September 2017 and June 2018 alone, 'farmer-herder violence left at least 1,500 people dead, many more wounded and about 300,000 displaced'. Out the figures for displacement, 'an estimated 176,000 in Benue, about 100,000 in Nasarawa, over 100,000 in Plateau, about 19,000 in Taraba and an unknown number in Adamawa'. In its own report, Amnesty International (2018: 16) reported that the conflicts had resulted in '406 injured, 5,000 houses burnt down and 182,530 people displaced' across 22 states and the Federal Capital Territory (FCT), Abuja between 2016 and 2018.. In Nasarawa state, IDP camps were opened in Awe, Kanje and Lafia LGAs where I visited in the course of my fieldwork.

The reality of humanitarian crisis is in conformity with the position of FGD participants. They agreed that it affected all of them. As one person puts it, 'it affects all of us negatively. It makes farmers not to go to their farms, it affects us negatively. Both the people that are involved in such conflicts and those outside that are not involved. It affects all of us both the community'. Another noted: 'there was loss of lives, property, people lose their shelter'. Another FGD participant in Awe LGA reported that:

> I left my village in Goje. I am right now in Awe town. You know when these things happen, we were inside our house in the village here, in the night, we just saw some people coming on machine not even knowing what they were coming to do. Later they stopped their machine, opened bullet and we started running for safety. They killed one of our sons in

> the village so people ran away. I left my machine (Motor bike) inside my house and ran away and left everything. The following day before I could come, my machine got lost. Because everybody in the village scattered I could not stay there again. I ran to Awe town from where I now come to school. Apart from my house rent, I pay N200 for transportation to come to work every day. It has not been easy.

The conflicts also had severe consequences for women and children in the state. ICG reported appalling conditions in the IDP camps it visited in Benue state, the same conditions applied to Nasarawa state as attested by KIIs. In these camps:

> IDPs, mostly women and children, had severely inadequate shelter and food, and were at risk of communicable disease'... The camps are overcrowded and lack safe drinking water; poor sanitation is compounded by open defecation... in some cases, up to 100 people are jammed into a classroom while others sleep in the fields, at the mercy of rains and mosquitoes. In early April, at least seven children died from an outbreak of measles at the sprawling Abagena camp on the outskirts of the Benue state capital, Makurdi, which houses an estimated 35,000 people. Others have died of malaria and diarrhea... Women and children are particularly hard-hit ... Some were raped by attackers... Thousands of pregnant women and nursing mothers in IDP camps have little or no health and sanitary facilities. As most camps have no perimeter fencing and sleeping spaces are not gender-segregated, girls and women are exposed to the risks of sexual harassment, assault and rape, both by outsiders and by fellow IDPs, and vulnerable to desperate survival mechanisms involving sexual exploitation. Many women and children are traumatised by the killings, raising concerns for their mental health, with possibly long-term effects (ICG, 2018: 12)

Though the above conditions were made with reference to Benue state, they also applied to Nasarawa state. Some of the interviewees reported cases of loss of pregnancy by some women as a result of stress and psychological trauma. Issues of malnutrition especially for children were also reported. In one particular instance, a participant at one of the FGDs expressly captured these dimensions when he submitted that 'by the time they are running for their lives, some children died, some pregnant women had miscarriage. Some will die because of lack of food and health facilities in the camps. Some women after delivery there will be nothing to care for them, both the mother and the children'. Another impact of the conflicts on women has to do with attendant hardship. For instance, at Kanje village participants at the FGD lamented herdsmen who seized and occupied their farmlands were also chasing away their women from the only stream where they fetch drinking water.

The conflicts have also had dire consequences for education. While this cuts across all levels of education (primary, secondary and tertiary), primary education were the worst hit. The ICG (2018) noted how 'children's education has also been badly hurt'. It also reported how 'armed attacks and the establishment of IDP camps have forced over 35 primary schools to close, interrupting the education of thousands of children' (ICG, 2018: 12). In Imon and Ihumon, participants showed me schools that had been closed for at least seven (7) months as a result of herder-farmer conflicts. In Imon Obi village, people reported that both the primary and secondary schools in the village had been closed for almost a year as a result of the conflicts. As one of the FGD participants explained: 'It is almost a year now that both primary and secondary schools have been abandoned. Because people were displaced—they ran away with their wards and children'.

The security implications of the conflicts were many. They include physical attacks and reprisal attacks, perpetual fear of attack, loss of freedom, food crisis and general insecurity. A more serious dimension relates to the proliferation of small arms and light weapons in the state. Almost all the participants in the FGDs and KIIs consented to this reality. It agrees with the findings of other empirical studies, one of which posits that;all of those interviewed agreed that weapons are becoming increasingly common on all sides, and that they are more and more sophisticated' (Blench, 2010: 8). A participant in the FGD at Imon Obi captures these tendencies thus:

> Yes, because where you go to pack your farm produce for use, those people are chasing you with ammunitions, you hardly escape. That's one area. Another area is that there are so many living witnesses in the village, people attacked with cutlasses. Some were left lame as a result of such attacks. You now find people living in perpetual fear. Another area in terms of security, there was a time like this, where people were lying down in their compound and suddenly we heard gunshots -two/three times. It resulted to a grown up girl been killed, she was shot in the belly. She eventually died on the way to the hospital and the father was injured, with broken bones. This happened just a few metres from where we are sitting (along this road). There is a lot, this has created a lot of insecurity, so that for

> the fear of an unknown, you find people packing their loads and ran away from this place.

Concerns have also been raised about the health implications of the conflicts. Apart from those already highlighted under the humanitarian challenges, particularly in IDP camps, one of the people interviewed at Imon Obi village, a retired medical practitioner, drew attention to the health implications of cow dung. According to him:

> Where herdsmen are roaming the street with their animals, the danger of it looking from the Medical Personnel perspective, is the risk of having animal dung in our premises. It has health implications because animal dung has different types of organism. You could find women dry their corn or cassava in front of their compound, and then cows come to pass their dung there. This is not hygienic. And anytime you are not happy about that you find a cutlass raised against you and if you are not careful your hands will be chopped off. This thing persists. If you like to have eye witness, we can move around and see cow dung in the compounds. This is risky for health.

The conflicts also contributed to the increase in crime rate in the state. Crimes such as armed murder, robbery, kidnapping, banditry and so on has intensified in the state. The conflicts also raised some human rights issues, especially with the securitization of official responses to the conflicts. Studies have documented these cases (Amnesty International, 2018; Nwanko, 2021; Omotola and Oyewole, 2024).

Management of Herder-Farmer conflicts in Nasarawa state

There have been official (governmental) and unofficial (non-governmental) responses to managing herder-farmer conflicts in the state. Governments at various levels have intervened using various methods, including the deployment of security, panel of inquiry, establishment and management of IDP camps, the provision of relief materials, attempts at demilitarization and amnesty, and peace education. At the unofficial level, NGOs/CSOs have invested in peace education, persuasion and advocacy, dialogue and conflict resolution, provision of humanitarian aid/assistance and facilitating the safe return, resettlement and reintegration of victims of displacement, among others.

FGDs and KIIs reveal some of what the specific interventions of government in managing the problem. Participants noted that 'they sent military men, security men like our village now, people started coming back but government now put some police there, they are always there. Some of us stated coming back'. Another said that the government 'sometimes they bring clothes, foodstuffs something to give us being IDPs in Awe'.

However, official interventions may have been hampered by the problem of corruption. As one FGD participant noted:

> The young person talking in terms of food, actually there is no food. The government supply but you understand the Nigeria factor. The food is sent through one person to this person, the real people that were affected will get little or nothing because just like the middlemen this one will take his share and these people that are really affected will not get. The people that represented them will make gain.

An interviewee, Dan Embega, Dan Embega, Executive Director of Shelter Life Environmental Initiative, one of the leading NGOs that have been involved in responding to the conflicts in the state, was much more critical of the role of government in handling the situation. According to him, the government did not live up to expectations:

> Government has not done enough so far. They set up a committee to look into the matter but nothing is done thereafter. I attended their last meeting but nothing concrete happened there. ... If you were accused of keeping Fulani herdsmen and there was nothing done, no investigation. The people who did this are Fulani, did you address them? Did you warn them? There was nothing like that. It is just to say we want peace but nothing beyond that. They will set up a committee, talk and then go away. The leadership of the Fulani people know that the government is siding with them and whatever you say at the meeting then they will be there, they will plead to the people that are in charge and ignore you.

Different non-state actors have also been credited with some helpful interventions. In some places, churches, traditional rulers and some individuals were said to have made facilities available for people to sleep. Churches and traditional rules reportedly provided food and shelter for some IDPs. Traditional ruler in Ihumon was also said to have organized peace meetings between herders and farmers to mediate in the conflict.

Vigilantes not only provide night watch services, but also device a means of alerting the people early enough in the event of impending dangers or attacks. As one of those interviewed said:

> … in another way you see these vigilantes as they are these young people come in group to play at night and people do come to watch so that if there is anything they alert people that are asleep so that they will wake up and run. But if any of them is caught with arm they know it is a serious one. But those ones that come from the bush (herdsmen) they move freely with arms.

At a much more organised level, some NGOs have made some other interventions. In 2015, for example, Shelter Life Environmental Initiative, in partnership with Global Priorities Solution, USA, held a workshop at the Ministry of Information in Lafia, where they brought the Minister of Information and many other stakeholders to discuss options for sustainable peacebuilding. Also in 2016, the same organization held another event to sensitise the youth of the state on the need to eschew violence and embrace peace. Most of these sensitization and peace education programmes drew participants from across stakeholders, including farmers, herders, District Heads, religious leaders, youth leaders and women leaders.

In another assessment of the role of these actors, one participant noted the inadequacy of official and unofficial responses. As she noted:

> In the first place, when the herdsmen destroy your crops and you ask question, it result to them killing you at the bush and when the farmers take up the matter to the traditional leaders they will say they themselves don't have anything to do, the herdsmen are more than what they can handle. But to the government, the government always snubs the news insisting that it is armed robbers. Whenever you complain that it was the herdsmen, the government will insist that it was armed robbery.

The assessment of the management of herder-farmer conflicts at both the official and unofficial levels by the participants in the FGDs and those interviewed was largely negative. The people seemed generally dissatisfied with the performance of state and non-state actors. Overwhelming majority (78.3%) of the respondents said that the actors did not live up to expectations in the management of the conflicts. Participants in the survey lamented the terrible conditions of the IDP camps to illustrate the failure. Issues raised include acute shortage of food leading to hunger and health challenges. They also alluded to poor sanitary conditions, especially for women, girls and children, poor security, and others. One interviewee at Kanje village aptly described the frustration thus:

> One thing is that we heard that the government announced that people should come back to their places that the crises have finished. But that was not correct. *We decided to come back and die in our community because we were fed up with the terrible state of life in the IDP camp* (Emphasis mine).

Many reasons were adduced for the ineffectiveness of interventions. These include the dominance of state and the marginalization of non-state actors, political interference, corruption and extortions of the locals, and failure to act proactively using early warning signals/reports, leading to late deployment of security personnel. In more specific terms, the inadequacy of management strategies was attributed to problems associated with regulatory frameworks (73,3%), poor response to early warning signals (86.4%), failure to arrest and prosecute perpetrators (79.8%), poor responses by the government (83.5%), failure of CSOs/NGOs to live up to expectations (74.8%) and the ethnicization and politicization of the conflicts (72.9%).

Corruption and poor control also contributed. Though not peculiar to it alone, it is a problem that is deeply rooted among security agents. Amnesty International (2018: 55–56) gave a harrowing narrative that depicted a clear case of how corruption in the security sector has been a major clog in the wheel of progress in addressing herder-farmer conflicts in the state that warrants extensive quotation. The report noted:

> Some residents of villages from Nasarawa... and Kokona LGAs and Agwada, Udege, and Loko Development Area Councils, all within Nasarawa State, on 10 March 2017 wrote a petition to the Chief of Army Staff seeking help against what they described as incessant attacks by Fulani gunmen on their communities... The army wrote a letter to the Inspector General of Police (IGP), attaching the petition, asking the IGP to "look into the petition with a view to taking necessary action to remedy the situation"... The IGP forwarded the letter to the Deputy Inspector General of Police in charge of Force Criminal Intelligence and Investigation Department for investigation... The villagers told Amnesty International that the policemen sent from the Nigeria Police Force Headquarters asked them to pay N150,000 ($411 in 2019), for logistics, which they paid in cash,

> because the policemen did not want to leave any trace of the funds to them. But only three policemen were sent to Nasarawa LGA. The policemen then went to the police station in Agwada town... between the 25 and 27 May 2017, where they asked people from the affected villages to come and write statements... According to a resident of one of the villages, the policemen refused to go to the villages,... complaining of bad road and that the Fulani gunmen had better weapons than them.

VII. Lessons for Peacebuilding

Some key lessons for peacebuilding are discernible from the study. These lessons are mainly derived from the major causes and management strategies of the conflicts as articulated in the chapter. First, there is a strong case was made for paying more attention to early warning signals by 79.7% of the respondents. Others include the need for a clear and focus regulatory framework (77.8%), greater interface between state and non-state actors (75.9%), more space and roles for non-state actors in the management of herder-farmer relations (74.4%), and the need to uphold effective regulation of the social media (66.2%) to combat the phenomenon of fake news.

Other key lessons established during FGDs and KIIs include:

- The need to pay attention to the question of late deployment, early withdrawal or reduction in the number of security agents deployed for peacekeeping in affected areas. This challenge was noted across the state by participants in the study. The challenge has turned out to be inimical to sustainable peacebuilding. The lesson here is that there is need for early and adequate deployment of security agents not just in number, but also in terms of the equipment, including communication gadgets and motivation (welfare). The government should not always be in a hurry to withdraw security agents on such missions at the slightest sign or sight of ceasefire by the warring parties.
- Better management of returnees matters, including issues of their safety, resettlement and reintegration. Reconstruction, rehabilitation, security, empowerment, confidence buildings are also important. They are critical to sustainable peacebuilding. A situation whereby IDPs hurriedly returned to their communities, either voluntarily or not, only to be confronted with the gory pictures of destroyed and/

or burnt houses and properties is not healthy for peacebuilding. In some of the LGAs visited for the field work, especially Awe and Obi, this was the situation. Houses and schools destroyed remained unattended over a year after. Yet, the returnees were allowed to return empty handed, meaning there was little or nothing to restart with upon return to their communities. Returning to meet those facilities in their terrible state reincarnated the gory tales and memories of the conflicts. This has implications for the healing process and should be avoided.

- Better management of IDP camps is pertinent. The significance of this can be located in the confession of some of the returnees that that they returned not because the environment was conducive for that. Rather, they made the hard choice between staying in the IDP camps and die of hunger and starvation, or risk returning to their communities and start whatever they could to eke a living. The main lesson here is that both state and non-state actors need to do more in their management of the IPD camps. If they had given adequate attention to the welfare needs of IDPs, including security, food, health and sanitary requirements, the premature urge to return to their communities, despite unfavourable conditions that could engender future conflicts, could have been avoided.
- Sustainable peacebuilding also demands investment in demilitarisation, especially of society. This is important in the wake of not just the massive proliferation and use of SALWs in these conflicts, but also the escalating rate of crimes across the state. As the findings of the study reveal, previous efforts aimed at tracking and withdrawing SALWs have not been productive. All actors need to do more in this regard.
- There is need for sustainable peace education through CSOs, media, religious houses (Churches and Mosques) and schools. The peace message should emphasise the need to eschew violence and embrace peaceful coexistence.
- The question of the accountability of security agents is also important.

Conclusion

This chapter has engaged herder-farmer conflicts in Nasarawa state, Nigeria. It placed emphasis on trends, manifestations, causes, management, consequences and lessons for peacebuilding. The chapter shows that the problem is longstanding, but has assumed changing form and character in contemporary times. Again, the conflicts are connected to a number of factors, notably environmental scarcity, migration and competition for scarce natural resources, complicity of security agents and other actors, and the poor management of the conflicts by both state and non-state actors. The passage of the Anti-Open Grazing Law by Benue state government was also very decisive, forcing herders from the state to migrate *en mass* to Nasarawa state, thereby putting addition pressure on already scarce natural resources in the state. The conflicts had negative consequences for both state and society, including their effects on national and human security, deaths, displacements, and loss of sources of livelihood. They also have gender implications, including rape, assaults, loss of pregnancy and miscarriages by women in IDP camps. While both state and non-state actors made diverse interventions to manage the conflicts, some with overlapping activities, these responses, though not without some positive impact, were generally considered to be inadequate or ineffective. Some of the reasons offered for this include the reliance on poor regulatory frameworks, dominance of state and the marginalization of non-state actors, political interference, corruption and extortions of the locals by security agents, and failure to act proactively using early warning signals/reports, leading to late deployment of security personnel. The critical lessons for sustainable peacebuilding derived from these finding include collaboration between state and non0state actors, prompt deployment of security agents based on early warning reports, avoiding premature withdrawal or reduction in the number of security agents deployed for peacekeeping in conflict affected areas, better management of returnees and IDP camps, demilitarization and continuous peace education.

References

Aderinto, A. and Achem, V. 2019, 'A concentric approach to understanding herderfarmer clashes in Benue and Nasarawa states, Nigeria', *International Journal of Sociology and Anthropology*, 11(4), pp. 37–42. https://doi.org/10.5897/IJSA2019.0803.

Adigun, O. W. 2019. 'A critical analysis of the relationship between climate change, land disputes, and the patterns of farmers/herdsmen's conflicts in Nigeria', *Canadian Social Science, 15*(3), pp. 76–89.

Akov, E. T. 2017, 'The resource-conflict debate revisited: Untangling the case of farmer–herdsman clashes in the North Central region of Nigeria', *African Security Review, 26*(3), pp. 288–307.

Amnesty International. 2018. 'Harvest of death: Three years of bloody clashes between farmers and herders in Nigeria' (available at: www.amnesty.org/en/documents/afr44/9503/2018/en/).

Atelhe, G. A. and Okoli, A. C. 2014, 'Nomads against native: A political ecology of farmers/ Herders conflicts in Nassarawa state, Nigeria', *American International Journal of contemporary Research, 5*(3), pp. 123–134.

Blench, R. (2010). Conflict between pastoralists and cultivators in Nigeria. Kay Williamson Educational Foundation Cambridge.

Ejiofor, P. F. 2022, 'Beyond ungoverned spaces: Connecting the dots between relative deprivation, banditry, and violence in Nigeria', *African Security, 15*(2), pp. 111–141.

Eke S. 2020, 'Nomad savage' and herder–farmer conflicts in Nigeria: The (Un) making of an ancient myth', *Third World Quarterly, 41* (1), pp. 745–763.

ICG. 2017. *Herders against farmers: Nigeria's expanding deadly conflict*. https://www.crisisgroup.org/africa/west-africa/nigeria/252-herders-against-farmers-nigerias-expanding-deadlyconflict.

ICG—International Crisis Group. 2018. 'Stopping Nigeria's spiralling farmer–herder violence' Africa Report No. 262, 26 July. Brussels: ICG (www.crisisgroup.org/africa/west-africa/nigeria/262-stopping-nigeriasspiralling-farmer-herder-violence).

Kwaja C. M. A. and Ademola-Adelehin, B. U. 2017, 'The implications of the open grazing prohibition & ranches establishment law on farmer-herder relations in the middle belt of Nigeria'. Available at: https://globalsentinelng.com/2018/02/09/global-sentinel-ffarn-publishes-policy-brief-solution-herders.

Kwaja, C. M. A., & Ademola-Adelehin, B. I. 2018a, *Responses to conflicts between farmers and herders in the Middle Belt of Nigeria: Mapping past efforts and opportunities for violence prevention*. Washington DC: Search for Common Ground.

Kwaja, C. M. A., and Ademola-Adelehin, B. I. 2018b, *Seeking security and stability: An analysis of security responses to farmer-herder conflict in the Middle Belt Region of Nigeria*. Washington DC: Search for Common Ground.

Liman, S. H. and Wakawa, A. S. I. 2012, 'Muslims of Nasarawa state: A survey, Nigeria Research Network (NRN)', *Background Paper No. 7,* Oxford Department of International Development, available at https://www.qeh.ox.ac.uk/sites/www.odid.ox.ac.uk/files/BP7Liman.pdf.

Madu, I. A. and Nwankwo, C. F. 2021, 'Spatial pattern of climate change and farmer-herder conflict vulnerabilities in Nigeria', *GeoJournal, 86*(6), pp. 2691–2707.

Mohammed, M., Ekhmheye, S. and Ibrahim G. M. 2021, 'The Impact of Herders and Farmers Conflicts on Agricultural Activities in Nasarawa State', *International Journal of Advanced Academic Research, 7*(10), pp. 319–335.

Ndubuisi, C. I. 2018. 'A critical analysis of conflicts between herdsmen and farmers in Nigeria: Causes and socio-religious and political effects on national development', *HTS Teologiese Studies/Theological Studies, 74*(1), pp. 50–65.

Nwankwo , C. F. 2024. 'From ejecting the herds to hidden dangers: Farmer-herder conflict and criminality in ungoverned forests along the Benue-Nasarawa-Taraba border', *Trees, Forests and People, 17*(1).

Nwankwo, C. F. 2021. 'Discursive construction of the farmer-pastoralist conflict in Nigeria', *Open Political Science,* 4, 136–146.

Okoli, A. C., and Ogayi, C. O. 2018. 'Herdsmen militancy and humanitarian crisis in Nigeria: A theoretical briefing', *African Security Review, 27*(2), pp. 129–143.

Okunade, S.K. and Kohon, H.S. 2023. 'Climate Change and Emerging Conflict Between Herders and Farmers in Nasarawa and Plateau States, Nigeria', In *Contemporary Issues on Governance, Conflict and Security in Africa*. Palgrave Macmillan, Cham.

Olumba, E. E. 2024. 'The politics of eco-violence: Why is conflict escalating in Nigeria's middle belt?' *Terrorism and Political Violence, 36*(2), pp. 180–197.

Olumba, E. E., Nwosu, B. U., Okpaleke, F. N. and Okoli, R. C. 2022. 'Conceptualising eco-violence: Moving beyond the multiple labelling of water and agricultural resource conflicts in the Sahel', *Third World Quarterly, 43*(9), pp. 2075–2090.

Omotola, J. S. 2007. 'Democratisation, sub-ethnic identities and intra-group relations among the okun of Kogi State, Nigeria', *The International Journal of Regional and Local Studies*, Series 2, *3*(1), pp. 81–93.

Omotola, J. S. 2008. 'Democratisation, identity transformation and rising ethnic conflicts in Kogi State, Nigeria', *Kasarinlan: Philippine Journal of third world studies, 23*(1), pp. 72–91.

Omotola, J. S. 2021a. 'Nigeria: Has This House Truly Fallen?', Text of Paper Presented at the 4th Annual Democracy Lecture Day, 12 June, Department of History and International Studies, Kogi State Univfersity, Anyigba, Nigeria.

Omotola, J. S. 2021b. 'Insurgency, Armed Banditry and Ethno-religious Conflicts in Central Nigeria', Lead Paper Presented at a National Conference Organised by the Department of History and International Studies, Federal University Lokoja in Honour of Professor Toyin Falola, as Part of the 5th Convocation Ceremony of the University, 10 November.

Omotola, J. S. 2024a. 'Traditional institutions and the management of Herders-Farmers conflicts in Nasarawa state, Nigeria', in Ehrhardt, D, Umar, S. and Alao, D, eds. *Traditional Authority and Security in Contemporary Nigeria*, London: Routledge, pp. 169–190.

Omotola, J. S. 2024b. 'SADC and Peacebuilding in the Southern African Region', in Bereketeab, R. ed., *Supranational Institutions and Peacebuilding in Africa: The African Union and Regional Economic Communities*, London: Routledge.

Sabo, S. N. Y. 2022, 'Implications of Herdsmen and Farmers Conflict on Food Security in Doma Local Government Area of Nasarawa State, Nigeria' *Humanus Discourse, 2*(3).

Shettima, A. G. and Tar, U. A. 2008, 'Farmer-pastoralist conflict in West Africa: Exploring the causes and consequences', *Information, Society and Justice*, *2*(1), pp. 163–184.

Tade, O. and Yikwabs, Y. P. 2020, 'Conflict triggers between farming and pastoral communities in Nasarawa State, Nigeria', *Journal of Aggression, Conflict and Peace Research, 12*(3), pp. 101–114.

Yikwab, P. Y., and Tade, O. 2022, 'How Farming Communities Cope With Displacement Arising from Farmer-Herder Conflict in North Central Nigeria', *Journal of Asian and African Studies, 57*(4), pp. 667–677.

CHAPTER 7

Women in the Shadow of the Conflict in the Farming and Herding Communities in Plateau State, Nigeria

Abosede Omowumi Babatunde

Introduction

This chapter focuses on the gendered nature of the farmer-herder conflict, by examining the roles of women in the conflicts and the impact on the peace process. It illustrates the largely invisible roles that women have played as actors in the conflict and how their roles have undermined the peace processes. While some scholars considered the nomadic and semi-nomadic pastoralist as violent males and the oppressors, the farmers (both male and female) are perceived as the victims (Kwaja and Ademola-Adelehin, 2018). Most studies have framed the youth who are regarded as male as the perpetrators of violence in the conflict, whereas the female youth are seen as the victims of gender-based violence (Ogundairo and Ijimakinwa, 2020; Brottem and McDonnell, 2020). In fact, studies on the farmers and herders' conflicts in Nigeria, Central Darfur, Chad and

A. O. Babatunde (✉)
University of Ilorin, Ilorin, Nigeria
e-mail: bose_babatunde@yahoo.co.uk; babatunde.ar@unilorin.edu.ng

J. S. Omotola (ed.), *Herder-Farmer Conflicts in Africa*,
https://doi.org/10.1007/978-3-031-80821-0_7

Central African Republic have projected the notion of masculinity in profiling the actors involved in cattle raid, encroachment and destruction of farms and crops and cross-border attacks that contributed to the violent nature of the conflict (Sørbø, 2010; De Waal, 2014).

Krause (2019) noted that women involvement in armed conflicts are often downplayed, while their experience of victimization and roles as peacemakers have dominated gender discourses. Ademola-Adelehin, et al., 2018) found that women have directly participated in the farmers and herders' conflict as primary, secondary and shadow actors. Women are directly and indirectly affected by the conflict outcome and can indirectly influence the dynamics of the farmer-herder conflict. In a related study, Krause (2019) observed that women have played pivotal role in community mobilization for violence in the ethno-religious and political crises in Plateau State.

Despite that some studies have established women active roles in the ethno-religious conflict in Plateau State, there is scant scholarly analyses of the roles that women have played in the complex, destructive and intractable conflict in the farming and herding communities. This chapter builds on existing studies in illuminating the gender nature of the farmers and herders' conflict in Africa, focusing on the case of Plateau State, one of the epicenters of the violent farmers and herders' conflicts in North central Nigeria. In doing so, this chapter will offer perspectives on how women roles in resource-based conflict in Africa contribute to the protracted conflict and impede the peace processes. While feminist scholarship has highlighted the roles of women in liberation struggles, civil wars, insurgencies and political conflicts in diverse contexts in Africa and across the world (Barry, 1996; Viterna, 2013; Matfess, 2020), the roles that women played in resource conflict in polarized context have not been sufficiently interrogated in gender discourses.

While there have been peace initiatives to resolve the conflict, including the peace commissions established by state governments in Kaduna, Adamawa and Plateau States between 2016 and 2018; the accountability forum, community resilience forum, and youth and peaceful coexistence in community initiative for fostering dialogue among pastoralists and farmers in Benue and Plateau States; and the peace efforts of some state-based civil society organisations such as CLEEN Foundation, and international NGOs such as Mercy Corps, the conflict has remained intractable (Kew, 2021; Ojewale, 2021). At the same time, this chapter contends that the lack of consideration for the visible or invisible roles played by women in resource-based conflict have profound implications for the peace processes geared towards achieve lasting peace.

This chapter utilized qualitative data generated from fieldwork conducted in 2019 in selected communities where the farmers and herders' conflict has been protracted and violent in Plateau State. The qualitative data is complemented with up-to-date literature, and relevant policy reports on the farmer-herder conflict. Qualitative method involved the use of key informant interviews, Focus Group Discussions (FGDs), and direct observation of the everyday realities in the selected communities Four communities comprising of diverse ethnic and religious groups including Doruwan Babuje, Mararraban Kantoma, Daffo, and Bokkos were selected. The research subjects were purposively selected based on criteria such as age, occupation, gender, leadership position and stakeholders in the conflict. The respondents include traditional leaders, community elders, herders, farmers, leaders of Miyyetti Allah, religious leaders, vigilante groups, women and youth, as well as officials of local NGOs. In-depth and key informants' interviews were conducted with 80 respondents in the four communities on the basis of 20 key informants and in-depth interviews per community. In addition, FGDs were conducted with women and youth groups in all the four communities.

Feminist Political Ecology Perspectives on Women Roles in the Farmers and Herders conflict

The theoretical analysis of women roles in the farmers and herders' conflict in Plateau State is situated within the feminist political ecology lens. Political ecology considers the complex relations between nature and society through a careful analysis of the politics of access and control over resources and their implications for the environment (Peluso and Watts, 2001). Political ecologist views the main sources of the farmers and herders' conflicts to transcend issues of resource contestation to encompass the power relations associated with the politics of access to and control over the resources in which those tasked with the management of the resources privilege some groups and marginalize others (Turner, 2004; Mkutu, 2019). In a related study on Eastern Ethiopia, Kenee (2022) observed that the predatory behavior of political elites driven by the quest for financial or political gains influence the complex and violent nature of the farmers and herders' conflict.

Feminist political ecology lens is useful for analyzing the gender issues interacting with class, caste, race, culture, and ethnicity that influence the processes of ecological change, resource access and control (Schroeder, 1993; Rocheleau and Ross, 1995). It helps in understanding the social, economic, environmental and political processes that determines access to and control of natural resources and how resource access and control influence gender issues, conflict and violence (Pe˅sa and Ross, 2021).

Feminist political ecology offers a relevant analytical framework for understanding the contextual issues that influence women involvement in resource contestation and conflict and the implications for the peace processes. It helps us to dissect some critical questions relating to the why and how women are involved in the farmers and herders' conflicts in Plateau State. It also raises questions about the nature of women's involvement in the conflict and how their participation impacts the peace process. Since feminist political ecologist focuses on the experience of women and other that are marginalized by neoliberal, colonial or patriarchal systems in extractive or other contexts (Cole, 2016), it provides relevant analytical framework for understanding the gendered nature of the farmers and herders conflict in polarized contexts like Plateau State.

Women's experiences of threat to their livelihood, survival and security instigates struggles, conflict and activism as forms of resistance to the inequity and injustice in accessing natural, environmental and economic resources needed for their survival. In case of the farmers and herders' conflict in the ethnically and religious diverse Plateau State, women are able to express resistance against the constraints in accessing natural resource through the invisible roles they played as instigators and supporters of violence. Women's involvement in the conflict ultimately aggravates their victimization, undermines their livelihood, survival, and wellbeing of their families and communities at large.

Gender Perspectives on Farmers and Herders Conflict

Gender discourse has increasingly acknowledged the distinct gender dimension of armed conflict and peacebuilding (Goldstein, 2001; Viterna, 2013; Sjoberg, 2016). Scholars observed that armed conflict can impact in multiple and dynamic ways on gender relations, leaving behind some enduring legacies that can empower or marginalize women after the end of the conflict (Wood, 2008; Krause, 2019). While feminist scholars have acknowledged women capacity for aggression and violence in situation of conflict, rejecting the essentialist assumption that women are more peaceful and less aggressive than men, they also emphasized that women and men are mobilized differently into armed groups and in varying numbers (Viterna, 2013; Cohen, 2013). Parkinson (2013) found that in civil wars, women have provided crucial logistic support for male fighters even when they were few numbers of female combatants.

In the literature on pastoral conflicts in Africa, women are mostly perceived as victims of gender-based violence (Brottem and McDonnell, 2020). Citing the case of South Sudan, Kircher (2013) described the systems of polygamous marriage and bride wealth that is paid in livestock as an incentivizing factor in cattle raiding and as a form of gender-based violence that exposed women to early marriage and intimate sexual violence. In Nigeria's Adamawa, Gombe, and Plateau States, the cycle of retaliatory violence between farming and pastoralist communities have been characterized by gender-based violence perpetrated against women (Ademola-Adelehin, et al., 2018). A related study focusing on northern Central African Republic found that pastoralists committed several sexual assaults on women (Brottem and McDonnell, 2020).

The prevalence of sexual and gender-based violence in the conflict between farmers and herders is attributed to the weakening of the community-based structures and local institutions, thereby making women and girls vulnerable to rape as an increasing tactic used by actors in the conflict (Akov, 2017; Ademola-Adelehin, et al., 2018; Ryle and Amoum, 2018; Kew, 2021). In fact, Ojo (2020) found that in Nigeria's North-Central and North-West regions, rising incidences of killings, kidnappings, cattle rustling, rape and abduction of women, destruction of farmlands and villages, are linked to the Fulani militias and bandits who used deadly weapons to attack farming populations dominated by Christians. Yet, it is important to note that both the farmers and herders are implicated in the violence.

Brottem and McDonnell (2020) emphasized that there is little scholarly analysis of women's economic roles in the farmer-pastoralist conflict, despite haven played very distinctive roles in producing and selling animal products. The disruptive effect of the conflict on trade and marketing disproportionately affects women from pastoral and farming communities. In a related study, Ademola-Adelehin, et al. (2018) explained that women who constitute about 60% of smallholder sustenance farmers in North-central Nigeria are affected by the destruction of crop, theft of farm produce, and the attack and theft of cattle. Yet, the conflict is also driven by threat to livelihoods due to resource scarcity and the inequitable access to land and water resource. The violent conflict also led to closure or disruption of market where women trade in farm produce, milk products such as locally produced milk, nono yogurt, during period of attacks and due to the state of insecurity linked to the conflict. It has also led to breakdown in intergroup relation between farming and pastoral women who had hitherto jointly celebrated ceremonies, and intercultural festivities (Ademola-Adelehin, et al., 2018).

Traditional leaders or local systems can pose a risk to groups with less political power, including rural women because under the customary laws, women lack rights to own or manage land and they may have few opportunities for representation within existing resource management or conflict resolution institutions (Brottem and McDonnell, 2020). In the case of South Sudan, Kircher (2013) found that pastoralist women lack decision-making authority even within their own households and face disadvantages in both customary and statutory judicial systems. By contrast, across the Sahel region, pastoralist women have power within their households and rights within their communities that they use effectively to meet their households needs (Flintan, 2008). Women can also use such influence to support and encourage act of violence. The case of Chad also showed that pastoralist women play dynamic, and empowered roles in redefining Mbororo cultural identity (Ibrahim, 2013). In Nigeria, Guinea and East Africa, women in pastoralist communities benefited from self-help groups, economic associations or cooperative for empowerment (Brottem and McDonnell, 2020).

The negative impacts of the conflict on women's livelihoods make them vulnerable to economic hardship and also fuels grievance that can incentivized them to play active roles in the violence. Women also experience mental stress and trauma linked to death of husbands and children in the violent farmers and herders conflicts. The loss of family member may fuel the desire for revenge through violent action. The mental health challenges linked to the loss of husband placed women as breadwinners, and imposed additional burden of care for the children. It also undermined women's capacity to adequately take care of their children and prevent anti-social activities of their youth (Ademola-Adelehin, et al. (2018).

Apart from the youth, the women have been implicated in the illicit use of drugs in the farming and herding communities. Owonikoko, et al.

(2021) described the case of Adamawa State where women in polygamous marriage are expected to serve as laborer for their husbands in their farms. If these women lack the rigor or power to tackle the farming activities, they face risk of being retired as malijwagi by the husband who will then marry another wife capable of doing the rigorous work on his farm. In their quest to boost their power for farm activities and prevent their husband from marrying another wife, some of the women use drugs and substances. The use of illicit drugs by women is perceived to incite aggressiveness, irritation and violent behavior which can lead to confrontation with herders when cattle encroach on their farms. It was reported that some of the women acting under the influence of drugs have perpetrated domestic violence against their husbands (Owonikoko, et al., 2021).

Studies on the ethno-religious conflict in Plateau state, showed that women have played pivotal role in community mobilization for violence, providing logistics for fighting by cooking for hundreds of men when they assembled from different villages for coordinated attacks (Human Rights Watch, 2013; Krause, 2019). Women provided security for men who needed to hide from security forces, while some women and girls have assisted the men with bullets, stones, and machetes (Krause, 2019). Research has identified some female perpetrators of violence in the 2001 ethno-religious conflict in Plateau State (Higazi, 2008). Women have also supported perpetrators of violence in the quest to eliminate perceived enemies, chanted war songs to encourage and motivate male fighters and shaming of those not involved in fighting; and have acted as spies and informants on movement of opponents and emissaries to transport arms (Ademola-Adelehin, et al., 2018). Women were also reported to spread false news, rumors and hate speech that deepens ethno-religious sentiments, cleavages and conflict (Krause, 2019).

Ademola-Adelehin, et al. (2018) argued that women and children are regarded as the vulnerable group and victim while men are perceived as largely the perpetrator of violent in the conflict between farmers and herders. This kind of assumption fails to recognize the fact that women are crucial stakeholders in agriculture and livestock production who are affected by the conflict and who experience grievances and threat to their livelihood as farmers and cattle breeders. Studies have identified three categories of women's involvement in the conflict between farmer and herders in the North-central region of Nigeria—women as primary party and direct actors in the conflict; secondary party that are interested in the outcomes, and as shadow party working behind the scene to influence the dynamics of the conflict (Ademola-Adelehin, et al., 2018).

In whatever form that women's participation in the conflict may take, it has significant implication for their roles in promoting peace in their communities. Scholars have noted that women are essentialized as peaceful and their peace activism often involved distinct forms of collective mobilization to facilitate peaceful relations and co-existence (Goldstein, 2001; Berry, 2018). Women have contributed to peace processes by appealing to men to shun violence and embrace reconciliation and peaceful dialogue (Ademola-Adelehin, et al. (2018).

These peace promoting roles that women have played sharply contrast with the roles they played in the conflict, such that their participation in the conflict inevitably undermines their peacemaking roles and capacities. At the same time, women face structural constraint in participating in the peace processes due to their limited involved in local decision-making process (Krause, 2019). Despite this, market women have been identified to play a key role in maintaining close communication and rumor-control in the ethno-religious crises in Plateau State (Bonkat, 2014). It was reported that individual women also served as messengers between community leaders unwilling to meet each other officially and display unity across the religious divide (Krause, 2019). Women have also engaged in protest to clamor for justice, over the violence that led to the death of women, children and their men. Through the support of some civil society groups, and traditional leaders, women in Plateau, Gombe and Adamawa States have established centres for legal, medical and trauma healing for women post-conflict situations, and participated in interfaith/interethnic dialogue and mediation of the farmers and herders' conflict (Ademola-Adelehin, et al., 2018). While some women have demonstrated the capacities to serve as peacemakers and advocates, others have shown their capacity to engage in violence. Yet, women's varied roles in the conflict and peace processes depend on their experience and reaction to the conflict issues as well as the support they derived from the state and local leaders and civil society groups.

Women roles in the Farmers and Herders Conflict in Plateau State

The farmers and herders' conflict in Plateau State is inextricably embedded in the preexisting ethno-religious and political crises, which has been protracted in the State since the early 2000s (Best, 2007; HRW, 2013; Madueke, 2019; Oosterom, et al, 2021). The farmers and herders conflict also manifests as division over indigene rights between the predominantly Christian communities and the predominantly Muslim Hausa-Fulani, regarded as 'indigene'; and 'settler' or migrant respectively (Angerbrandt, 2015; Krause, 2019). The conflict over land and water resources between the farmers and indigenous groups such as the Berom, Anaguta, and Afizere, and the pastoral and migrants' groups, the Hausa-Fulani, reflects contestation for territorial and political rights and control (Madueke, 2019).

The contestation over identity, political and economic rights and benefits shaped the nature and sources of the farmers and herders' conflict as well as the roles of women in the conflict. While the resource conflict between the farmers and herders relates to access to land and water resources for their livelihood, the schism along ethno-religious and indigene and settler dichotomy have influenced the intensity of the conflict in terms of the cycles of violent retaliatory attacks in the selected communities in Plateau State.

The accounts of the respondents indicate that the farmers and herders conflict escalated during the ethno-religious and political crises. According to the traditional ruler in Doruwa Babuje, a predominantly Muslim, and pastoral community, inhabited by those regarded as Hausa Fulani, the conflict emerged in 2000 as a split over of the ethno-religious and political crises. Also, a Muslim religious leader, known as Imam observed that since 2010 the conflict intensified and led to destruction of lives and properties, burning of shops, houses, mosques, vehicles, and farms in their community. A similar account from the leader of the vigilante group suggests that the conflict rapidly spread from one community to another. In Mararraban Kantoma, a Christian dominated and farming community, inhabited by the Berom Christian indigenous group, the community head, Damaje told me that since 2010, they have experienced series of sporadic attacks allegedly from the Hausa Fulani herders. In Bokkos and Daffo communities, inhabited by a mix of the indigenous farmers and the pastoralist's migrant, the Miyetti Allah, the leader of the cattle breeders observed that since 2013, the conflict permeated most of the communities in the Bokkos LGA areas.

While the farmers and herders' conflicts across these communities involved violent attacks and counter attacks from the diverse ethnic and religious and indigene and settlers' groups, the main perpetrators of violence are perceived to be the male youth. The statement of the respondents in Doruwa Babuje suggests that most of the spontaneous attacks by the Berom on their community were carried out by the Berom youth. Most of the respondents attributed the cause of the violent attacks in their communities to retaliation over incidents of cattle rustling and damage to farms.

The women in the FGD sessions in Doruwa Babuje perceived that the attacks on their community allegedly perpetrated by the Berom Christians was driven by the quest to sack them from their community because they are regarded as invaders due to their migrants' position. The fear of displacement is alleged to have influenced the women to support their youth to defend their community and counter attacks from the Berom. While some of the women claimed that they encouraged their youth to shun violence or retaliatory attack on the farming communities, others expressed their anger over the unfair treatment they experienced from the government officials and security agents who they perceived to support the Berom's invasion and attack on their community. This incentivized the aggrieved women to influence and encourage their youth and men to carry out violent retaliation as an act of self-defense to protect their territory from the Berom. It is worth noting that the women leader in Doruwa Babuja claimed that their youth always adhere to their directive. This suggests that they are able to influence their youth, either positively or negatively.

The accounts of most of the respondents suggest that conflict occurs frequently during the planting and harvesting season. As one farmer narrates "The herders often direct their cattle to our farms while we are planting or harvesting crops." The women leader and FGD respondents in Doruwa Babuje who are farmers alluded to the claim that herders' cattle often encroach on farms and destroy the crops such as maize, yam and cassava that they planted or were in the process of harvesting. A respondent described the case of a women farmer who was a victim of attack by a herder whom she confronted for the invasion of her farm by the cattle and the damage to her crop. The herder allegedly stabbed the women in the stomach, and she died. The death of the women provoked reprisal attack on herders living in the community and neighboring communities. This also led to a counterattack by the herders on the farming communities. The case of the female farmers highlights the fact that women as farmers are direct actors in the conflict, while also positioned as victims. At the same time, women's experience of victimization can be the driving force behind the cycle of reprisal violence.

The diverse formidable roles that women played in the lingering ethno-religious and indigene/settler conflict (Higazi, 2008; Krause, 2019), that intertwined with the farmers and herders' conflict also make them implicated actors in the resource-based conflict. The unresolved animosity linked to ethno-religious, and indigene and settlers' crises have shaped contestations for dwindling land spaces. While the indigenous farming communities struggle for land spaces, the herding communities search for grazing land for their cattle. For instance, the indigenous people in Bokkos, the Ron, Mushere and Kulere are mainly farmers. In the case of Bokkos, increasing land scarcity fuels intense contestation for land spaces for farming and grazing between the farmers and herders (settlers) living in Bokkos communities. While the farmers lay claim to the land as the indigene, the settlers also demand a right to the land which had been inhabited for centuries by their forefathers. The situation is magnified because of the lack of clearly defined grazing routes as the cattle routes created since the early post-independence period (1960–1966), through the Nigerian Grazing Reserve Act of 1964 have disappeared or taken over by farmers or construction activities (Amaza, 2018). A related study on the farmer-herder conflict in Plateau and Gombe States, found that women are the majority of farmers, and they allegedly encroached on cattle routes due to human settlement on farmland (Ademola-Adelehin, et al., 2018).

The threat to the livelihood of both the farmers and herders influenced the roles of women in the conflict. In fact, the Miyetti Allah in Bokkos explained that the Fulani women have influenced the youth to perpetrate violence against the farming communities because of their grievance over threat of their husband, youth and their own livelihood. Studies have established that perceived threat to access to resources and livelihoods fueled sense of victimhood and exclusion which provoked violent reaction in the farmers and herders (Majekodunmi, et al., 2014). While the men have directly responded through violence, women have reacted indirectly through their support and encouragement for their men and youth to engage in violence. The statements of most of the respondents suggest that women have been the unseen and invisible actors in the acts of violence perpetrated by the men.

While studies have shown that the Fulani herders are most often the aggressor, and the farmers are mostly the victims of violence (Kwaja and Ademola-Adelehin, 2018), this research found that both groups have been engaged in violent attacks on each other. The account of a respondent, a community leader in Daffo, illustrates that farmers have instigated unprovoked attacks on the herders. The respondent reported a particular incident in Daffo community in 2018, where a farmer barricaded a route to obstruct passage for the Fulani herder and his cattle. About six cows died in the process of attempting to pass through. The herder confrontation with the farmers incited the farmer to hit him with a hoe and he died. The farmer fled the scene, but the death of the Fulani herder led to reprisal attack on the farming communities.

Moreover, the farmers have also been alleged by the Fulani herders to have been incentivized to poison the river that is the main source of drinking water for the cattle and the Bokkos community. Some of the herders in the FGD sessions in Bokkos alleged that the farmers poisoned the river. This claim was confirmed by the Miyetti Allah and FGDs respondent, a herder in Bokkos who alleged that some cattle who drank the water from the poisoned rivers died. The deep-rooted animosity between the farmers and herders have made them to lose all sense of consideration for the fact that both the farmers and herders would be affected by the poisoned river which is the main source of drinking water for the whole community. Related research suggests that in some part of Nigeria's Middle Belt, the farmers have even poisoned crops they know the cattle will feed on, thereby destroying the value that would have been generated from the crop or the poisoned cattle by the farmers and the herders alike (SB Morgen, 2019).

The accounts of most of the respondents in Bokkos and Daffos suggest that the farmers' action is partly linked to the herders' attack on the female farmers and some young girls from the farming communities who were reportedly raped along the farms by the young herders. Thus, the act of rape or gender-based violent against the women can incite the farmers to attack the herders who are perceived as the perpetrators. This kind of attack on the herders magnified the violence because it leads to retribution from the herders that further lead to cycle of reprisals, and a climate of insecurity in the affected communities.

Another act of retaliation by the farmers is the burning of farm residuals during dry or fallow season to prevent herders' cattle from grazing. In Mararraban Kantoma, the youth in the FGD sessions expressed the notion that their confrontation with the herders is linked to the trespass on their farms by the cattle and the damage it caused to their crops. On the other hand, most of the Fulani herders interviewed accused the farmers of trespassing on grazing route and also burning of farms to prevent cattle from grazing during dry season. This account correlates with existing studies which showed that in Adamawa State, some farmers have been burning their post-harvest crop residue as an act to prevent the herders from grazing on their lands (Brottem and McDonnell, 2020).

In the case of the Mararraban Kantoma community, the farmers' decision to burn farm residuals can be attributed to grievance over incessant surprise violent attack on their community by those perceived to be the herders. In fact, the surprise attack on Mararraban Kantoma community in July 2018, allegedly by the herders was carried out in the midnight leading to the maiming, killing and displacement of many of the community members. The women in the FGD sessions explained that some of them fled their community with their children and relocated to Jos, and Mangu which are considered safer for their children to continue their schooling. While most of the women in the community have not returned back from the IDPs camp at Rwuruk village in Barki Ladi LGA, most of those who participated in the FGD session indicated that they had supported the action of their men to burn the farm residuals to prevent the herders' cattle from grazing. Some of the women expressed frustration and anger at the attack on their community and perceived the herders as their ach enemy who should be eliminated by any means available to them.

Another conflict issue is intricately linked to the use of underage boys to herd cattle, and the problem of drug abuse. Most of the farmers explained that the herders use underage boys of 8 to 12 years who allowed their cattle to wander into farms and damage crops. In Bokkos, the respondents expressed the view that some of the underage boys are given about 200 to 300 herd of cattle. They apparently lacked the capacity to effectively manage the herds. The farmers alleged that these boys consume narcotic drugs to boost their capacity to control and manage the large herd of cattle. Thus, they act aggressively under the influence of drugs when they are confronted by the herders for encroaching on their farms. The underage boys have been accused of sexually molesting the girls from the farming communities, thereby provoking the aggrieved women from the farming communities to support their men to violently attack the herders. In fact, the women leader in Bokkos described how the Fulani herders who are fully armed and intoxicated with narcotic drugs have attacked and raped unarmed women and girls in their farms. Ademola-Adelehin, et al. (2018) reported the rising rates of rape of women and girls from the farming and herding communities whereby suspected herders targeted and raped females from the farming communities while working on the farm or logging firewood in the forests, and women and girls from pastoral communities have been victims of rape by males suspected to be farmers while walking through lonely path to get to school or sell in the village markets. This pattern of sexual molestation of women and girls is perceived by most of the respondents as retaliatory attacks by youth from both farming and herding communities.

At the same time, research found that women farmers in Adamawa used illicit drugs to enhance their power or rigor to cope with the hard labor involved in farming activities (Owonikoko, et al., 2021). The use of drugs by the female farmers may also lead to aggressive behavior and violent attack on the herders when their cattle trespass on farmlands. However, the account of respondents indicates that women farmers have not been involved in direct act of aggression or violence against the herders. Although they have confronted the herders when their cattle encroached on farmlands, the women have been at the receiving end of violent attacks by the herders.

The indirect support that the Fulani women provided for their youth and men to attack the farmers who are both men and women make them implicated actors in the violence. The attack on the female farmers, women and girls including sexual molestation, physical injury and death can also be discerned as an indirect violence perpetrated by women against their fellow women. In their study, Ademola-Adelehin, et al. (2018) found that Fulani women in Adamawa are alleged to act as informants who spy on farming communities, and have been involved in illicit trade of arms which is hidden in fishes and other produce that they sell. In contrast, this research found that women played largely indirect roles in the violence that characterized the farmers and herders' conflict in Plateau State. Studies have shown that women played critical roles in mobilizing their men for violence and in providing logistic support in the ethno-religious and political crises in Plateau State (Human Rights Watch, 2013; Krause, 2019). Since the farmers and herders' conflict is inextricably linked to the ethno-religious and political crises, it is plausible that the logistic support provided by the women have contributed to the violence that characterized the farmers and herders' conflict. Nevertheless, most of the respondents confirmed that women have assisted the youth who perpetrated violent attacks on the other group to hide from security agents and to escape from arrest or prosecution. In fact, a community leader and the Miyetti Allah in Bokkos suggest that women have provided money for their youth to escape from been arrested by the police for act of violence they perpetrated. This account corroborates Krause's (2019) study that showed that women have assisted their men to hide from security forces after they perpetrated acts of violence. Ademola-Adelehin, et al. (2018) observed that women have defended their action of hiding male perpetrator of violence and withholding information because of their distrust of the security agents and the fear of harassment if they could not produce concrete evidence to substantiate the information shared.

Moreover, the Miyetti Allah in Bokkos considers that women played negative roles in the violence because they capitalize on their closeness to their children to influence them to perpetrate acts of violence. The women's sense of grievance overrides consideration for the risk they exposed their men and youth to and the possibility that their male and female folks could be killed during the crises. The leader of the cattle breeders also noted that only few of the women, estimated at 30 percent are not supporter of violence. Some of the women denied that they are supporting their youth acts of violence. The women leader in Daffo lamented that the Fulanis and Rons youth hardly listen to their mothers. The respondent expresses it thus "some of the youth acting under the influence of drugs beat up their mothers whenever they appeal to them to desist from violent acts." The statement of the women leader confirmed the view of the Miyetti Allah that some of the women are not supporters of violence. Nevertheless, it indicates that the complicity of many of the women in the violence have influenced most of the youth asocial behavior of drug abuse.

In the case of Doruwa Babuje, the traditional leader expresses the notion that their women have played positive roles in appealing to their children to shun acts of violence. Similarly, the women leader explained that they usually punish their youth found to engage in acts of violence by beating them. She narrates "whenever the children sense that we mothers are upset or angry with them, they tend to show remorse and apologize to us, but when they disobey us and are not remorseful, we report them to the Imam to preach to them." Most of the women in the FGDs sessions in Doruwa Babuje disclosed that they encourage their youth to engage in viable work because their idleness influences their involvement in violence.

In Mararraban Kantoma, the women in the FGD session explained that they talk to the youth to exercise caution and not to react violently to the Fulani, while they also appeal to their community leader and chief for peaceful means of addressing the conflict. In addition, the leader of the vigilante in Doruwa Babuje expressed the view that women play limited role in the conflict because their religion practices, Islam requires that women are confined to the home while the men move around. Yet, women's confinement does not preclude that they can directly influence their male folks and their youth.

The statements of the respondents suggest that the women influence on their youth varies. While some of the respondents in Bokkos, Doruwa Babuje and Mararraban Kantoma, perceived that women have mostly played positive roles in the conflict; they tend to downplay the impact of women's experience of sexual molestation, rape, and direct target of violent, loss of family members and relatives in the crises on women's conflict behavior. This suggests that some respondents trivialized the roles that women played in supporting their men's violent attack on the other group. It is important to note that the action of women as supporter of violence tend to inculcate culture of violence in the youth, thereby making them not have any sense of accountability for their acts of violence and its negative consequences. This has adversely impacted on women's motherly roles in imbibing peaceful attributes in their children and capacity to play mediating roles in the conflict.

The theft of cattle depicts the criminal dimension of the conflict between the farmers and herders. Cattle rustling affects both the farmers (because some of them also breed cattle and goats) and the Fulani herders. Studies confirmed that women in herding communities' rear cattle, goat and chicken as well as engaged in selling of cattle milk (nono), butter (man-shanu) and or local cereal (fura) as their primary source of livelihood (Ademola-Adelehin, et al., 2018). The farmers and herders perceived one another as the culprit in the theft and raid of cattle. Some of the farmers in herders in Doruwa Babuje explained that attack on cattle is carried out at midnight and they were able to identify the rustler as Fulani through their spoken language. Yet, some of the respondents in the FGD sessions claimed that the Berom Christians in the farming communities are the cattle rustlers. The role of women in cattle rustling is unclear. Nevertheless, cattle rustling contributed to cattle trespassing on farmland because when the theft of cattle occurs, the herds scatter and in the process encroach on farms. Also, the rustlers pass through farmlands and damage crops. The farmers usually perceived that the herders' cattle trespassed on their farms and destroyed their crops, so they retaliated by attacking the herders. Thus, cattle theft that result in encroachment on farms and damage to farmlands belonging to women have also contributed to their support for their youth and men to attack the herders.

The Impact of Women Roles in the Conflict on the Peace Processes

Women varied roles in the farmers and herders' conflict have important implications for the efforts to resolve and achieve peaceful resolution of the conflict. Women are portrayed as peacemakers based on their attributes as mothers, wives, and caregivers (Goldstein, 2001; Viterna, 2013; Berry, 2018). While women have peaceful attributes, Peˇsa and Ross (2021) observed that women experience of inequalities shaped their perceptions of and reactions to environmental and socio-economic changes. In the case of resource conflicts like the farmers and herders, threat to women's livelihood provoked aggressive reaction and shaped women's varied roles in the conflict. The roles of majority of the women in the conflicts invariably undermined the key roles they have or could have played in promoting peace.

While women's roles as caregivers are vital to the wellbeing of their family, their roles as implicated actors in the conflict undermine the well-being of their families. This suggests that women participation in the conflict which contribute to the cycle of reprisal violence that characterized the conflict led to a climate of insecurity that make it difficult for women to play the important roles that they have hitherto played as care givers and nurturers for their families and communities. For instance, some of the women in Mararraban Kantoma, suggests that the incessant outbreak of violence led to their internal displacement.

The accounts of some of the respondents in Doruwa Babuje and Mararraban Kantoma, indicate that women cautioned their youth not to engage in violence, encouraged them not be idle and to engage in viable jobs, and discouraged them from use of illicit drugs. In fact, the women leader in Doruwa Babuje expressed the view that they appeal to their community leader and chiefs to find peaceful ways of resolving the conflict between the farmers and herders. The respondent added that they have a religious group known as the Muslim women group which advocate for peace, but these group has dispersed because some of the members have left the communities. Ademola-Adelehin, et al. (2018) found that women were alleged to have exchanged gifts and participated in religious ceremonies of the other religious groups in their efforts to build peaceful social relation. The accounts of the respondent showed that the Muslim women group is no longer functioning since many of the members have left the community. This account suggests that the insecurity impacted on women's role as peacemakers. It also illuminates the negative impacts of women roles in the conflict. While few women have positively contributed to the efforts to promote peace, the negative roles that most of the woman played in the conflict significantly eroded the positive contribution of the peace promoting women.

The statements of some of the women in Mararraban Kantoma, signify that women often call peace meetings with their fellow women. Apparently, such peace meetings have not dissuaded many of the women from participating as supporters of violence. This is perhaps linked to the deep-rooted sense of grievance, distrust and suspicion of the other groups which override women's intrinsic peaceful attributes. In addition, the negative roles that most of the women played in the conflict make them to abdicate their responsibility of being good role models for their youth. The FGDs respondents in Bokkos explained that when the paramount ruler was murdered on the way to his farm, the women wore black attires, and they carried out a protest as a demonstration of their pain at the loss. Yet, it remains to be seen if the loss of the paramount ruler led them to reconsider their negative roles in the conflicts and what danger it portends for their families and communities.

Nevertheless, studies have reported that incessant violent confrontations between the farmers and herders have made women to rally together to protest to call for the arrest of the attackers and justices for the victims. It was also reported that in 2018, women from Irigwe community in Miango District, Bassa LGA, Plateau state embarked on protests against the killing of women and children during the attacks to demand for the arrest of attackers, response by government and security actors and justice for the victim (Ademola-Adelehin, et al., 2018).

It is important to note that women peace initiatives cannot achieve any meaningful impacts, if the local and religious leaders, political elites, government officials and security agencies are not playing credible and complimentary roles. Research on the farmers and herders in part of Sahel region, Nigeria, Ghana and Sudan showed that where the State and local leaders have played credible and constructive roles in resource management, conflict management and peacebuilding, there exist more cooperation than conflict between the two groups (Tonah, 2006; Moritz, 2010; Kwaja and Smith, 2020; Brottem and McDonnell, 2020). Some studies observed that in some communities in Plateau and Gombe States, the support of traditional council have strengthened the capacity of some women leaders and role of other women in peacebuilding processes and they were also able to provide trauma healing services, known as Hope Center, to support women (Ademola-Adelehin, et al. (2018). While the Plateau State government established a peace commission in 2016 in the effort to mitigate the farmers and herders conflict, as well as the protracted ethno-religious, and political crisis in conjunction with local governments, traditional institutions and security agencies, there was lack of political commitment to the peace intervention process (Kew, 2021). The Plateau State peace commission was also tasked with building early warning and early response systems and developing grassroots conflict resolution infrastructure such as mediation and restorative justice units and processes. Apart from the lack of credible peace actors to champion the peace processes, poor funding and undue interference from the state government (Kew, 2021), the failure to engage local women in the peacebuilding process also undermined the effectiveness of the peace efforts. The accounts of the local women suggest that they were not carried along in the government peace intervention efforts.

In the case of Daffo community, one of the women in the FGD sessions disclosed that the women had initiated a meeting with the local chief to request for a peace dialogue with the conflict parties, but the chief refused to act on their request because of the fear they he might be targeted for attack, by those who have insisted on violent retribution. The account of the respondent corroborates the claim of the local leader in Mararraban Kantoma, that some of the local leaders from the farming communities in Berom have been against any appeal to desist from violent confrontations. The woman in the FGD session added that they had protested out of frustration about the lack of response and positive action from their local leader.

Moreover, in localized contexts, where women play limited role in local decision making and are excluded from the peace process, it would be difficult for them to significantly influence the peace process. Yet, it is important to consider that if women can influence the conflict despite their limited inclusion in local decision making and peace processes, they also can influence the peace process. In fact, while the leader of the vigilante in Doruwa Babuje indicated that women in the Muslim communities are mostly confined to the house, some of the women leaders told me that women under the aegis of the Christian Association of Nigeria (CAN) and the Jamma'at Nasirul Islam (JNL) women wings come together to dialogue on peaceful means of arresting the farmers and herders' conflicts. These women wing of the religious institutions also brainstorm on how to curtail violent and reprisal attack in their communities and also deliberate with the CAN/JNL Chairman, the government officials and the men wing of the religious groups in their communities.

The extent to which the efforts of these religious women paved way for peace is also determined by the complementary roles played by the head the religious institutions. Yet, most of the youths in the FGS sessions accused the religious leaders of instigating their followers against adherents of other religion. In contrast, the account of the religious leaders suggests that they played positive roles in promoting tolerance and peaceful coexistence between the people of the different faith. The claims of the religious leaders seem implausible, taking into cognizance the frequent occurrence of major religious crises in the State and how the intense religious division contributed to the violent conflict between the farmers and herders. One of the religious leaders, the Imam in Doruwa Babuje observed that the division along religious lines is more pronounced than that of ethnic schism. Some of the Berom Christians have allegedly attacked people of other ethnic groups, as well as the Berom Muslim. Some respondents have narrated cases of cattle rustling allegedly perpetrated by Berom Christians in which the Berom Muslims were the victims.

The women also mentioned that they have ethnic association and market women association who dialogue together and take resolution to the community leaders or tribal leaders. However, the frequent outbreak of conflicts between the farmers and herders in the communities suggest that the efforts of some women in appealing for peace through consultation with their men have failed to yield any positive impact. Ademola-Adelehin, et al. (2018) observed that market women in

Gombe and Plateau States played major roles as observers who monitored and reported to the security agents about the mopping up of machete in a market and non-opening of shops for particular ethnic identities, and that women have acted as early warners by signaling potential danger and alerting other women in inter-group marriage to return back to their place of origin, before the outbreak of 1997–98 Mangu-Bokkos violent conflict.

The women respondents have complained that the lack of adequate support and empowerment from local NGOs also undermined their capacity to contribute to the peace process. The respondents in Bokkos explained that while many of their youths have benefited from NGOs training and empowerment programmes, only a handful of women were beneficiary. The women added about 25% of their female youth participated in NGOs initiated empowerment programme. In fact, the officials of some of the local NGOs like the Institute of Governance and Social Research (IGSR) and the Centre for Peace Advancement in Nigeria (CEPAN) interviewed suggest that they consider increasing the numbers of women participants in future programmes. The support of the local NGOs for the women would inevitably boost their capacity in the peace process and can also influence them to desist from the indirect roles they have played in the violent conflict. The relevance of the support of NGOs in strengthening women's capacities is highlighted in studies that showed that the assistance provided by some civil society organisations like Search for Common Ground, West Africa Network for Peacebuilding and others, increased the skills of women in contributing to interfaith/ interethnic dialogue and mediation of the farmers and herders conflict at the community level (Ademola-Adelehin, et al., 2018).

Conclusion

This chapter analyzed the experience and roles of women in the farmers and herders conflict in polarized context, focusing on Plateau State, one of the hotspot of the violent contestation between two groups in the North-central Nigeria. Plateau State has been battling preexisting ethno-religious, indigene and settler and political crises. The identity division and political crises inexorably influenced the violent nature of the farmers and herders conflicts. It also shaped the experience and roles of the women in the conflict between farmers and herders. While studies have established the active roles that women have played as supporter and perpetrator of violence in the identity division and political crises, this chapter showed that women have played largely invisible roles as supporters of violence in the conflict between farmers and herders.

This chapter demonstrates that women in the selected communities have encouraged and supported their men and youth to perpetrate act of violence against the other group. Women farmers have been in direct confrontations with the herders over encroachment on farms and damages to crops. Some of the female farmers have been attacked and in extreme case, killed by the herders, while some have been raped. The attack on the women farmers have led to cycle of reprisal attacks in many communities. It has also incentivized the farmers to deny the herders' cattle access to farm residuals during fallow season, while some farmers were alleged to have poisoned rivers that provide water for the cattle and the community, thereby leading to the death of some cattle. While youth are seen as the main perpetrator of violence, they have been encouraged and supported by the women in their violent acts. Some women have also shielded their youth from the security agents to prevent them from been arrested and prosecuted for acts of violent they have perpetrated.

It is important to understand the roles that women played as supporters of violence and the negative impacts on the peace process. While women have traditionally played important roles in promoting the wellbeing of their families and communities as caregivers, nurturers and peacemakers, their roles in the conflict have negatively impacted on their capacities as peacemakers. Although some women have not been implicated in the conflict, their capacities to contribute to peace and wellbeing of their families and communities is undermined by the negative roles that other women have played in the conflict which breeds a cycle of violence and insecurity. This amplified the threat to women's livelihood, while the loss of their husband and children in the conflict placed additional burden on women and undermined their wellbeing and capacities to care for their families and communities. Women's roles in the violence also worsens gender and sexual-based violence in which women are the major victims. Thus, women have indirectly contributed to the act of violence perpetrated against their fellow women.

It is equally important to note that some women have played key roles in the peace processes through nonviolent protest to demand for an end to the cycle of violence, accountability and justice, peaceful dialogue between the farmers and herders, and collaborations with some traditional and religious leaders and civil society groups. Women capacities in the peace processes are undermined by the lack of credible traditional and religious leaders and the negative roles of the political elites in the conflict. At the same time, the limited support from civil society groups has undermined women's capacities due to lack of socio-economic empowerment that can boost their capacities in the peace process. Thus, the roles of credible state and local leaders, political elites as well as complementary roles of civil society organizations are critical to efforts to build women's capacities in peacebuilding, and mitigate the negative roles they can play in resource-based conflict.

References

Ademola-Adelehin, B.I., Achakpa, P., Sulieman, J., Donli, P., and Osakwe, B. (2018). The Impact of Farmer-Herder Conflict on Women in Adamawa, Gombe and Plateau States. Search for Common Ground, August.

Akov, E. T. (2017). "The Resource-Conflict Debate Revisited: Untangling the Case of Farmer–Herdsman Clashes in the North Central Region of Nigeria." African Security Review. Vol. 26, 3: 288–307.

Barry, D. (1996). Women and Political Insurgency: France in the Mid-Nineteenth Century. Palgrave Macmillan; 1996th edition.

Benjaminsen, T.A., and Boubacar Ba (2021). Fulani-Dogon Killings in Mali: Farmer-Herder Conflicts as Insurgency and Counterinsurgency. African Security.

Best, S. G. (2007). Conflict and Peace Building in Plateau State, Nigeria. Ibadan: Spectrum Books.

Berry, M. E. (2018). War, Women, and Power: From Violence to Mobilization in Rwanda and Bosnia-Herzegovina. Cambridge University Press.

Bonkat, L. (2014). Survival Strategies of Market Women and Violent Conflicts in Jos, Nigeria. Journal of Asia Pacific Studies, Vol. 3: 281–299.

Brottem, L. and McDonnell, A. (2020). Pastoralism and Conflict in Sudano-Sahel: A Review of the Literature. 1st Edition, Washington DC: Search for Common Ground.

Cohen, D. K. (2013). Female Combatants and the Perpetration of Violence: Wartime Rape in the Sierra Leone Civil War. World Politics, Vol. 65: 383–415.

Cole, S. (2016). A gendered political ecology of tourism and water. In: Mostafanezhad, M., Thompson, A., Norum, R. and Shelton, E., eds. Political Ecology of Tourism: Community, Power and the Environment. Routledge.

De Waal, A. (2014). "When Kleptocracy Becomes Insolvent: Brute Causes of the Civil War in South Sudan." African Affairs. Vol. 113, 452: 347–369.

Goldstein, J. (2001). War and Gender: How Gender Shapes the War System and Vice Versa. Cambridge, UK: Cambridge University Press.

Flintan, F. (2008). Women's Empowerment in Pastoral Societies. (World Initiative for Sustainable Pastoralism, Global Environment Facility, International Union for Conservation of Nature and United Nations Development Programme, 2008). https://www.iucn.org/sites/dev/files/import/downloads/gender_format.pdf
Higazi, A. (2008). Social Mobilization and Collective Violence: Vigilantes and Militias in the Lowlands of Plateau State, Central Nigeria. Africa. Vol. 78: 107–135.
Human Rights Watch. (HRW, 2013). "Leave Everything to God: Accountability for Intercommunal Violence in Plateau and Kaduna States, Nigeria." New York.
Ibrahim, H. (2013). "Le Rôle des Femmes Dans la Viabilité Economique Et Sociale Des Sociétés Pastorales: Le Cas de la Société Mbororo Au Tchad" (La Contribution De L'elevage Pastoral A La Securite Et Au Developpement Des Espaces Saharo-Saheliens, N'djamena, Association des Femmes Peuls Autochtones du Tchad (AFPAT).
Kew, D. (2021). Nigeria's State Peacebuilding Institutions: Early Success and Continuing Challenges. Special Report No. 496, June. United States Institute of Peace www.usip.org
Kenee, F.B. (2022). "Pastoralists and Violent Conflict along the Oromia–Somali Border in Eastern Ethiopia: Institutional Options toward Peacebuilding." African Studies Review. Vol. 65, 2: 404–429.
Krause, J. (2019). "Gender Dimensions of (Non)Violence in Communal Conflict: The Case of Jos, Nigeria." Comparative Political Studies. Vol. 52, 10: 1466–1499.
Kwaja, C.M.A., and Smith, K. (2020). Transnational Dimensions in the Western Sahel and Lake Chad Basin of Conflict between Farmers and Herders in the Western Sahel and Lake Chad Basin. Search for Common Ground. April.
Kwaja, A. M.C. and Ademola-Adelehin, B.I. (2018). Responses to Conflict Between Farmers and Herders in the Middle Belt of Nigeria: Mapping Past Efforts and Opportunities for Violence Prevention. Search for Common Ground Publication.
Kircher, I. (2013). Challenges to Security, Livelihoods, and Gender Justice in South Sudan: The Situation of Dinka Agro-Pastoralist Communities in Lakes and Warrap States. London: Oxfam.
Madueke, K.L. (2019). "The Emergence and Development of Ethnic Strongholds and Frontiers of Collective Violence in Jos, Nigeria." African Studies Review. Vol. 62, 4: 6–30.
Matfess, H. (2020). Brokers of Legitimacy: Women in Community-Based Armed Groups. RESOLVE Network. Community Based Armed Groups Series. June.
Mkutu, K. (2019). Pastoralists, Politics and Development Projects Understanding the Layers of Armed Conflict in Isiolo County. BICC Working Paper, 7.

Morgen, S. B. (2019). "The Pastoral Conflict Takes a Deadlier Turn." SBM Intelligence.
Moritz, M. (2010). "Understanding Herder-Farmer Conflicts in West Africa: Outline of a Processual Approach." Human Organization. Vol. 69 2: 138–48.
Ogundairo, J.A., and Ijimakinwa, F. (2020). Pastoralism and Politics of Exclusion in Ibarapa, Oyo State, Nigeria. African Studies. Vol. 79, 4: 428–443.
Ojewale, O. (2021). Violence is Endemic in North Central Nigeria: What Communities are Doing to Cope. June 23, 2021. Conversation Africa.
Ojo, J.S. (2020). Governing "Ungoverned Spaces" in the Foliage of Conspiracy: Toward (Re)ordering Terrorism, from Boko Haram Insurgency, Fulani Militancy to Banditry in Northern Nigeria. African Security, Vol. 13, 1: 77–110.
Oosterom, M., Sha, D.P., and Dowd, C. (2021). Commissions of Inquiry and Pathways to Accountability in Plateau State, Nigeria. Journal of Modern African Studies. Vol. 59, 4: 439–462.
Owonikoko, S.B., Suleiman, J.B.A., Maibaka, W.K. and Tasiu, N. (2021). "What a Man Can Do, a Woman Can Do Better: Women Farmers, Livelihood and Drug Abuse in Adamawa State, Northeastern Nigeria. Journal of Ethnicity in Substance Abuse.
Parkinson, S. E. (2013). Organizing Rebellion: Rethinking High-Risk Mobilization and Social Networks in War. American Political Science Review. Vol. 107, 418–432.
Peluso, N. L. and Watts, M. (2001). Violent Environments. Ithaca: Cornell University Press.
Peˇsa, I., and Ross, C. (2021). Extractive Industries and the Environment: Production, Pollution, and Protest in Global History. The Extractive Industries and Society. Vol. 8: 100933.
Rocheleau, D. and Ross, L. (1995). Trees as Tools, Trees as Text: Struggles Over Resources in Zambrana-Chacuey, Dominican Republic. Antipode. Vol. 27: 407–428.
Ryle, J and Amoum, M. (2018). Peace is the Name of Our Cattle-Camp Local Responses to Conflict in Eastern Lakes State, South Sudan. Kenya: Rift Valley Institute.
Sørbø, G. M. (2010). Local Violence And International Intervention In Sudan. Review of African Political Economy, Vol. 37, 124: 173–186.
Sjoberg, L. (2016). Women as Wartime Rapists: Beyond Sensation and Stereotyping. New York: New York University Press.
Turner, M. (2004). "Political Ecology and the Moral Dimensions of 'Resource Conflicts': The Case of Farmer–Herder Conflicts in the Sahel." Political Geography. Vol. 23: 863–889.
Viterna, J. (2013). Women in War: The Micro-Processes of Mobilization in El Salvador. New York: Oxford University Press. 288.

Wood, E. J. (2008). The Social Processes of Civil War: The Wartime Transformation of Social Networks. Annual Review of Political Science. Vol. 11, 539–561.

CHAPTER 8

Considering Gender Issues in Farmer-Herder Conflict Resolution in Darfur Region, Sudan

Fatma Osman Ibnouf

Background Context of Darfur Conflict

In 2003 fighting broke out in the Darfur region of Sudan as a struggle between two of insurgent movements and Sudanese military force. However, the root causes lay more deeply as an old conflict between sedentary farmers and nomadic herdsmen. Farming and pastoralism are the two traditional systems of livelihood in Darfur Region, and the relations between these systems often described as nomad-sedentary relations, were highly integrated and together formed a wider livelihood production system that covered the Region (Abdul-Jalil 2014). Sudan, like the rest of Africa drylands zone, suffered from the increasing frequency and severity of drought from the 1980s upwards. Since then, conditions have steadily changed and in the course the nature of that farmer-herder relationship has transformed from complementarity to conflict (Abdul-Jalil 2014), exacerbated by the weakening of customary institutions—native

F. O. Ibnouf (✉)
Development Studies and Research Institute (DSRI), University of Khartoum, Khartoum, Sudan
e-mail: fatma_ibnouf@hotmail.com

J. S. Omotola (ed.), *Herder-Farmer Conflicts in Africa*,
https://doi.org/10.1007/978-3-031-80821-0_8

administration, poor governance and the growing security threats particularly due Darfur war. De Waal (2005: xiv–xviii) adds that the violence and atrocities that have intensified in Darfur have complex causes but, the role of four factors is crucial in understanding the origins of the present conflict, (namely: land, settlement of disputes, national policies, and ideology).

Darfur occupies the far west of Sudan and shares international borders with four countries: Libya, Chad, Central African Republic, and South Sudan—such neighboring and geographical conflict environment is increasingly facilitating the violence in Darfur. The intensity of the conflict has also been attributed to the influx of more sophisticated arms and weapons linked to cross-border attacks from Chadian militias and militias from Central African Republic and the flow of weapons from Libya particularly after the collapse of Gaddafi regime in 2011. Since then, more actors involved in the Darfur armed conflict include Government forces for e.g., Armed forces, Popular Defense Forces, Janjaweed[1] and its Rapid Support Forces (RSF) and on the other side the armed opposition groups i.e., Sudan Liberation Movement (SLM) and Justice and Equality Movement (JEM) in addition to many splinter factions from the main groups (SLM and JEM). These developments have cumulatively affected on the farmer-herder conflict in Darfur, make matters worse and further complicated and thorny matters for farming and pastoral communities.

During the last three decades of the twentieth century, Darfur witnessed more than thirty armed bloody conflicts in both settled and grazing communities (Takana 2016), which also resulted in gross poverty through the loss of livestock and land, human rights abuses and forced displacement. The continuing violence in Darfur has led to the consensus that addressing the root causes of the protracted conflicts is crucial if peace is to be secured. Noteworthy, one of the governmental mechanisms still in place for dealing with farmer-herder conflict is engaging the military or/and police forces—as government often treats incidents as security problem. That is one of the major hurdles to peace between pastoralists and farmers.

Darfur war has claimed thousands of lives and led to thousands of internally displaced persons (IDPs) (Abdul-Jalil 2014; De Waal 2022).

[1] Janjaweed militias were turned into the RSF to fight armed rebellion in Darfur. Human Rights Watch calling them "men with no mercy".

The United Nations has described war[2] in Darfur as "the world's worst humanitarian crisis". The western news media widely point to the war in Darfur as it has been started in 2003 as an ethnic conflict between 'Arabs' and 'Africans'. It should be noted, although the population of Darfur is ethnically diverse, however, in Darfur tribes often self-identify as Africans or Arabs more by lifestyle than any features difference; while African tribes are farmers, Arabs are generally herders. Even if there is a little difference along this line, there are also African tribes that are herders, for instance the Zaghawa group is primarily herders and this group is on the African side of the African/Arab dichotomy.

The farmer-herder conflict is not about ethnic differences and the two groups are not racially different. Ethnic cleavages have been used to obtain short-term political gains, but the creation of tribal militia has fostered deep-seated enmities which are coming to the fore today (Pantuliano 2010). In Darfur many pastoral groups have practiced the tradition of seasonality north–south movement as a livelihood strategy over the centuries. Nonetheless, farmer-herder two group-communities have coexisted side by side peacefully and they have been intermingled with marriage, social and economic interactions. The drought since the mid-1980s drove local tensions, as livelihoods were failing in the drought (Bromwich 2018). It is noticeable that the herder-farmer conflicts over natural resources—diminishing resources—in turn breeds further poverty and natural resource degradation, continuing a vicious circle of poverty and instability, which then aggravates existing conflict. Consequently, Darfur communities remain vulnerable to the continuous stream of climate, conflict and other shocks that have affected them throughout their lifetimes (Young and Ismail 2019). Although many of the same problems that led to the herder–farmer conflicts in the first place persist, however there are a number of aspects concerning the political dimension interact to shape the dynamics of the farmer-herder conflict in Darfur.

Darfur conflict has become, and continues to be, a focus of conflict management efforts by international and regional agencies and actors to end the conflict that began in 2003. These efforts have failed to achieve

[2] In some instances, war and conflict are often used interchangeably. However, for the purpose of this study Darfur war refers to the armed conflict between governments and a number of insurgent movements, which started in 2003, while Darfur conflict is the farmer-herder conflict.

even negative peace, that's absence of direct violence.[3] As pointed-out by Srinivasan (2021) the conflicts in Darfur still burned, despite peace initiatives that toured through Nigeria, Libya, Ethiopia and Qatar. Peace processes primarily focused on wealth and power-sharing arrangements (Ellerby 2013), which are considered to be the root causes of war. The main weaknesses of the peace processes are the lack of coherence as it was the result of work of different consultants and organizations without efforts being made to establish considering the ground realities. Gender issues are never considered to be factors even in the sharing of power and wealth. Sexual and gender-based violence continues to be reported by UNAMID as a "pervasive" feature of the conflict in Darfur (Linke 2018).

Important developments have taken place in Sudan following the Sudan revolution in December 2018 and a new transitional Government has been established. Restoring long-term stability to Darfur is the ultimate goal of the transitional government, as it has been said by the officials. While many are optimistic about the recent Juba peace agreement signed on 3rd of October 2020 between the transitional government and the Sudan Revolutionary Front (SRF) 'SRF is a coalition of rebel groups from the Darfur, Kordofan and Blue Nile'. Nonetheless, nothing substantial has been changed and the Juba agreement has still not pacified conflict in Darfur. Most of these agreements are externally-brokered peace agreements between the Sudanese government and some rebel groups although rejected by other rebel-groups which have continued to fight. Netabay (2009) argues that the Darfur peace process has failed due a number of factors, among them is inconsistent strategy of participation. It may worth mentioning some agreements even generate further violence, in particular between pastoralist groups and farmers. Even during the revision process of this paper fighting has been erupted on 31st of December in Zalangi locality—the study area. Peace actors and institutions continue to support peace-processes that only benefit a few, instead of envision a more just future. Building peace is about profit share for the many rather than fulfilling greed of few—as

[3] The Darfur peace efforts include, but are not limited to, the N'Djamena peace negotiations in 2003 and 2004, the two years of internationally mediated efforts in Abuja started shortly after the N'Djamena agreement from 2004 to 2006, and then Sirte, Libya peace talks October 2007 and peace agreements took place at Doha, Qatar, in 2011—almost all these efforts did not success—internet sources.

it has been said. Resolution of farmer-herder conflict requires enhancing peaceful co-existence among these two groups.

The sustainable peace in most farmer-herder conflicts affected areas remains elusive, despite all the aforementioned efforts/initiatives that have been made. The complexity of a perennial conflict between farmers and herders calls for all concerned peace-related actors to re-examine the factors, which have undermined the peace efforts. Most of these efforts are not commensurate with diversity of actors (with gender-aware), their local peculiarities and the traditional conflict resolution mechanisms. The people-affected by conflict are closest to the challenges to drive the appropriate solutions and to exercise their rights and voice their needs. Men's and women's efforts have an impact on the conflict resolution process' outcome, as they work toward a single common objective with diverse perspectives and different experiences.

Researching Gender Issues in Farmer-Herder Conflict Context–Specific

Women and men have often experienced the conflict differently—because they play different roles and enjoy different statuses. Women's contribution to conflict resolution and peacebuilding processes has received increasing scholarly attention over the last two decades (Adjei 2019). However, scant attention has been paid to gender issues in farmer-herder conflict resolution efforts. In the farmer-herder conflict resolution women have been marginalized by mistakenly assuming women have marginal role in these communities, which is a form of gender bias. In such situation gender issues can be understood as continuously produced through and connected to the realities of the multiple and context-specific experiences and every-day practices. Importantly women were understood only as victims in conflict, this narrow conception of women as victims is both a cause and effect of a competing peace process for women (Ellerby 2013). In this sense, women-as-victims were excluded from negotiations because they were not considered 'legitimate' actors to the conflict (ibid). Consequently, the suffering and experiences of women are largely missing from talks table and are often overlooked in conflict resolution. Some argued that woman is not merely victim of the conflict, but instead she can be combatant herself or perform combat roles such as hidden male family members. It is however beyond the scope of this study to discuss combat roles. The question remains of how to think through the link between gender issues and conflict resolution, in specific farmers and herder's conflict contexts. **These points generate some important questions, which beg to be answered:** How complex and diverse men's and women´s roles can be in farmer-herder conflict times. How women are perceived, experienced and dealt with such protracted conflict to mitigate its effects as a tool towards conflict resolution. What enables women to participate in conflict resolution and what limits their participation.

This study focuses on how women based on their assigned gender roles can impact farmer-herder conflict resolution and how is it work. The case study (Darfur, Sudan) attempts to advance understanding of the different tasks, responsibilities, and experiences of women in conflict context, which have challenged their traditional roles in both communities. The case study is also an attempt to explore different ideas, actions and insights, and gain a better understanding of the women potential to contribute to conflict resolution. This study also seeks to generate information that could be used by conflict resolution practitioners, and many others concerned with address farmer-herder conflict more effectively. This will pave the way for how peace processes incorporate the realities on the ground to ensure that when peace builds, it works to the present and future benefit of all, women and men—it offers opportunity for peace from the ground up.

The study is structured as follows: the background context gives a brief clarification of the background of the conflict in Darfur of western Sudan and its impact and peace efforts. Then the second part of the section throws light on the researching gender issues in the specific-context of the farmer-herder conflict. The next section provides insight into the extant studies on the gender issues and peacebuilding. The following section explains the study area and the method for generating primary data for the study. This is followed in successive sections by an analysis of the farmers and herders' conflict in Central Darfur state of Darfur region of western Sudan provides a presentation of the study findings and discussion of these findings on the light of the position of gender issues in conflict resolution. The very last sections of the paper contain the concluding remarks and implications for conflict resolution and then some recommendations are provided.

Gender Issues and Peacebuilding in the Existing Literature

Over and above all, peace that does not recognize the gender issue is not a "gendered peace just". To ensure that conflict resolution processes and outcomes are gender-just, feminists identify the need for theorists and practitioners to build theories and methodologies that can identify and address context-specific gender norms, identities, and power structures in sites of conflict, and also recognize the 'practical' and 'strategic' gender interests of women situated in conflicted contexts (McLeod and O'Reilly 2019). This is supported by a growing amount of literature. Feminist literature on women's involvement reveals that war has moved from an emphasis on how women are victimized during wars to an agency-oriented approach (Begikhani et al. 2018). Attention is paid to the ways in which women are not only victims, but also active agents and participants in war, and how war situations can be transformative for women's position in society also after war has ended (ibid).

Many studies on conflict and peacebuilding analyze the dominant constructions of femininity, portraying women as victims, weak and essentially peaceful by nature (Hendricks 2011). Men are not naturally born aggressive and prone to war and killing, and not all women are naturally prone to have what seems a natural aptitude to make peace. This idea is said to reproduce gendered dichotomies and power hierarchies (Confortini 2006). Several feminist researchers point out, that viewing men as more violent by nature can serve as an argument to maintain women's subordination as well as keeping women out of influential political and military positions (Confortini 2006).

Peace is conceived as far more than simply the end of violence, but rather as a process that transforms multiple structures of exploitation and injustice, including gender hierarchies (Olivius et al. 2022). Men's dominant position in peace process is encouraged by gender expectations that push the concept of traditional gender roles into higher meaning. Literature on peace as male-dominated fields is considerable. Adeogun and Muthuki (2017), who studied the case of South Sudan, stated that "it is instructive to know that the bottom-up approach with the effective support of top-down approach via descriptive and substantive representation of female advocates in decision making will bring sustainable peace building in the new nation". Despite the peace processes leading up to the peace agreements in many farmer-herder conflict affected-African regions there have been gaps and challenges. It is the question how far the peace agreements in general meet the expectations and needs of the women in the war-affected communities? Most of Darfur agreements never once mentions gender and is silent on the most pressing issues facing women and girls in the conflict affected-area, such as sexual and gender-based violence. Such gender biases led to gender inequality in most of these peace accords. Shepherd (2015) reveals armed conflict is not a gender neutral event; therefore, the dispute resolution process designed to resolve armed conflict should not be neutral toward gender. Considering gender in peacebuilding also increases the chances of successful planning, implementation and institutionalization of a post-armed conflict order (Hudson 2009).

The United Nations have set a number of resolutions to include women equally on peace negotiations and peacebuilding. The United Nations Security Council adopted Resolution 1325 "Women, Peace and Security" (UNCR 1325 in 2000) appears to be established on a significant body of feminist scholarship. The Resolution 1325 shows that the exclusion of women from the peace process is a threat to the peace itself (Bell and O'Rourke 2010). But the UNCR 1325 and its followed further resolutions have not so far fully implemented. However, the criticisms of the content and politics of Resolution 1325 speak to the assertion that "the problem [with women's participation] is not so much the absence of relevant international standards, but the lack of implementation and respect for them" (Bouta et al. 2005: 83).

Gender issue is one of the forgotten dimensions of the herder–farmer conflict resolution in Sudan and elsewhere in Africa. For instance, existing literature on African pastoralism only marginally reported issues on women in pastoral societies, particularly their socioeconomic roles and contributions to livestock production; in contrast, men's activities and roles are often reported by scholars as if women are idle in pastoral societies (Onyima 2019). Women have a dynamic political and social influence in pastoral and farming communities, even where they do not have opportunities for full and equal participation (Brottem and McDonnell 2020). As far as the gender issues are concerned, this constitutes the best entry point to address the deep-rooted gender structures.

Some scholars found that there has been a change in traditional gender due to war, El-Bushra's (2003) indicates that conflict has undoubtedly given women greater responsibilities, and with them the possibility of exerting greater leverage in decision making and increasing their political participation. This may be attributed to that the crises are usually removed social barriers and traditional patriarchal patterns thus open opportunities for increasing of women in 'male' activities. The roles of women alter and expand during conflict as they participate in the struggles and take on more economic responsibilities and duties as heads of households (Arostegui 2013).

Worst still, if there are structural barriers, then attain gender equality becomes a challenge. Women experienced the impact of conflict is closely intertwined with structural gender issues in their community. Violence against women rates rise during conflict and may remain high afterwards in a culture accustomed to violence. It is also a ubiquitous issue and has been generally recognized as an abuse of gendered relations of power. Women suffer from gender-based war crimes which damage their reproductive and sexual health and rights. Some scholars highlight the interplay between culture and the interpretation of violence against women, rendering it 'heroic, justified, reasonable, or at least acceptable' (Merry 2009). Research indicated a significant linkage—empirical as well as theoretical—between gender equality and security and lasting peace (Hudson et al. 2012). With equality, both men and women can be able to participate in the peacebuilding processes and each would have a voice on decisions taken with regards to priorities and needs. The women inclusion is imperative to reaching inclusive peace agreements that lead to positive and sustainable peace (Sweetman 2005 cited in Speake 2013). Although fighting is a direct threat to women's lives, however women are usually involved in the everyday activities of struggling for the survival of their family during conflict. 'Whether it's daycare, water, sanitation—it is peacebuilding, and every peacebuilding act is also an act of healing' (Liepold 2010 cited in Noma et al. 2012).

Study Area, Data and Methods

Darfur region is one of larger and more densely populated regions in Sudan. Sedentary farming and pastoralists' practices are the most common livelihood activities in Darfur region. Darfur Regional Authority is divided into five federal states; namely North, East, West, South and Central Darfur States. Darfur region has been battled with farmer-herder conflict since the great Sahelian drought of the 1970s. The Central Darfur State borders other Darfur states and shares international borders with Chad and the Central African Republic. The State is generally covered by the various agricultural and pastoral lands. The frequent droughts and the deterioration of pasture areas have forced many tribal pastoral groups to seek grazing resources outside their recognized area, therefore competing with sedentary farming groups and leading to conflicts in the State. In the Zalangi Locality, the expansion of cultivated areas by farmers encroached on the forests and on the lands which are traditionally used for grazing has further increased the conflict in frequency and intensity with increased presence of herding-tribes. Thus, Zalangi Locality in the Central Darfur State (see the map) has been chosen as the case study area. Zalangi is heartland of the Fur African group (sedentary farmers) and there are other African groups such as the Burgo, Tama, Zagawa who practiced farming and Arab ethnic groups who practiced nomadic as a way of life, Bani-Hussien, Nawiaba, Misseriya, Khozam, Abala, Tarjam, Jalul, Mahriya, Bani-Halba (Dawoud and Hassan 2015). The competition of farmers and herders over use of the land and water resources in the same spaces continues to lead to almost constant conflicts between these groups. The cases of standoffs between herders and farmers over access to land and water resources are often recorded by the daily newspapers. A combination of factors has undermined the former integration between farming and pastoralism and their livelihood institutions (Young and Ismail 2019) (Fig. 8.1).

The case study is mainly used qualitative research methods. The qualitative research has been associated with a feminist sensitivity, as it best allows "women's voices to be heard" (Bryman 2008: 369). Qualitative data were obtained from focus groups discussions, and key informant interviews, and in-depth interviews to collect primary data from women, men and multiple actors, who are involved in farmers-pastoral conflict at different levels—living in the areas or involved in the conflict resolution. The interview participants selected partly through targeted sampling informed by University of Zalangi staff members and local individuals in positions of influence. The interviews, both individual and focus group, were recorded, transcribed, and then translated from Arabic to English language. Interview transcripts and written notes were analyzed systematically through iterative and repeated re-reading of them. This study also reviews of literature to provide an overview of gender issues and conflict resolution and peacebuilding processes. These sources offered benchmarks for comparison with the study findings.

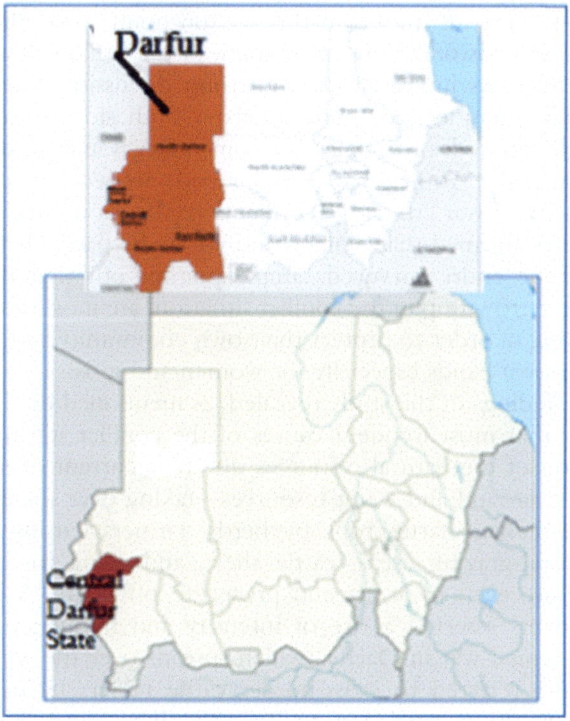

Fig. 8.1 Map of Central Darfur (the study area)

Insight from Darfur: 'Making Gender Issues Work' for Conflict Resolution

This section provides the synopsis of the case study of Zalangi of Central Darfur State. The case study focuses on nature, causes, trends, and consequences of farmer-herder conflict. The effects of conflict on women, whose situation is not as well researched as those women in the other parts of Darfur affected by the civil war. It discusses also how do women characterize their roles in the quest for conflict resolution.

a. **Nature of Herder-Farmer Conflict—Causes and Consequences**

The participant quotes in this section point to conflict between farmers and pastoralists is an ongoing dispute that still affects their daily's lives. As indicated during group discussions the impact of conflict is considerable 'hundred from both sides were killed, or physically injured, or displaced as some villages and nomadic camps were burned'. Women have been raped, abused and experienced gender–based war crimes. Participants of the group discussions and interviews affirmed that women and youth are particularly targeted. Almost the entire surveyed sample pointed-out that their youth, who have grown-up in the conflict situation, are most often engaged in fighting in order to protect their own community and take justice by their own hands especially for women and girls.

The findings of the study revealed, as mentioned by the surveyed sample, that most frequent causes of the conflict still in place are: depletion of the natural resources due to recurrent droughts, skirmishes over land and water resources—taking over somebody else's land –, damage farm-crops by herds, farmers cutting new fields in pastoral-grazing areas, cattle theft, and using force to do it, and failure even to arrest and prosecute offenders. A majority of respondents asserted a rise of intensity and frequency of conflict due to armed-war in Darfur, which spreads over the whole region. They also referred to cross-border cattle raiders by herders from Chad and the Central African Republic. The research participants have attributed the increased of the violently of the conflict to the increased availability of modern weapons and recurrent situations of instability in Sudan and neighboring countries. Surveyed sample criticized the local government because '...they're not take appropriate measures to make basic services and farcicalities available, adequate, and equitably accessible'. While the farmers participants blamed the herders for intentional destruction of their farmlands and crops, nonetheless, the pastoral respondents accused the farmers for preventing them to access grazing land and water points. They quoted '...the pastures areas and the livestock routes are sometimes completely blocked'.

The structure of the conflict has been more complex with more actors involved in the conflict for example the local leaders and some armed-groups such as Janjaweed milia. The needs and interests of both farming and pastoralists' groups are changed over time that make the conflict more complicated. Regarding how land resources are allocated and managed, farmers feel increasingly threatened by herding-groups. Some interviewees reported that in recent years the balance of power has been shifted –favoring pastoralists over farmers. According to the key informant from Fur-tribe the local government has allocated land to some herding-tribes –due to their allied with the central government– at the expense of sedentary farmers, which continue to pave the way to refuel clashes between two groups and in fact have exacerbated the conflict to unprecedented levels of disputes.

b. **Effects of the Conflict on Women**

An undeniable fact farmer-herder conflict has been and continues to affect men's and women's daily lives in various ways. Indicated by other studies 'farmer-herder Conflict has its economic and social impact on women (Ademola-Adelehin et al. 2018). As long as the farmer-herder conflict is the frequent recurrence, men are preoccupied with cattle raiding and fighting and the like. Domestic violence, maternal death, and other incidences of social exploitation are part of the experiences of women and girls in the conflict affected-area. Nonetheless, women have to deal their own suffering like the traumatic impacts of the war, experiences of loss, and limited resources while responding to such stressful experiences, including birth, rape, and abuses.

Gender based violence intend to hurt both women and men. In the case of the latter, the goal of the enemy group is to humiliate the men who are related to the women victims of violence. Many studies indicated that sexual violence is being used as a weapon to humiliate the enemy. Akinsulure-Smith (2014, p. 678) cites scholars have documented the worldwide use of sexual violence against women throughout the ages and across cultures, calling it a weapon, strategy, instrument, and tool. Women are raped, abducted, humiliated, and endure forced pregnancy, sexual abuse and are at high risk of contracting AIDS/HIV. The perceptions of women interviewed regarding gender-based violence against women: Many women had experienced some form of sexual or physical assault during this ongoing conflict. The dominant culture of the social gender norms, women and girls are assumed to accept acquiesce, to be silent about their experiences of violence. Many interviewees spoke about how the feeling of shame of victims of sexual violence to bring forward their complaint The insecurity of many women's livelihoods leaves them open to multiple forms of abuse. Rape continues to permeate pastoral and farming communities and even in IDPs, the members of the both communities are the main perpetrators. Such violence not only results in serious physical, sexual impacts, mental hardships and sometimes death, but increases a feeling of insecurity, and affecting women and girls' access to resources and overall quality of life. Some victimized women have become isolated from communities due to the stigma associated with sexual abuse or rape '…it is still surrounded by silence'. These gender discrimination practices that blame women, naturalize violence, and contribute to aggressors' impunity. It is unlikely that the crimes against women during conflict will be adequately addressed unless women will be included from the very first stages of the conflict resolution process. Women reported that they endure sexual violence at the hands of all those involved in the conflict … A woman said in low voice "*I'm a victim of sexual abuse and was going to take my secret to my grave until I no longer could hold my silence … it's unfathomable suffering faced by many women here*". Women often have disproportionately borne their brunt ever, when women's' victims of sexual violence step forward, they are ostracized. The victims suffer in silence, because they have no right to object due to gender cultural barriers … giving voice to these experiences can render visible what is often hidden. The research participants were united in their belief that experiences of sexual violence must not be silenced to help inform appropriate justice responses.

To tailor services to women needs in conflict situation instead of a one-size-fits-all approach to services … There is often a gap of support of women efforts. During group discussion women have raised concerns on absence of basic services, the reproductive health services, among others. Not much has been done to ending the violation of women human rights in conflict-affected areas and the problem has not yet received proper attention on the official level. However, when one right lacks, it is more likely that the other rights are more fragile, with a higher risk of them not being enjoyed. There are some isolated efforts by aid and support nongovernmental organizations (NGOs) and civil society organizations (CSOs) to address the violation of women human rights problem and support victims. But they do not respond to the all needs of women victims, nor do reaching all of the women who have experienced violence.

c. **Women and Conflict Resolution Mechanisms**

Most women's problems in such conflict-affected areas are related to women's gender identity and social roles. The conflict resolution efforts continue to ignore or inadequately account for gender issues. The peacebuilding processes have often gone through an extensive elites or foreign experts' consultation where the affected-population, in particular women are not made part of the processes. The local ownership of the conflict resolution processes is of monumental importance. Where women feel they have been excluded, the peace process may even exacerbate discriminatory gender norms.

Power is in the hands of men, whereby masculinity is taken to mean open exercise of force and violence. For some women respondents, women equipped with less power at all levels, are thought to be prone to peaceful solutions to conflict situations. Women during group discussion narrated: '*we have the right as men to be listened to, and have our views considered regarding all issues that affect our lives in this situation we both live in*'. Women and girls have seen little change in their lives and traditional gender status, and continue to fall victim to conflicts and violence, patriarchal culture and social norms and practices. The women respondents also drew attention to that: our situation is still far from ideal. 'Both farmer and pastoral women share common experiences: Women are often overlooked. They have been socialized into traditional gender roles in such both patriarchal societies ... Although the work women do is very essential for the survival of their family and community during conflict'... Because of gender construct, women work is not recognized as contribution to peacebuilding. Similarly, this tradition is going on since ages '*even if initially our role supporting and care of the families, during conflict we are now doing more than we're used to do*' ... '*Above all it is crucial that we go beyond a stereotype perception of women as wives and caregivers and men as perpetrators and peacemakers*'. ... Women have often been excluded from participating in peace processes (formal and tradition) because they are viewed as incompetent and lack capacity.

Women participants critiqued what they perceived as the exclusion of women from conflict resolution processes. Participants spoke about patriarchy when she said "*wherever there are systems that have power over, there is exclusion from conflict resolution*". The interviewed women indicated '*If peace is achieved it may well be at the expense of women's rights … our knowledge and insights about our rights and needs remain untouched'*. Women reported the situation during conflict is very difficult *'we unarmed; we're instigators of these clashes; we were unable to defend ourselves'*. Nonetheless, women indicated through interviews that *'we're all take part to achieve peace on the ground … We're predominant men community which gives us a bigger feeling of unity, which forms the basis for solidarity between us …. Peace is needed to be felt and experienced by everyone daily life*. Women struggle to make ends meets, particularly with lack of state support and gap in humanitarian agencies response. One of woman interviewees summarized the women perspective in her comment '*In peace talks we should be represented by ourselves not on behalf … then conflict resolution will be achieved*'. As aforementioned discussion, there is clear evidence that women suffer atrocities during conflicts. Even within these different societies—farming and pastoralists, the biggest thing that draws women together is a shared experience of being at a disadvantage due to their societal gender structures.

In famers and pastoral communities where women are limited by the gender roles in their society to participate in formal peacebuilding, they use these gender roles as informal actors to achieve peace at local level or as a way to work towards peaceful society. Women envision the peace they would like to achieve in conflict affected areas, when the daily life is maintained. These involved their quotidian arrangements for the provision of necessities to ensure the daily survival, caring for children, elderly, injured, disabled, themselves to substances for their independents. Women perform these works with neither the resources nor the institutional resources to help them through such adverse conditions. In Darfur conflict affected-areas women have taken on increasing importance as household leaders and cultivators, although this has little impact on their social or political standing (Linke, 2018). To deal and cope with such risky situations, women indicate they adopt greater diversity and enormous flexibility alternatives. The everyday lives of experiences of women are a key to understanding conflict resolution practices.

Survey women participants in interviews and focus group discussions respond to the question whether they consider that their daily work create the capacity for peace in their communities. Women have been asked to provide some concrete examples of the ways they usually adopt to build peace in their community within traditional culture. Women participants indicated that they present and engaged in many tasks, which are not only following the normative gender roles of women but all types of peace. For example, in the following quotation, a group of women respondents indicated that their foremost priority is to save lives of their children and family, as long as the killing is underway: which they called "survival efforts"—conflict is being part of life itself. *'Life here is about survival'* as one of the women respondents put it. During group discussion, women are said to be faced with greater responsibilities as most of them have to work harder to provide for their family—as sometimes single breadwinner, "the everyday life realities". The risk of being killed or rape on the way, women are confronted to get survival livelihoods. women take on the tasks previously performed by men, both in agricultural production and pastoral activities like trade of animal and farm products. Women could internalize their assumed gender roles, but they just feel more themselves when they perform other non-traditional roles. Women often take responsibility for the care of their dependents as the main caregiver and nurturer. Current situation demands a new approach that goes beyond the existing conflict transformation process to address what knowledge exists that can be useful for peacebuilding. The gender issue is a dimension that sorely overlooked in many peacebuilding efforts. The case study of Darfur has shown that women have unique responsibilities and roles related to grow up their children at ages in which they are most vulnerable to fall victim to violent ideas.

Darfur case shows that there is a high level of social cohesion reflected by the widespread of intercultural farmers/herders' marriage. Such intercultural marriage within the IDP populations (for those who are lived in displaced camps) is one way of bonding two rival groups in the process of peacebuilding and conflict resolution. Through marriage, kinship relationships can be established between clans as well as ethnic groups (Pretty and Ward 2001 cited in Tadesse et al. 2010). Through intermarriage women shape reform movements bridge ethnic divides and foster alliances in service of creating a just and multi-farmer and herders' communities. For the farmer woman married to a herder man from other tribe this is in terms of social security and stability for their families, and for farmer-herder' community at large. It is in terms of the demographics of society, a large change in which could stop/prevent conflict and hence stabilize Darfur as a whole.

Traditional justice, in particular judiya is variably formal justice and reconciliation mechanisms that Darfurian use in addressing conflict (Tubiana et al. 2012). The case study found that there are still indigenous conflict resolution mechanisms (Judiya and Rakoba), which sometimes leading to practical agreements that creating conducive environments where herders and farmers can be able to live together peacefully. As indicated by Elsanousi (2017) Judiya is the main mechanism for traditional mediation, reconciliation and justice in Darfur in Sudan. These conflict resolution mechanisms stances are in favor of men. Customary institutions entrench conservative cultural norms which constrain women's participation, politically, socially and economically. Consequently, women face disadvantages in these indigenous conflict resolution systems. Some men interviewed groups identified women '… are not qualified enough, are naturally weak, emotional, lack experience and leadership skills to participate in these conflict resolution mechanisms'—traditional descriptive stereotypes. They need someone wise and strong, their men, to make the decisions for them. What do women know about Judiya and Rakoba? Their position or place is in the kitchens. Some men narrated '*Judiya and Rakoba aren't a woman's place to sit at a table discussing things she doesn't understand and she knows nothing about*'. Men added '*we are the ones with a long experience … it is very difficult to reason with women*'. They concluded '*women don't opt for such roles*. This shows how some men, through their words, deny women the space to contribute positively in conflict resolution.

d. **Women's Coping Strategies**

The case study brought out experiences of gender issues being reinforced as a result of the farmer-herder conflict. As a result of the reality of conflict, each man and woman have to re-adapt to changed roles. Men often leave their homes and in practice women start to take on men's roles in their absence.

Women have crossed the gendered division of labor to take on more male responsibility. Conflict left women with extra duties to do at the home besides their usually day to day activities of providing for the family. They have to become more active in informal markets in order to provide for their families. This is a shift in traditional assumed gender roles. However, from the women´s perspective, things are not perceived as a choice but as a given situation, as a consequence of conflict. While conflict may provide women with a measure of new social and economic opportunities, little evidence existed for a change in the prevailing patriarchal attitudes—including access to land, credit, and support services. The farmers and herders' traditional societies are loathing altering customs. The gender discrimination in land ownership remains up to now an unresolved and volatile issue in both customary and official systems. Traditional leaders are often settled most inheritance disputes in favor of men, according to traditional practices—as indicted by interviewees from the governmental institutions.

Women's respondents report that they are used to supplement farming and livestock-based activities with survival livelihood diversification, such as selling of farm and milk products and by-products. These activities have a role to play in ensuring food security and peaceful household, and in turn community. Through these diverse actions and responsibilities, women contest and reconfigure gender. If it were not for women, the suffering of many individuals (especially children and elderly and disabled) would have been much greater as the conflict went on.

Women constitute a relatively powerful sector of both farming and pastoral communities with regard to their productive and economic role in the family. Many of the women interviewed spoke about their desire maintaining stability in the home and to their community. The following quotes affirm these points: '*we're part of this community, and we definitely feel its pain and we keep doing the best we can to rise to continuous challenges and to fit our community's needs'... We're undertaken considerable risks in order to provide for our children and family, even when fighting is going on ...*'.

In Zalangi locality there are a very limited number of non-state organizations, which are working to address women issues. One of the supportive women's organizations has been established by women activists to response to women needs in pastoral and farming communities. Through organization women have been equipped with literacy education and handicrafts making skills. The women's organizations during group discussion argued: '... *we've seen women outnumbering men … some of these women eager to attend literacy classes where they can learn to read, write, account for the first time … and learn craft and sewing skills, which increase their opportunities for earning income*'. Capacity building programming through literacy and handicraft classes is widely recognized even among respondents as the gateway to economic security. Access to learning means also raise women awareness and improve their capacity to stand up for their rights. Thus, in turn contribute to provide women independence and agency, whereupon women are able to act on their capabilities when the opportunity arises to get rid of the myths that women are not competent for the opportunities that become available. A 'farmer-pastoral women group' was initiated as a forum for these victimized women to advocate for their rights and needs but it is hardly functional.

To sum-up: Yet, even with the women role changes during these ongoing conflicts, patriarchal attitudes still prevail in farming-pastoral communities, to the detriment of women. There is a need for some elements of change around the culture of hegemonic masculinities and subordination of women—to tackle deep-rooted, systemic challenges in inclusion women in the peace resolution work. In farmer–herder conflict-affected areas, due to the injustice imposed upon women, they know the price of suffering and can probably deal with it more effectively than men—as indicated by surveyed sample.

Concluding Remarks and Implications for Conflict Resolution

Gender issues have never been considered to be factors in peace resolution and security in all Darfur peace agreements so far. Even women's views, opinions, wishes and aspirations were not represented at the negotiating table and as a result, the fragile Darfur Peace Agreement has failed to ensure full protection of women and girls (Shai and Vunza 2021). The formal conflict resolution mechanisms assumed to be gender neutral reify, even traditional mechanisms as well. Judiya is the main term for traditional justice and reconciliation mechanisms in Darfur, while a rakoba is a customary precedent between two parties, normally set by a successful past judiya that is applied to future disputes between the same parties

(Tubiana et al. 2012: 37). Even these customary conflict-resolution mechanisms (Judiya and Rakoba) remain male-dominated and they have often been gender blind. During Doha Document for Peace process neither traditional leaders nor the leaders of armed conflict parties—who are all men—were very receptive to the idea of women's participation in the peace talks (Linke 2018). Thus, women have been tokenized during the negotiations and peacebuilding processes. Nonetheless the clear message from Darfurian woman who was interviewed by De Waal, in 2009 "... if women are convinced with the peace process, it is going to happen". Meaningfully engaging different local actors and their diversity of experiences and their suffering, particularly the less visible farming and pastoralists' women, in the building and implementation of peace is a worth to be considered. That will lead to more affective policy that holds the promise of empowerment of women and achieve of gender equality.

This Darfur case study indicates that women in pastoral and farming communities involve in several informal peace practices through their lived experience of conflict. Women's experience is often not visible within this conflict and their perceptions of conflict largely remind ignored in conflict resolution. For Elisabeth Porter, therefore, a more just and secure world will result from peace processes that are more inclusive of women (Klot 2011). The study indicates that the different activities women do, from the struggle to survive conflicts, to preparation of foods, performing of care-work, to community ties all are critical elements of building peace. As indicated by this study and affirmed by Gizelis (2011)women are involved in many different peacebuilding processes at the community level, as well as providing day-to-day and emergency support for their communities.

The study findings corroborate those of others (see Akinsulure-Smith 2014). Conflict itself is gender violence against women, as sexual violence is used as a weapon of conflict. However, with the rising tendency to use rape and other forms of sexual violence against women as a weapon, there should be an effort in all conflict situations not to ignore gender issues.

The gender issues are framed within interactions between a variety of circumstances and influences. Gender issues influence experiences of conflict, exposure to conflict-related crimes, access to resources and assets, and participate in day-to-day survival work, and many determinants of conflict resolution. Holding women's experience up to the light is crucial because without doing this, we cannot fully understand shifting gender identities, roles, and power relationships in situations of conflict (Thompson 2006).

The conclusion of the study argues for inclusion of the gender issues to make a difference to resolution processes, where their effect has been obvious, and address the barriers to implement gendered approach to peacebuilding. The study findings aligned with the arguments by scholars such as (Speake 2013) a truly gendered approach to peacebuilding and conflict resolution must have a comprehensive analysis of the variety of roles that women play in society. In addition to Björkdahl (2012) cited '...research indicates that the presence of women and the incorporation of a gender perspective in peacebuilding efforts have a favorable effect on the peace processes'. Invisibility of gender issues in conflict resolution are meant a loss of the opportunity for women to break through the gender inequality arising from the prevalence of a gender–biased tradition. Durable peace is generally more likely in countries with higher levels of gender equality (Gizelis 2009). This study deduces that gender issues should be recognized in a fundamental way in any attempt for conflict resolution, importantly it should "best fit" such specific context. In this way society can be rebuilt for all, and the unequal structures can be addressed outright.

Lessons for Peacebuilding: Gender Issues Matter in Addressing Herder-Farmer Conflicts

Nonetheless, there are many unanswered questions that need more comprehensive understanding of farmer's and pastoralists' women roles in resolution of such conflicts. Yet, the findings of this case study have profound implications for policymaking and influence on how gender issues can be counted in conflict resolution. Making this happen requires peacemakers will, and bottom-up approach matched with a willingness to make it a reality, to cite but a few examples. Thus, the case study provides recommendations based on the findings, the major areas of concern are:

- Collecting, analyzing, and publishing gender disaggregated data that inform policies are needed in recognition of the role play by both men and women in building and sustaining peace.

- Developing evidence-based gender policies that leave no one behind; and that can accelerate gender related objectives—as with the implementation mechanisms of legal provisions, reform of the laws, the security sector and other government institutions.
- Gender issues considerations must be included in broader frameworks of farmer-herder conflict resolution. The gender different set of priorities and needs of women should be heard and addressed, that's to address entrenched gender norms, stereotypes and gender-based violence
- Strengthening national sector systems with greater emphasis on gender, women inclusion, and security. Policy response requires addressing special needs of women to ensure women emerge resilient from the effects of violent conflict considered to be culturally 'appropriate'.
- Challenging patriarchal ideologies through education and awareness raising campaign. The women need to be prepared and enabled—education is first and foremost—to claim her right of equality then. *Where most considered it a waste of time for girls to attend school*
- Formulating multi-dimensional polices that touch on addressing gender issues to be integrated into post-conflict programs and activities. Such as ensuring the needs and concerns of women and girl survivors from conflict gender-based violence are reflected in programs and planning to ensure they are effectively addressed. The protection of survivals/victims who suffer from discrimination due to rape should be the paramount concern, with psychosocial and legal services.
- Pay attention to gender equality in all programs to achieve gender equality previously set by national and international instruments. Special attention needs to be placed on critical sectors, such as health, the ownership of land, education governance, and infrastructure where disparity between men and women is apparent. Building the capacity of the institutions that concern of gender and women issues.

References

Abdul-Jalil, M. A. (2014). Nomad-sedentary Relations in the Context of Dynamic Land Rights in Darfur: From Complementarity to Conflict. In

J. Gertel, R. Rottenburg, & S. Calkins (Eds.), Disrupting Territories: Land, Commodification & Conflict in Sudan (pp. 102–120). Woodbridge; Rochester: Currey.

Ademola-Adelehin, B. I. Achakpa, P. Suleiman, J. Donli, P. and Bridget, O. (2018). *The Impact of Farmer-Herder Conflict on Women in Adamawa, Gombe and Plateau States, Nigeria*. Search for Common Ground (SFCG), Nigeria.

Adeogun, T. and Muthuki, J. M. (2017). "Only the Person Who Wears the Shoes Knows Where the Shoes Pinch": Reworking Bottom-Up Approach in South Sudan. *Women's Studies International Forum*, 62 (1), 83–90

Adjei, M. (2019). Women's Participation in Peace Processes: A Review of Literature. *Journal of Peace Education*, 16 (2), 133–154.

Akinsulure-Smith, A. M. (2014). Displaced African Female Survivors of Conflict-Related Sexual Violence: Challenges for Mental Health Providers. *Violence against Women*, 20 (6), 677–694.

Arostegui, J. (2013). Gender, Conflict, and Peace-Building: How Conflict Can Catalyse Positive Change for Women. *Gender and Development*, 21 (3), 533–549.

Bell, C. and O'Rourke, C. (2010). Peace Agreements or Pieces of Paper? The Impact of UNSC Resolution 1325 on Peace Processes and Their Agreements. *The International and Comparative Law Quarterly*, 59 (4), 941–980.

Begikhani, N. Hamelink, W. and Weiss, N. (2018). Theorising Women and War in Kurdistan: A Feminist and Critical Perspective. *Journal of Kurdish Studies*, 6 (1).

Björkdahl, A. (2012). A Gender-Just Peace? Exploring the Post-Dayton Peace Process in Bosnia. *Peace & Change*, 37 (2), 286–317.

Bouta, T. Frerks, G. and Bannon, I. (2005). *Gender, Conflict, and Development*. Washington, DC: The World Bank.

Bromwich, B. (2018). Power, Contested Institutions and Land: Repoliticising Analysis of Natural Resources and Conflict in Darfur. *Journal of Eastern African Studies*, 12 (1), 1–21.

Brottem, L. and McDonnell, A. (2020). *Pastoralism and Conflict in Sudano-Sahel: A Review of the Literature*. Search for Common Ground (SFCG).

Bryman, A. (2008). *Social Research Methods*, Third Edition. Oxford: Oxford University Press.

Confortini, C. (2006) Galtung, Violence, and Gender: The Case for a Peace Studies/Feminism Alliance. *Peace & Change*, 31 (3), 333–367.

Dawoud, A. A. and Hassan, T. A. (2015) The Dynamics of Pastoralist Livelihoods in Central and West Darfur States as a Result of Darfur Conflict. *Journal of Agricultural Science and Engineering*, 1 (2), 83–88.

De Waal, A. (2022). *The Conflict in Darfur, Sudan: Background and Overview*. Fletcher School of Law and Diplomacy, Tufts University https://sites.tufts.edu/.

De Waal, A. (2005). *Famine that Kills: Darfur, Sudan*. Revised Edition Oxford: Oxford University Press.

De Waal, A. (2009). *The AU Panel and Civil Society: 'There Is Nothing to Do but to Sit around the Table'*. African Arguments, available online at https://africanarguments.org/.

El-Bushra, J. (2003) Fused in Combat: Gender Relations and Armed Conflict. *Development in Practice*, 13 (2–3), 252–265.

Ellerby, K. (2013). *The Tale of Two Sudans: Engendered Security and Peace Processes*. Washington, DC: United States Institute of Peace. Available at http://www.previous.usip.org/files/academy/case-studycompetition/20130322-The-Tale-of-Two-Sudans.pdf.

Elsanousi, Y. E. A. (2017) Traditional Judiya Leaders in Sudan as Actors of Humanitarian Diplomacy: Are They Eligible to Fulfill These Roles in the Darfur Humanitarian Crisis? *Pyrex Journal of African Studies and Development*, 3 (2), 13–23.

Gizelis, T. I. (2011) A Country of their Own: Women and Peacebuilding. *Conflict Management and Peace Science*, 28 (5) (Sage Publications).

Gizelis, T. I. (2009) Gender Empowerment and United Nations Peacebuilding. *Journal of Peace Research*, 46 (4), 505–523.

Hendricks, C. (2011). Gender and Security in Africa: An Overview. Discussion Paper, 1104–8417; 63. Uppsala: Nordiska Afrika Institutet.

Hudson, H. (2009). Peacebuilding Through a Gender Lens and the Challenges of Implementation in Rwanda and Côte d'Ivoire. *Security Studies*, 18 (2), 287–318.

Hudson, V. M. Ballif-Spanvill, B. Caprioli, M. and Emmett, C. F. (2012). *Sex and World Peace*. New York: Columbia University Press.

Klot, J. F. (2011). A Review of Peacebuilding: Women in International Perspective. *Peace Review*, 23 (2), 263–267.

Linke, J. (2018). *Women in Peace and Transition Processes: Sudan: Darfur (2009–2017)*. Geneva, the Graduate Institute of International and Development Studies, Inclusive Peace & Transition Initiative. Available online at https://www.inclusivepeace.org.

McLeod, L. and O'Reilly, M. F. (2019) Critical Peace and Conflict Studies: Feminist Interventions. *Peace-building*, 7 (2), 127–145.

Merry, S. E. (2009). *Gender Violence: A Cultural Perspective*. Malden, MA; Oxford: Wiley-Blackwell Publisher.

Netabay, N. (2009). *The Darfur Peace Process: Understanding the Obstacle to Success*. Unpublished M.A. Thesis University Notre Dame.

Noma, E. Aker, D. and Freeman, J. (2012) Heeding Women's Voices: Breaking Cycles of Conflict and Deepening the Concept of Peacebuilding. *Journal of Peacebuilding & Development*, 7 (1), 7–32.

Onyima, B. N. (2019). Women in Pastoral Societies in Africa. In Yacob-Haliso O., Falola T. (eds) *The Palgrave Handbook of African Women's Studies*. Cham: Palgrave Macmillan.

Olivius, E. Hedström, J. and Phyo, Z. M. (2022). Feminist Peace or State co-optation? The Women, Peace and Security agenda in Myanmar. *European Journal of Politics and Gender*, 5 (1), 25–43.

Pantuliano, S. (2010) Oil, Land and Conflict: the decline of Misseriyya Pastoralism in Sudan. *Review of African Political Economy*, 37 (123), 7–23.

Shepherd, C. K. (2015). The Role of Women in International Conflict Resolution. *Hamline University's School of Law's Journal of Public Law and Policy*, 36 (2), 53–67.

Shai, K. B. and Vunza, M. (2021). Gender Mainstreaming in Peacebuilding and Localised Human Security in the Context of the Darfur Genocide: An Africentric Rhetorical Analysis. *Journal of Literary Studies*, 37, (2), 69-84.

Speake, B. (2013). *A Gendered Approach to Peacebuilding and Conflict Resolution*. E – International Relations.

Srinivasan, S. (2021) *When Peace Kills Politics International Intervention and Unending Wars in the Sudans*. London: Hurst & Company Publishers Ltd.

Tadesse, B. Tesfaye, Y. and Beyene. F. (2010). Women in conflict and indigenous conflict resolution among the Issa and Gurbura clans of Somali in Eastern Ethiopia. *African Journal on Conflict Resolution*, 10 (1).

Takana, Y. S. S. (2016). *Darfur: Struggle of Power and Resources, 1650–2002: An Institutional. Perspective*. Bergen: Chr. Michelsen Institute.

Thompson, M. (2006). Women, Gender, and Conflict: Making the Connections. *Development in Practice*, 16 (3/4), 342–353.

Tubiana, J. Tanner, V. and Abdul-Jalil, M. (2012). Traditional Authorities' Peace-making Role in Darfur. Washington DC, United States Institute of Peace, available at https://www.files.ethz.ch/isn/155469/PW83.pdf.

Young, H. M. and Ismail, M. A. (2019) Complexity, Continuity and Change: Livelihood Resilience in the Darfur Region of Sudan. *Disasters*, 43 (S3), S318–S344

CHAPTER 9

Herder-Farmer Conflicts in Togo

Richard Alemdjrodo

Introduction

Transhumance is one of the oldest forms of feeding animals in extensive breeding (based on grazing). Since the 1950s, the nomadic people of the Sahel (especially the Fulani herdsmen coming from the Fouta in Guinea) have always sought to move toward the greenest areas of coastal countries. But the expansion of their pastoral activities to the coastal countries creates every year territorial bloody conflicts. UNOWAS (2018: 23–24) documents how movement of pastoralists from Burkina Faso to Togo has become an issue in recent times. Environmental constraints such as climate change and desertification in Burkina Faso are pushing many pastoralists southwards into neighbouring countries, including Togo. This trend of 'migratory drift' from the drylands to (sub-)humid areas, resulting in permanent relocation of pastoralists has continued unabated. The conflicts between farmers and pastoralists are a recurring problem in many West African countries. This paper deals with the case of Togo, with a particularity linked to the will of the herdsmen to settle in the country. Though indigenous pastoralists abound, this chapter focuses on migrant

R. Alemdjrodo (✉)
School of Law, University of Lome, Lomé, Togo

J. S. Omotola (ed.), *Herder-Farmer Conflicts in Africa*,
https://doi.org/10.1007/978-3-031-80821-0_9

pastoralists in Togo partly due to their activities and associated consequences, including heightening competition for scarce natural resources (IOM 2017; Herbert and Birch 2022).

The conflicts between already established pastoralists on Togolese territory and farmers are exacerbated each year by the arrival of breeders from the Sahel with their herds. Like all coastal countries, Togo faces the transhumance of pastoralists from Sahel countries, and the cohabitation between farmers and these pastoralists gives rise to conflicts which sometimes result in deaths. The local populations are confused by the fact that Togolese authorities do not oppose the entry into the national territory of nomadic herders. But the Togolese government could not have acted otherwise because transhumance is a legal obligation for West Africa countries. Indeed, Togo is bounded by agreements with other countries in the region.[1] This agreement is justified by the fact that the Economic Community of West African States (ECOWAS) considers transhumance in the ECOWAS region as an essential activity for safeguarding and increasing agricultural production and livelihoods as an integral part of the region's agriculture, food security, and poverty reduction policy[2] The Togolese authorities wish to strengthen cooperation with countries of origin to enforce the periods of transhumance (January 15–May 15). The government had also proceeded with the redefinition of entry points on the territory and specified authorized transit and grazing corridors (see IOM 2017).

It is undeniable that clashes between pastoralists and farmers have a significant impact on human, national and regional security[3] As such, they have become a source of growing concern for Togolese authorities and the civil society, with each party trying to strengthen local mechanisms for conflict resolution through dialogue. There are therefore good local

[1] Heads of states Decision A/DEC.5/10/98 regulating transhumance between ECOWAS members. Faced with recurring conflicts, and to prevent clashes that often occur between herdsmen, trans-border authorities and even farmers, ECOWAS urged, on March 30, 2017, herdsmen in the region to obtain among other measures, the community's International Transhumance Certificate (ITC) whenever grazing movements are to be embarked upon: https://www.ecowas.int/ecowas-stresses-the-need-to-obtain-international-transhumance-certificate.

[2] https://ecpf.ecowas.int/wp-content/uploads/2016/01/Decision-1998-English.pdf.

[3] Study by the United Nations Office for West Africa and the Sahel (UNOWAS) August 2018: https://unowas.unmissions.org/fr/pastoralisme-et-s%C3%A9curit%C3%A9-en-afrique-de-l%E2%80%99ouest-et-au-sahel.

practices that could be held to be a pertinent consideration for conflict prevention and peaceful coexistence. However, in recent years, efforts to resolve these conflicts have come up against a new development, namely the tendency of transhumant herders to get closer and closer to the coast and, above all, to the capital Lomé and to stay in its surroundings beyond the date of the end of the transhumance period. The government issued repetitively decrees asking pastoralists—mostly from Fulani tribe—to leave the country. Apparently, the threat of removal, deportation or exclusion was not deterrent enough for the herdsmen. The government was adamant to remove the herdsmen, because the month of June marks the beginning of both the rainy season and farming. The violence between the populations is then inevitable. Moreover, because of the proliferation of weapons in the region, the government fears that the conflicts will become even bloodier. The region is also plagued by trafficking of illicit goods that generates unprecedented profits, acts of banditry and theft (including of animals). The arrival of Al Qaeda in Islamic Maghreb and the possible consequences of the recent events in Libya (Marty 2011) or the terrorist attacks in Burkina Faso in 2016 further complicate the problem, with effects on transhumance in West Africa (FAO 2012).

It is in the context of these new behaviors likely to multiply the conflicts between farmers and breeders that this study was conducted. The chapter focuses on finding explanations for the conflicts, their management and lessons for sustainable peacebuilding. In the lines that follow, we will successively discuss the method of data collection for this study, the Historical and Contemporary Manifestations, the causes and consequences of the conflict, the management of the conflict by the local and governmental authorities of the country, and finally lessons that can be learned for peacebuilding in the country.

Study Area, Data and Methods

Togo is subdivided into five Regions: Maritime, Plateaux, Centrale, Kara and Savanes. For an effective study of the effects of transhumance, the fieldwork focused on the regions most affected by the phenomenon: the Kara region, the central region and the plateau region.[4]

[4] See an official map of the reception regions for transhumant, https://www.researchgate.net/figure/Localisation-des-couloirs-de-transhumance-officiels-de-la-region-des-Savanes-du-Togo_fig2_357187787, Reception areas for transhumant herders are designated

Two communities mainly have retained our attention in the Kara region, namely Yade-bohou and Kemerida because of their strategic position for the study. For the central region, Kpeyi Hezouwe in the canton of Tchebebe in Sotouboua prefecture was selected. But for the Plateau region, fieldwork could not be done until the first week of January 2019. Indeed, following political unrest, the massive presence of the military on this territory did not encourage people to participate in our research. However, we eventually conducted the fieldwork in the region. The population of study were the population involved in conflicts including herders and farmers. The major difficulty in this area was the visit on the way to herders, who live far from villages, in some areas difficult to access. But the exchanges with them took place in local languages, thanks to a student at the University of Kara who speaks the languages. Other challenges encountered during the fieldwork include hostility from a segment of the population, because of the Togolese political context. This population feels abandoned by politicians and anyone who comes from Lomé is quickly interpreted as a politician, Illiteracy was also an issue. But we struggled to get some reasonable number of respondents, whose responses were cogent enough to help address our research questions and objectives.

In line with overall methodological frames of the study, primary data were collected using structured and semi-structured in-depth interviews, Focus Group Discussions (FGD), key informant interviews, direct observation and questionnaires administered on purposefully selected respondents and stakeholders in the selected communities in ways that ensured the fair representation of critical constituencies, including farmers, herders, women, youth, government and non-governmental actors, as well as spatial representation.

In the Kara region, the questionnaires were administered in the town of Kara, but also in the villages of Lama and Lama-Kpedah, Kemerida-Lama, Ketao, and Lama-Pkeda. In the central region, in addition to the city of Sotouboua, respondents were found in the localities of Lassa, Lassa-Houde, Matchatom, Tchare, Yade-Bohou. Finally in the plateau region, respondents were found in the town of Notsé, as well as in the

in these regions by the Ministry of Agriculture, Animal and Fisheries Production. Example, the reception area of Dimori (Kara region), Yanda (Plateaux and Central region) and Tetetou (Plateaux region) which should make it possible to limit conflicts with local populations.

localities of Kpeyi Hezouwe, Kpove, Kpove-Marché, Kpove-village and Kpove Detokpo. Overall, the herdsmen and farmers met were very reluctant to participate in the survey. In the Kara region, the questionnaires were administered to 20 individuals and 10 individuals were interviewed; in the central region 17 people were gathered for the focus group and 9 individuals were interviewed; and in the plateau region, 16 respondents participated in the surveys, while 7 people were interviewed. For the focus groups, the age of the respondents varies between 15 and over 55. In this sample of 53 people, 20 are farmers, 10 are transhumant pastoralists, 11 people are students living in the regions, 3 representatives of NGOs, 5 teachers, 2 civil servants and 2 individuals without occupation.

Historical and Contemporary Manifestations

At the heart of the conflicts between herders and farmers is the problem of pressure related to land and land overexploitation[5] that Togo is facing due to strong population growth[6] According to the National Institute of Statistics and Economic and Demographic Studies (INSEED), Togo had a population of 7,886,000 inhabitants on January 1, 2021.[7] In the north, increasingly violent conflicts between peasants and herders are reported (FAO 2012).[8] Historically, decrees n°2006–033/PR and n°2007–089/PR indicate the creation of a national committee and prefectural transhumance committees. It should be noted that the cohabitation between the herdsmen coming from Burkina-Faso and entering through the Savannah region in northern Togo goes back a very long time, and as Sokemawu (2009) pointed out, strong friendships had been woven between the two groups. This friendship is expressed through diverse forms of assistance, such as food support, donations of food or livestock products, and visits

[5] According to Tamou, the agricultural front tends to reduce pastoral areas in favor of cotton cultivation. See, Tamou C. 2002. Etat des lieux spatialisé et quantitatif de la transhumance dans la zone périphérique d'influence du Parc National du W (Bénin). Rapport de maîtrise d'écologie). Cotonou: Université de Cotonou, p. 67.

[6] The annual population growth rate is 2.4%: https://www.worlddata.info/africa/togo/populationgrowth.php.

[7] https://inseed.tg.

[8] La transhumance transfrontalière en Afrique de l'Ouest Proposition de plan d'action, Document FAO 2012.

during cultural events such as baptisms, weddings and funerals.[9] The peaceful relationship between the two groups led to the installation of transhumant and nomadic herdsmen in all the localities of the savannah region, and beyond, and to their sedentarization thereafter.[10]

The majority of herders entering Togo come from Burkina Faso[11] Togo has taken measures to regulate the influx of these breeders, by establishing a quota of 50,000 animals authorized to enter each year from other West African countries, and a tax of 5000 CFA per head of cattle when herders cross the border[12] Beyond its ability to produce animals for its local market, Togo has today acquired a strategic position in the livestock trade. Despite the reduction of pastoral spaces (advancement of agriculture, advancement of urban areas, expansion of National Parks), its territory serves as a reception area for many transhumant people. It is very difficult to have reliable statistics on cross-border transhumance. They are estimated at several tens of thousands of heads per year. Animals generally head for the Plateaux Region via the Savannah, Kara and Central Regions (Fig. 9.1). Coming from Burkina, sometimes from Niger and Benin, herders flee the dry season in their area of origin.[13] They usually arrive in January. At this time the harvest is over and there are few problems of cohabitation with agricultural activities. On the other hand, during the ascent in June, the space is closed and the conflicts are numerous insofar as even the cattle tracks, in theory secured, are cultivated. The table of frequency (Fig. 9.2) shows that it is in Sotouboua and its surroundings that, according to the respondents, the conflicts are more recurrent.

[9] Sokemawu K. (2009): Relation paysan-foulani dans la Région des Savanes au Togo: une cohabitation complexe et des problèmes majeurs. In: Revue de Géographie du Laboratoire LEÏDI, N°7, Université Gaston Berger, Saint-Louis, pp. 99–106.

[10] Sokemawu K. (2015), Gestion des conflits entre paysans et éleveurs peulhs de la région des savanes au Nord-Togo dans le processus d'un développement durable, In Revue de Géographie Tropicale et d'Environnement, n° 2, 2015, pp. 26–39.

[11] Stenning, D. J. (1957), 'Transhumance, Migratory Drift, Migration: Patterns of Pastoral Fulani Nomadism', *The Journal of the Royal Anthropological Institute of Great Britain and Ireland*, 87 (1): 57–73.

[12] Pastoralisme et Sécurité en Afrique de l'Ouest et au Sahel – Vers une coexistence pacifique, Étude du Bureau des Nations Unies pour l'Afrique de l'Ouest et le Sahel (UNOWAS), 2018.

[13] Corniaux C., Actualisation des données sur le commerce du bétail au Togo: Circuits, marchés et consommation de viande bovine, Rapport CIRAD, 2012.

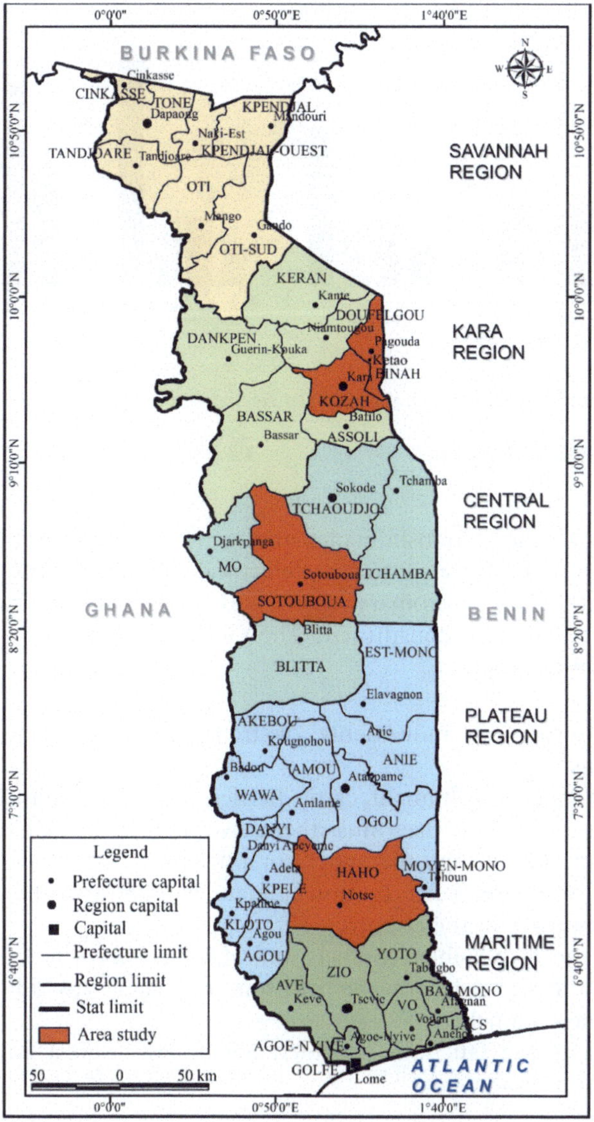

Fig. 9.1 Map of the study areas (*Source* National Institute of Statistics and Economic and Demographic Studies [INSEED])

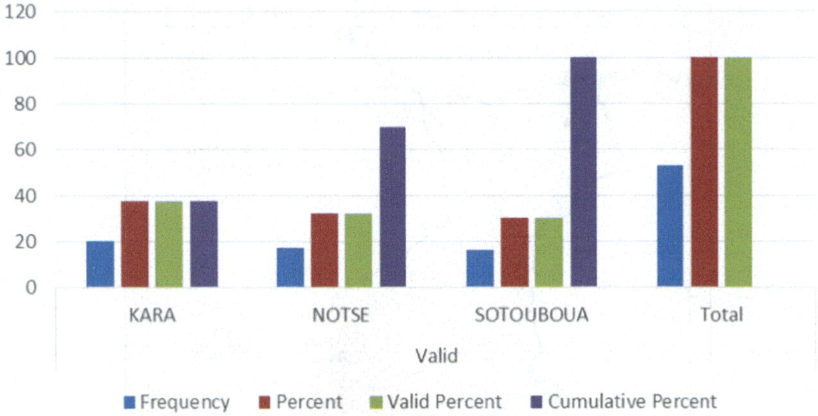

Fig. 9.2 Table of frequency

In Togo, a national transhumance management committee has been set up; at the level of the prefectures, a prefectural committee with the administrative authorities, customary chiefs and sedentary and transhumant Fulani chiefs has been constituted. The said committees are responsible for the following:

1. To control the movements of transhumant herders and their animals;
2. To channel transhumant cattle herders and their animals towards grazing areas that they must themselves define, so that the animals do not pass through the agricultural fields;
3. To ensure compliance by transhumant herders with the regulatory texts in force in the country;
4. To settle, if possible, conflicts amicably between third parties and transhumant herders on the occasion of damage caused by the latter and their animals;
5. To apply the sanctions provided for by law against any offender against Togolese laws.[14]

[14] La transhumance transfrontalière en Afrique de l'Ouest Proposition de plan d'action, Document FAO 2012.

The Savannah Region is the gateway for transhumant herders and, as such, it has a strategic geographical position. It is at the crossroads between the transhumance and livestock marketing routes of northern Ghana, eastern Burkina and northern Benin. It also corresponds to an area where cattle breeding is still possible, especially in its eastern part (Kpendjal prefecture[15]). But the space is shrinking and the number of transhumant people is increasing (seasonal or commercial movements). Aware of the risk of conflict and the economic importance of the sector, the Prefecture of Kpendjal was designated as a transit zone in an interministerial decree dated May 22, 2008 on the organization of the transhumance movement in Togo[16] However, this order is difficult to enforce. Like cattle production, it faces increasing conflicts of interest[17]:

- Agricultural colonization linked to population growth and based on animal traction which has resulted in a saturation of space in recent decades. Agricultural clearing leads to a narrowing, or even a closure, of passageways used for transhumance and for the marketing of livestock;
- A serious problem of access to water points (rivers, dams, ponds) for watering animals on marketing routes oriented towards Ghana and in the Oti prefecture (to Lomé, Benin and Nigeria). Herders often have to negotiate with farmers;
- A closure to the south by the wildlife reserve and the Kéran National Park. This leads the transhumant to go towards the east of the Region where the forest authorities maintain a prohibition to circulate in the wildlife reserve. Transit to the transhumance areas of the Plateaux Region or on commercial circuits therefore becomes very problematic. The fines are numerous.

If statistical data on conflicts between herders and farmers are not available in Togo, the press reports serious cases of violence and deaths

[15] This locality has been the subject in recent months (June, July 2022) of several terrorist attacks which have caused the death of several civilians and soldiers.

[16] Décret No 2008–33 modifiant le décret No 2007–089 du 26 juillet 2007 portant création, composition et attributions du comité national et des comités préfectoraux de la transhumance.

[17] La transhumance transfrontalière en Afrique de l'Ouest Proposition de plan d'action, Document FAO 2012.

every year. On February 16, 2016, significant clashes took place between nomadic herders and farmers in the village of Tchalo in the central region. Two seriously injured were recorded among the farmers. In retaliation, about twenty oxen were massacred by young people from the locality who blocked traffic on the national N°1 for several hours between Sokodé and Sotouboua[18] A week after these events, a new clash between nomadic herders and farmers was reported in the canton of Agbélouvé. The events occurred not far from the villages of Ayakopé and Doglobo and resulted in the death of 4 people. According to the information, it was a Fulani herdsman who was grazing his herds in the field of a farmer who allegedly shot the latter. Surprised by another farmer passing by, the Fulani did not hesitate to repeat his package. Alerted, the local population went after the Fulani herders. There are finally 4 dead and several murdered animals.[19] Ultimately, the 2016 transhumance campaign was very tense in Togo. It caused five (5) deaths and three (3) injuries in the Maritime, Plateaux and Central regions, 239 cases of destruction of fields or crops, the cost of which was estimated at more than 12 million CFA francs (19 400 USD). In compensation for this destruction of fields, the transhumant farmers paid 7.9 million CFA francs (12 763 USD). In total, the herders lost 707 heads of animals in this violence[20]

More recently, specifically between 2019 and 2020, Kratli and Toulmin (2020: 24) reported incidents and fatalities connected to pastoralist-farmer conflicts in Togo between, based on ACLED data, as 32 and 10 respectively. It is, therefore, not surprising when the 2024 *Togo Country Report* of the TBI Transformation Index, notes that 'conflicts of transhumance between pastoralists and agriculturalists are still virulent beneath the surface'. The conflicts are reported to be widespread, occurring in about one-third of prefectures, notably in northern and central Togo. In 2020 alone, such conflicts reported accounted for '12 deaths and 14 injuries, displaced 1603 people, and 130 cases of land devastation with

[18] Source: Online journal Togo actualité: https://www.togoactualite.com/affrontements-a-tchalo-centre-pays-entre-agriculteurs-eleveurs-nomades/

[19] https://www.togoactualite.com/togo-affrontement-eleveurs-peuls-agriculteurs-A-agbelouve-4-morts-plusieurs-betes-abattues/

[20] Bilan officiel publié dans le journal en ligne 27avril.com: https://www.27avril.com/blog/affaires/agriculture/togo-fin-de-transhumance-2016-15-mai-bouviers-transhumants-s-en-foutent-royalement.

compensation for victims totaling XOF 10 million (BTI Transformation Index 2024).

But sometimes, the tension between herders and farmers provokes popular demonstrations. This was the case on May 19, 2020 in Tohoun, (about 148 km northeast of Lomé), when the farmers of this locality, very angry, came out in large numbers to demonstrate their frustration7 in front of the Mayor of the commune of Moyen-Mono 1. They complained about what they described as the "excessive invasion" of their villages by the Fulani herders and their cattle. They demanded, in addition, the final departure of the herders from their canton, unconditionally, threatening to act in place of the authorities if the latter did not take responsibility.[21]

It should be noted that the Togolese government, in its efforts to reduce violence between herders and farmers, was successful in 2019. Indeed, with the implementation of the operational transhumance management plan 2019, the number of conflicts linked to transhumance is experiencing a marked reduction, evidenced by the results of the 2019, 2018 and 2017 campaign in Togo. We note as results:—zero (0) fatal conflict in 2019 as in 2017 and 2018- 08 minor incidents against 09 incidents in 2018;—10,370 heads of cattle registered for a tax collection of 56,548,000 FCFA ($ 92,272) in 2019 against 30,077 heads of transhumant cattle in 2018 for a tax collection of 65,000,000 FCFA ($ 106,063). This suggests that this operational plan is already bearing fruit.[22] However, the lull was only short-lived, because according to the 2020 report, conflicts linked to transhumance caused in 2020 on Togolese soil, 12 deaths, 14 injured, 1603 refugees, 130 cases of devastation of fields. A sum of approximately 10 million FCFA ($ 16,317) was paid to the victims[23]

Causes and Consequences of the Conflict

According to our investigations in the field, it appears that the main reason for this vehemence is of an anthropo-sociological nature. The logics in which the activity of the farmers and that of the stockbreeders

[21] Source société civile: https://societecivilemedia.com/togo-transhumance-risques-daffrontement-tres-eleves-entre-peuls-et-agriculteurs-du-canton-de-tohoun/

[22] https://afrique-news.info/togo-lepineux-probleme-de-gestion-de-la-transhumance-au-coeur-du-12eme-forum-du-paysan-togolais-du-23-au-25-janvier-A-kara/

[23] http://www.ctoptogo.org/articlesSuite.php?id_art=325&id_type=2.

fit in differ considerably, which raises a major problem of understanding between the two communities. The study suggested a number of factors to the participants as potentially fostering conflict between the two communities. The first factor on the list is that of poor regulatory frameworks for herding. Half of the participants considered that the regulations constitute one of the major reasons for this conflict. It is not known that it is the regulations that are in question, but rather their ignorance. This is the place to give details on the regulation of transhumance in West Africa. This aligns with extant studies that underscore lack of proper knowledge of such laws and regulations, especially by the herders, as a major challenge (IOM 2017: 2017; RMB and Partners 2021: 10).

Each country has a legal system in this area which does not comply with Community regulations. This non-conformity of national laws does not contribute to improving conflict resolution. If the national texts adopted by the States for the implementation of the ECOWAS Decision of 1998 are generally harmonized with the said decision, by making explicit reference to it, it is however clear that certain texts are not in conformity with the said Decision. Thus, in Togo,, the requirement of prior information from the national authorities, of any Territorial Transhumance, 60 days in advance, the collection of multiple grazing taxes at often high rates, are not necessarily in conformity with the ECOWAS community provisions; such regulatory provisions are likely to hinder free territorial transhumance in the region. The imposition of these taxes has not slowed down the entry of transhumants into the territory (Fig. 9.3).

Generally speaking, there are shortcomings inherent in the 1998 ECOWAS decision:

- The obligation to indicate the routes of transhumant herders in the CIT constitutes a requirement that is unfavorable to the principle of strategic mobility used by herders. Transhumant herders do not plan their routes in advance, but take them as they progress, depending on the opportunities and constraints presented to them;
- In terms of dispute settlement, the ECOWAS Decision remains unfinished because the prior amicable settlement mechanism, the Conciliation Commission, is only competent for disputes between transhumant herders and farmers; the other categories of conflict (between transhumant herders and local herders; between transhumant herders and other users of natural resources) are thus ignored;

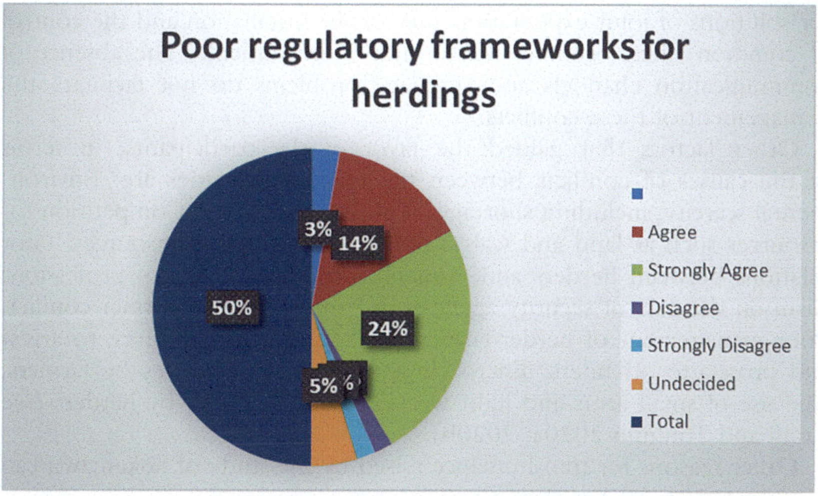

Fig. 9.3 Participant's response to the factor of poor regulatory frameworks for herdings

- The Decision does not contain any provision on cooperation between ECOWAS and ECCAS on the management of territorial transhumance while there are many cross-border movements of livestock between ECOWAS Member States and ECCAS States (Cameroon, CAR, Chad) and even COMESA/SADEC (Sudan). The Decision could have envisaged the conclusion of an agreement between ECOWAS and ECCAS as well as bilateral agreements between ECOWAS States and those of ECCAS (see Ezirigwe 2023, IOM 2017).

To appease and make cross-border transhumance sustainable, it is urgent to harmonize the regional legal framework and correct its shortcomings. Indeed, transhumance also drives pastoral groups away from home. They do not always follow exactly the same path. Often they are unaware of changes in local rules and although they exploit these spaces they generally do not participate in discussions on the management of these resources. The rules that are then decided are not their rules. From this moment on, the competition is exacerbated, quickly turns into conflict and the dialogue between the actors, essential for the search for solutions of joint exploitation and for the installation and the control of common rules, becomes increasingly more difficult. The absence of communication channels and language problems do not facilitate the management of these conflicts.

Other factors that gained the favor of the participants, in terms of the causes of conflicts between the two communities are: Environmental scarcity, including shortage of grasses and water; Competition for resources such as land and water; poor management of resources; Poor relations between herders and farmers associations; Lack of professionalism on the part of security agencies in handling herder-farmer conflict; Poor management of herder-farmer conflicts, including failure to arrest and prosecute offenders; Encroachment on grazing routes by farmers; The use of small arms and light weapons such as AK47 by herders (see Kratli and Toulmin 2020a, 2020b).

Other reasons for transhumance raised by the study of Sokemawu can be reported in the Togolese case:

- Ancestral prejudices; pastoralists being considered as landless people;
- The shortcomings of the interventions of the public services in terms of agricultural and pastoral development;
- Cases of unresolved or insufficiently resolved conflicts; in these cases, the victims hold a grudge and do not hesitate at the slightest opportunity to seek justice. Often, the authority (administrative, judicial or customary) is suspected of being in collusion with one or the other party.

The lack of mutual respect for pastoral and agrarian calendars gives rise to disputes. The products and by-products of the harvest are left at the level of the cultivation areas for more or less long periods depending on tradition or because of the work schedule. The regulatory measures aimed at giving periods for access to post-cultivation pastures show some limits; which can be understood because of the inter—annual variability that characterizes agricultural campaigns and the more or less early fodder deficits in the northern regions.

Historically, the main cause of conflicts between herders and farmers remains the damage caused by the herds. In this regard, there are some figures on the damage caused to households in Togo. A study showed that the herds of transhumant herders caused damage to 14% of farmersin both Togo and Burkina Faso[24] According to this study, this rate is not negligible, and it certainly explains the resentment of sedentary people towards transhumant herders, but it is not higher than for the damage caused by local herds, and it is certainly the combination of the two with around 30% of the households concerned, which makes it possible to take the dimension of the problem.[25]

In this conflict, Togolese farmers feel that local authorities tend to minimize the damage they suffer. The aforementioned study, however, affirms that a large proportion of households in Togo and Burkina-Faso have never had to suffer damage caused by herds in their crop plots (67% in Togo and 73% in Burkina -Faso).[26] But the feelings of those who suffer the damage are quite strong and this is enough to fuel resentment against transhumant herders.

Overall, these conflicts have led to deaths, displacement of persons, destruction of properties and loss of livelihood, mutual suspicion and distrust between the two groups with economic and social implications. As the 2024 *Togo Country Report* earlier reference reveals, 'Livestock in transhumance often ravages farmers' fields causing clashes that lead to injuries and deaths'. In 2020, such conflicts led to '12 deaths and 14 injuries, displaced 1603 people, and 130 cases of land devastation with compensation for victims totaling XOF 10 million'. The report projects that 'these conflicts will intensify in the future due to the effects of climate change on pastoralism and the stagnation of soil fertility, which will force farmers to plow fallow land or forest' (BTI Transformation Index 2024).

Management of the Problem/ Official and Unofficial Responses

Both governmental and non-governmental actors have responded to the problem in various ways. The government, for example, set up a body called the National Transhumance Committee[27] (CNT) responsible for

[24] See Document: PROTOCOLE D'ACCORD FAO—CIRAD, p. 127: https://agritrop.cirad.fr/597045/1/Prospective%20et%20pastoralisme%20Togo%20Burkina%20rapport%20final%20novembre%202020.pdf.

[25] Ibid. p. 127–128.

[26] Ibid. p. 127.

[27] *Journal Officiel République du Togo*, 1995–017-02.

managing the various disputes and supervising the actors concerned as well as possible. This committee, specifically, has the following role:

- Control by all appropriate means of the movements of transhumant herders and their animals throughout the national territory;
- The channeling of transhumant herdsmen and their animals to the reception areas selected for this purpose using the defined sanitary routes;
- The health monitoring of transhumant animals and the technical supervision of the breeders who accompany them;
- Ensuring compliance by transhumant herders with the regulatory texts in force in Togo;
- The amicable settlement of conflicts between third parties and transhumant herders on the occasion of damage caused by the latter or their animals;
- The application of the sanctions provided for by law against transhumant herders who refuse to respect Togolese laws.

This committee produces an annual report on transhumance and is also responsible for updating the maps of transhumance corridors in Togo on behalf of the Livestock Department of the Ministry of Agriculture, Livestock and Fisheries of Togo.

At the heart of the official answers to the question of the management of transhumance is the question of transhumance corridors which are not always well known to herders and which often have to be redefined. Thus, in 2020, for the Plateaux Region, work was done to set up a new transhumance corridor. The spaces, thus delimited for the passage of animals, extend over a distance of 39 km. Four companies had been retained for the execution of the works (in particular the tracing of the corridor, the installation of water points and veterinary posts). This passage zone was obtained thanks to the help of landowners in the region, who agreed to give up their properties. An NGO was called upon to ensure the agreement of the landowners, the NGO Enterprise Territory and Development (ETD), which was the initiator of the project. Discussions have taken place with the owners, we learn, to negotiate adequate compensation. However, the government has made a commitment to begin payment this year (2024) But the big challenge remains respecting the demarcated areas for peaceful transhumance.[28] Other official responses include:

a. Formulation of policies to benefit from the influx of pastoralists from neigbouring countries, with a quota of 50,000 animals per year permitted to enter from other West African countries, and a tax of 5000 FCFA per head of cattle when pastoralists cross the border (UNOWAS 2018: 24).
b. Establishment of a prefectural committee at the prefectural level, with administrative authorities, traditional leaders and chiefs sedentary and transhumant Fulani. Its mandates include to: (i) control the movements of nomadic herders and their animals, (ii) channel transhumant herdsmen and their animals to grazing areas that must define for themselves that animals do not pass fields, (iii) ensure respect by herders of the regulations in force in the country, (iv) if possible to settle amicably all disputes between third parties and herders on the occasion of damage caused by them and their animals, (v) apply the penalties provided by law against any offender against the laws Togolese (FAO and ECOWAS 2012: 37–38).
c. Directorate of Livestock and Fisheries (DEP) under the Ministry of Agriculture, Livestock and Fisheries (MAEP), replicated at regional and departmental levels with departments of Agriculture, Livestock and Fisheries attached to the APRM (FAO and ECOWAS, p. 61).
d. Development of a systems of "double transhumance", in which Sahelian livestock move into the the country during the dry season, whereas coastal livestock move north during the rainy season. These dynamics are reported to have multiplied the number of directions taken during transhumance (North–South, South–North, East–West) as well as increased the number of transhumance routes (Thébaud 2017; cited in IOM 2017: 5).
e. Impose an exit date for foreign transhumant herders (Thebaud 2017: 9&12).

According to the Network of Peasant Organizations and Agricultural Producers of West Africa (ROPPA), Togo is a textbook case

[28] https://www.togofirst.com/fr/agro/0309-6168-togo-vers-un-couloir-de-transhumance-dans-la-region-des-plateaux.

in the management of transhumance in the sub-region. For example, the Togolese Coordination of Peasant Organizations and of Agricultural Producers (CTOP) carried out one of the activities of the Regional Dialogue Project for Peaceful Transhumance in West Africa (PRODIATA). It was aimed at contributing in the long term to facilitating peaceful cross-border transhumance and improving the nutrition of coastal populations pastoralists. The organization offered to involve a delegation from the Ghana platform, Farmers Organization Network In Ghana (FONG) in the annual transhumance review meeting in Togo.

The Minister of Security, General Yark Damehane and his colleague for Agriculture, Livestock and Rural Development, Antoine Legba Gbegbeni, President of the National Transhumance Committee, took the opportunity to invite the prefectural committees to work to reverse the trend during the next transhumance campaign. They also invited the actors to respect the Operational Plan for the Management of Transhumance adopted by Togo and which advocates peaceful management through peaceful coexistence between the different communities.

The FONG delegation from Ghana was able, through this activity, to acquire knowledge that it intends to implement to better manage transhumance issues. For the same occasion, she immersed herself in the issues and mechanisms of animation of the CNT for an upcoming implementation of this instrument in their country. Also, the delegation exchanged with the CNT to know its origin, the process of establishment and its functioning, and developed a roadmap for the initiation of the process and the scaling up of the experience of the CNT of Togo. in Ghana. The CTOP for its part took note of the measures and decisions taken for the next campaign and submitted recommendations on the regulatory measures taken for the following campaign. All this will strengthen the participation of national and regional professional organizations in the decision-making of the National Transhumance Committees.

It should be noted that ROPPA has engaged in a multi-party partnership (APESS, RBM, CARE, SNV, HR) for the implementation of the Regional Dialogue Project for Peaceful Transhumance in West Africa (PRODIATA) which aims to contribute in the long term to facilitating peaceful cross-border transhumance and improving the nutrition of coastal and pastoral populations.

Following the results of the 2020 transhumance campaign, which saw the country record 12 loss of human life and 130 devastations of fields, a sum of 9,699,800 FCFA ($ 15,827) was paid to the victims for this purpose.[29] This damage occurs despite the adoption of the Operational Plan for the Management of Transhumance, which advocates peaceful management through peaceful coexistence between the different communities. As always, recommendations have been made by the CNT for a peaceful transhumance in 2021, in particular:

> commission an in-depth study on the extent of the spaces, the availability of fodder and water, etc. for ranching; acquire the areas for the cattle production development zones (ZAPB) in accordance with the state land code in force in Togo; mobilize resources to ensure the operation and sustainability of pastoral facilities and agro-pastoral infrastructure in the territories; involve the inter-profession in the management of transhumance; take into account the agro-pastoral activity in the strategic documents (Development Plan) of the Communes for a better socio-economic development of the territories.[30]

Despite the delimitation of transhumance areas, the participants in this study underlined their difficulty in controlling this delimitation. As this delimitation is often contrary to the 1998 ECOWAS Decision, it would be appropriate, for better management of entry areas, to one of the first strategic actions is to revise Decision A/DEC.5/10/98 relating to the regulation of transhumance between ECOWAS Member States. The main modification to be introduced is to leave the transhumant the free choice of adapting their itinerary while respecting the previously determined entry points. It will also be necessary to extend the powers of the Conciliation Commission to conflicts other than those arising between transhumant herders and farmers (conflicts between local pastoralists and transhumant pastoralists; conflicts between transhumant pastoralists and administrative authorities). It is necessary to take into account the cross-border movement of livestock between ECOWAS and ECCAS Member States by concluding, on the one hand, a partnership agreement between ECOWAS and ECCAS on TT to harmonize policies and the community instruments of the two organizations and by promoting, on the other hand, the conclusion of bilateral agreements between ECOWAS States

[29] https://agriculture.gouv.tg/bilan-de-la-transhumance-2020-et-perspectives-les-acteurs-appeles-a-assumer-leur-responsabilite-pour-une-gestion-plus-apaisee-des-prochaines-campagnes.

[30] Ibid.

and those of ECCAS. It is important to ensure that these changes are duly incorporated into the CIT.

In terms of the effectiveness of these responses, majority of of people who participated in this study (92%) expressed the view that governments at all levels have not lived up to expectations in handling herder-farmer conflicts. This percentage is very high and testifies to the distrust of the two communities towards the Togolese government authorities. In order to find solutions to these conflicts, review meetings are organized annually. Thus, for example, from November 19 to 21, 2020, a 2020 transhumance review meeting in Togo was held in the town of Kara in the Kozah prefecture. Organized by the Ministry of Agriculture, Livestock and Rural Development, this sub-regional meeting was held between the structures involved in the management of transhumance issues in Togo and the leaders of breeders' organizations and farmers from Togo and Ghana.

But such a poor rating og government responses should not be surprising because of the many challenges associated with the responses. These include failure to consistently implement the extant laws/ regulations, lack of proper knowledge of the law, especially by pastoralists, conrdatictions in ECOWAS' rulkes aimed at protecting hersers, which discourages modern livestock farming (Ezirigwe 2023), and herders' deep feeling of bias, marginalization, if not exclusion in decision-making institutions of the state, A herder in Togo expressed this frustration thus: 'The farmers are favoured quite simply because all the positions are held by their sons, for example the gendarmerie, the police, the deputies, the municipal councilors, so there is political and ethnic influence. Besides, the Peulh herders are considered as people from elsewhere' (quoted in RBM and Partners 2021: 10).

Lessons for Peacebuilding

Several lessons can be drawn from this study for a sustainable resolution of conflicts between transhumant herders and farmers. First, from the point of view of the historical trajectory, the government authorities need to show more pedagogy to put an end to the marginalization of which the pastoral populations of the Sahelian regions are victims. Pastoralism remains the object of prejudice in Togo. It is considered an archaic and outdated form of production and transhumant herders are very often pointed out as responsible for the damage caused by the herds, even if there are also sedentary herders whose herds can also sometimes be responsible for certain destruction of goods.The phenomenon of attempted sedentarization observed in Togo should make people think about alternatives to the transhumance system: for example, for better integration into the national economic system, consider sedentarization as a long-term solution.

Then, to correct the problems related to the roots of these conflicts, Togo set up a national transhumance management committee at the national level. But this organization extends to the level of the prefectures, with a prefectural committee comprising administrative authorities, customary chiefs and sedentary and transhumant Fulani chiefs. The said committees are responsible for: controlling the movements of transhumant herders and their animals; to channel the transhumant herdsmen and their animals towards the grazing areas that they themselves must define so that the animals do not pass through the fields; to ensure compliance by transhumant herders with the regulatory texts in force in the country; to settle, if possible, amicably conflicts between third parties and transhumant herders on the occasion of damage caused by the latter and their animals; to apply the sanctions provided for by law against any offender against Togolese laws. But this organization has shown its limits with the recurrence of conflicts. Even more decentralized conflict prevention mechanisms should also be put in place: among other things, pre-harvest meetings, creation of consultation committees, regulatory measures setting harvest dates. These mechanisms can be initiated by administrative authorities in conjunction with local authorities and traditional authorities. The participants in this study clearly expressed this need for a much more active involvement of grassroots populations in conflict resolution. As confirmed by a study of CIRAD,[31] when the populations are not associated with the search for a solution, we witness the continuation of these conflicts:

- The hardening of the reception conditions for transhumant people: distrust having taken hold of the populations, the stay or passage of new migrant herders leaves everyone on their guard. Exacerbation

[31] https://agritrop.cirad.fr/597045/1/Prospective%20et%20pastoralisme%20Togo%20Burkina%20rapport%20final%20novembre%202020.pdf.

of feelings of xenophobia, because more than 80% of the damage to crops would be caused by herds of "Peulh foreigners"

- The deterioration of the climate of good coexistence between resident breeders and farmers. Exactions are also frequent: local populations attack pastoralists who have settled in the area;
- Rejection of livestock or pastoral activities considered destructive;
- The fact that animals are also poisoned, injured and/or killed in retaliation;
- Rejection of administrative or court decisions; which constitutes a challenge to the authority of the State.

All of this contributes to disturbing peaceful inter-community coexistence. However, despite all the difficulties they encounter in neighboring countries, we are seeing more and more "leakage" transhumance because many breeders prefer to settle permanently in these countries with their livestock than to suffer exactions in their own country.

With reference to ECOWAS regulation of transhumance, its existing 1998 Decision, is outdated and requires revision to reflect the terms of new realities, as well as the needs of an effective implementation strategy of its operationalizing Regulation C/REG.3/01/03. To do this, the States must proceed, with the assistance of ECOWAS, to the implementation of the measures contained in the said Regulations. For this reason, it is important to develop and adopt a regional pastoral development plan and ensure its implementation.

Finally, regarding the implications of non-state actors, the authorities recognize the need to do everything possible to ensure that transhumant herders and farmers master the transhumance areas and the laws applicable in Togo. The participants in this study deplored the fact that the government does not involve non-state actors more for this work on knowledge of the regulatory texts in force in the country. Indeed, the effective involvement of non-state actors is a key success factor in the implementation of the political and legal framework. In particular, this involves ensuring their effective involvement in the process of revising and implementing community texts on pastoralism. Beyond this participation, it is for the States and ECOWAS to ensure on a permanent basis, information, sensitization, training of the actors at the base, in particular to: (i) lead in the countries of the ECOWAS space, an exercise of capitalization, updating, translation and popularization of texts relating to transhumance in order to put them within the reach of the actors most directly concerned; (ii) conduct campaigns to raise awareness and popularize texts on cross-border transhumance with a view to pointing out the dysfunctions and improvements to be made, and reporting this information at the regional level. Emphasis will be placed on the specificities of certain countries, which have had to integrate decentralization into their decision-making processes (closer presence of municipalities in the application of regulatory texts, and management of their application at their level).[32]

Conclusion

At the end of this study, we can say that the conflicts between transhumant herders and sedentary farmers remain a major concern, despite the brief experience of 2019, a year without major conflict. Ultimately, what seems to be the catalyst for the most recent conflicts is the fact that herders remain in the territory beyond June. This moment, which corresponds to the rainy season and the beginning of the planting season by farmers, is delicate for a cohabitation between Herders and farmers. Pastoralism policy has always been addressed by West-African countries and ECOWAS authorities in the spirit of conservation, because, on one hand it is a secular African tradition and, on other hand, it allows a better and efficient management of agriculture in the arid Sahel countries. Although pastoral livelihoods are a considerable source of wealth and allow creating strong economic interdependence between farmers and pastoralists, many conflicts are emerging in the wake of the herds. These conflicts usually fall under the competition for water and pasture. But they will take a more complex twist in the case that nomadic herders decide to give up their lifestyle and to settle on the coastal territory. If the conflict becomes more violent and more frequent, it is surely moving towards the simple closure of borders, which will be devastating for the Sahel, but if nothing is done conflicts will cause many deaths and destruction of property.

The authorities wish to strengthen cooperation with countries of origin to enforce the periods of transhumance (January 15–May 15). The government had proceed with the redefinition of entry points on the

[32] Note aux décideurs - Rapport de l'étude sur la transhumance transfrontalière et les conflits liés à l'utilisation des ressources naturelles en Afrique de l'Ouest. https://www.coraf.org/download/262/publication/18743/cadre-juridique-adapte-et-harmonise-pour-une-transhumance-transfrontaliere-durable-dans-lespace-cedeao.pdf.

territory and specify authorized transit and grazing corridors. In terms of resolving conflicts between communities, the Togolese authorities have created the CNT, which really takes into account extensive decentralization. Even if this committee is not yet perfect in the eyes of the participants in this study, it serves as a model in the West African subregion. The committees set up by the States have not been able, for several reasons, to contain the conflicts linked to transhumance. Significant shortcomings were identified in their operation. Indeed, these are dominated by the administration and oriented towards the resolution of conflicts when they have erupted.[33] Hence the importance of involving non-state actors in the management of these conflicts. The latter are not represented at the level of the decision-making sphere and there is therefore no consultation between actors for the identification of concordant objectives, conflicting objectives as well as common challenges, to make transhumance a mode of farming integrated into local or national economies and a factor of social cohesion. However, in Togo, the NGO like RAFIA participates in the management of major natural resource management projects and is part of the committees that have given a good place to actors and consultation. These efforts have had significant effects on reducing conflict.[34]

Such a multi-actor management experience can be implemented at the regional level where national and regional actors could collectively find solutions to key issues such as the need for innovation in transhumance practices, ecological challenges, epidemiological policies and institutions of transhumance. It is clear that in view of past experiences, the peaceful management of cross-border transhumance can only be achieved through inter-institutional arrangements at different levels which are integrated, in particular a regional platform, national platforms and local multi-actor platforms.

[33] Nederlof, S. Na d Pyburn, R., 2012. One finger cannot lift a rock. Facilitating innovation platforms to trigger institutional change in West Africa. KIT-CoSci-WUR.

[34] Ibid.

References

Bilan officiel publié dans le journal en ligne 27avril.com, https://www.27avril.com/blog/affaires/agriculture/togo-fin-de-transhumance-2016-15-mai-bouviers-transhumants-s-en-foutent-royalement

BTI Transformation Index. 2024, *Togo Country Report 2024*, https://bti-project.org/en/reports/country-report/TGO.

Corniaux C. 2012, Actualisation des données sur le commerce du bétail au Togo: Circuits, marchés et consommation de viande bovine, Rapport CIRAD.

Decision A/DEC.5/10/98 regulating transhumance between ECOWAS member: https://ecpf.ecowas.int/wp-content/uploads/2016/01/Decision-1998-English.pdf.

Décret No 2008–33 modifiant le décret No 2007–089 du 26 juillet 2007 portant création, composition et attributions du comité national et des comités préfectoraux de la transhumance.

Document online, https://www.coraf.org.

Document: PROTOCOLE D'ACCORD FAO—CIRAD, p. 127, https://agritrop.cirad.fr/597045/1/Prospective%20et%20pastoralisme%20Togo%20Burkina%20rapport%20final%20novembre%202020.pdf.

Ezirigwe, J. 2023, 'ECOWAS Rules to Protect Pastoralists Discourage Investments in Modern Livestock Farming', *The Conversation*, 8 October, https://theconversation.com/ecowas-rules-to-protect-pastoralists-discourage-investments-in-modern-livestock-farming-213493.

FAO and ECOWAS. 2012, *The Cross-border Transhumance in West Africa Proposal for Action Plan*, https://ecpf.ecowas.int/wp-content/uploads/2016/01/CrossBorder-Transhumance-WA-Final-Report-1.pdf .

Herbert, S. and Birch, I. 2022, *Cross-border Pastoral Mobility and Cross-border Conflict in Africa—Patterns and Policy Responses. XCEPT Evidence Synthesis*. Birmingham, UK: GSDRC, University of Birmingham, https://csf-sudan.org/wp-content/uploads/2023/01/gsdrc-pastoralist-mobility.pdf.

International Organization for Migration (IOM). 2017, *Regional Policies and Response to Manage Pastoral Movements within the ECOWAS Region*, Abuja: IOM, https://environmentalmigration.iom.int/sites/g/files/tmzbdl1411/files/documents/2023-09/regional-policies-and-response-to-manage-pastoral-movements-within-the-ecowas-region-2019.pdf.

Journal Officiel République du Togo, 1995–017–02.

Krätli, S. & Toulmin, C. 2020a, *Farmer-herder Conflict in Sub-Saharan Africa?* IIED. https://pubs.iied.org/10208iied.

Krätli, S. & Toulmin, C 2020b, *Farmer–herder Conflict in Africa: Re-thinking the Phenomenon?* Briefing. IIED. https://pubs.iied.org/17753IIED/.

Kwaja, C. M. A. & Smith, K. 2020, *Transnational Dimensions of Conflict Between Farmers and Herders in the Western Sahel and Lake Chad Basin*. Search

for Common Ground. https://www.sfcg.org/wpcontent/uploads/2020/04/SFCG_Policy_Brief_Transnational_Dimension_to_FH_Conflicts.pdf.
La transhumance transfrontalière en Afrique de l'Ouest Proposition de plan d'action, Document FAO 2012.
Nederlof, S. Na & Pyburn, R. 2012, One finger cannot lift a rock. Facilitating innovation platforms to trigger institutional change in West Africa. KIT-CoSci-WUR.
Note aux décideurs - Rapport de l'étude sur la transhumance transfrontalière et les conflits liés à l'utilisation des ressources naturelles en Afrique de l'Ouest. https://www.coraf.org/download/262/publication/18743/cadre-juridique-adapte-et-harmonise-pour-une-transhumance-transfrontaliere-durable-dans-lespace-cedeao.pdf.
Pastoralisme et Sécurité en Afrique de l'Ouest et au Sahel—Vers une coexistence pacifique, Étude du Bureau des Nations Unies pour l'Afrique de l'Ouest et le Sahel (UNOWAS), 2018.
Réseau Billital Maroobé (RBM) and Partners, 2021, 'Listening to Herders in West Africa and the Sahel: What is the Future for Pastoralism in a Context of Rising Insecurity?' *Synthesis Report*, Réseau des Organisations d'Eleveurs et Pasteurs de l'Afrique, https://www.maroobe.com/images/DOCS/Synthetic%20Report-Patoralism%20and%20Insecurity%20in%20the%20Sahel%20and%20West%20Africa-%20RBM.pdf.
Société civile, https://societecivilemedia.com/togo-transhumance-risques-daffrontement-tres-eleves-entre-peuls-et-agriculteurs-du-canton-de-tohoun/.
Sokemawu K. 2009, Relation paysan-foulani dans la Région des Savanes au Togo : une cohabitation complexe et des problèmes majeurs, in *Revue de Géographie du Laboratoire LEÏDI*, N°7, Université Gaston Berger, Saint-Louis, pp. 99–106.
Sokemawu K. 2015, Gestion des conflits entre paysans et éleveurs peulhs de la région des savanes au Nord-Togo dans le processus d'un développement durable, in *Revue de Géographie Tropicale et d'Environnement* (2), pp. 26–39.
Stenning, D. J. 1957, 'Transhumance, Migratory Drift, Migration: Patterns of Pastoral Fulani Nomadism', *The Journal of the Royal Anthropological Institute of Great Britain and Ireland*, 87 (1): 57–73.
Study by the United Nations Office for West Africa and the Sahel (UNOWAS) August 2018. https://unowas.unmissions.org/fr/pastoralisme-et-s%C3%A9curit%C3%A9-en-afrique-de-l%E2%80%99ouest-et-au-sahel.
Tamou, C. 2002, Etat des lieux spatialisé et quantitatif de la transhumance dans la zone périphérique d'influence du Parc National du W (Bénin). Rapport de maîtrise d'écologie). Cotonou : Université de Cotonou, p. 67.
Thebaud, B. 2017, *Pastoral and Agropastoral Resilience in the Sahel*. Nordic Consulting Group. http://www.inter-reseaux.org/IMG/pdf/afl_resilience_study_june2017_abridged_version.pdf.

Togolese Presse Online, http://www.ctoptogo.org/articlesSuite.php?id_art=325&id_type=2.
Togolese Presse Online, https://afrique-news.info/togo-lepineux-probleme-de-gestion-de-la-transhumance-au-coeur-du-12eme-forum-du-paysan-togolais-du-23-au-25-janvier-a-kara/.
Togolese Presse Online, https://agriculture.gouv.tg/bilan-de-la-transhumance-2020-et-perspectives-les-acteurs-appeles-a-assumer-leur-responsabilite-pour-une-gestion-plus-apaisee-des-prochaines-campagnes/.
Togolese Presse Online, https://www.togofirst.com/fr/agro/0309-6168-togo-vers-un-couloir-de-transhumance-dans-la-region-des-plateaux.
Togolese Presse, Online journal Togo actualité, https://www.togoactualite.com/togo-affrontement-eleveurs-peuls-agriculteurs-a-agbelouve-4-morts-plusieurs-betes-abattues/.
Togolese Presse, Online journal Togo actualité, https://www.togoactualite.com/affrontements-a-tchalo-centre-pays-entre-agriculteurs-eleveurs-nomades/.

PART III

Concluding Reflections

CHAPTER 10

Conclusion: Matters Arising in Herder-Farmer Conflicts and Lessons for Sustainable Security, Development and Peacebuilding

J. Shola Omotola

Introduction

This concluding chapter teases out the major findings of the various chapters of this book, highlighting convergences and divergences. Informed by the main research puzzle upon which this project is predicated ab initio, the chapter organises its critical reflections along the various subthemes of the study, notably historical trends, causes, consequences, actors and management of the problem, as well as lessons for sustainable security, development and peacebuilding. The chapter thus provides a basis for cross-national comparison and generalisation. But beyond these broad

J. S. Omotola (✉)
Department of Political Science, Federal University Oye Ekiti, Oye, Ekiti State, Nigeria
e-mail: shoal.omotola@fuoye.edu.ng; sholaomotola@yahoo.com

J. S. Omotola (ed.), *Herder-Farmer Conflicts in Africa*,
https://doi.org/10.1007/978-3-031-80821-0_10

issues, other salient elements such as the usage of the term herder-farmer conflicts also call for better clarity to eliminate possible misconception. We address these and related themes in this concluding chapter.

Matters Arising in Herder-Farmer Conflicts

The book throws up a number of pertinent issues that require highlighting and elaboration. This section highlights some of these matters, with illustrations from the various chapters of the book.

I. **The Definitional Challenge: What is the Herder-Farmer Conflict all About?**

One of the first issues of concern that came out from the book is the question about the meaning of herder-farmer conflicts. Ordinarily, such a question should not have arisen given the fact that the term herder-farmer conflicts has emerged as arguably one of the most talked about in academic, policy and advocacy circles in the last decade. It is a term whose everyday usage maybe unprecedented because of the trends, manifestations, consequences and contentions surrounding the management of the problem (Brottem 2021; Chukwuma 2020; Kwaja and Ademola-Adelehin 2017). Yet, its meaning remains contested. In fact, Kendrich and Sanders (2024) bluntly rejected the term, insisting that it should not be called 'herder-farmer conflicts'. This may not be unconnected to the fact that a lot of stereotypes and prejudices were often woven into the narratives (Bukari and Schareika 2015). Eke (2020) called herder-farmer conflicts 'ancient myth'. Hussein et al. (1999) referred to some of the issues in herder-farmer conflicts as mere claims, some backed by evidence and many others unsubstantiated. One of the contributors to this volume (Akachi –on Benue state, Nigeria), drawing from insight from his extensive field experience in Benue state, tend to share this perspective about the lack of clarity on the concept when he asserts that '…attacks by Fulani herdsmen were often against whole 'heterogeneous communities', few members of whom were farmers … Therefore, it needs to be made clear that *the oft-used notion of "farmers-herders' conflicts" is conceptually erroneous*' (emphasis mine). This is the crux of the matter.

Consequently, without necessarily dismissing the validity of these controversies regarding the concept we offered what we consider to be a much more nuanced and holistic definition of the term (Omotola, Chapter 2 in this book). This is pertinent because, as Omotola demonstrated in Chapter 2, different narratives have been weaved around the concept over the years. Again, the menace of what is generally categorized as herder-farmer conflicts is not static, constantly evolving and changing in complexion. Yet, attempts at forging a distinction between herders and farmers as if they are entirely distinct groups are questionable. They overlap in many ways. Conflict is also multidimensional. Any definition of herder-farmer conflicts must be done in recognition of these diversities. On these notes, we conceptualise farmer-herder conflicts as encompassing violent conflicts that directly involve herders and farmers resulting from various factors such as environmental scarcity, climate change, migration, resource completion (land, vegetation and water) and the mal-governance of these issues. Such conflicts may and may not be pastoralist in orientation and/or outlook. While pastoralist conflicts can embrace aspects of pastoralism, not all pastoralist conflicts are entirely herder-farmer conflicts. Anything beyond this risks falling into the pitfall of conceptual stretching, accommodating all varieties of conflicts that occur in herding and farming communities. Such a reading can be misleading (see Chapter 2 for more details).

II. **Old Problem, Changing Complexion**

Our study also reveals that the problem of herder-farmer conflicts is not new. It is an old problem that has transformed over the years, constantly evolving, mutating and putting on new complexions from time to time (many chapters in this book stressed this point: Chapters 4 by Ngalim, 5 by Akachi and 1 & 6 by Omotola). Though not always like this from the beginning, studies and evidence have shown that the problem is long-standing—it is neither new nor recent. In fact, these conflicts are regarded as one of Africa's oldest, most historically complex and very destructive and intractable conflicts. If anything has changed, it is the fact that it has intensified in contemporary times (Hussein et al. 1999).

The changing complexion oscillates in different directions. In specific terms, the changing form and character of the conflicts manifests in terms of increased frequency, higher intensity, including the use of deadly weapons and rising casualties/deaths and other humanitarian emergencies such as internal displacement of persons and refugees. Other noticeable trends include undue politicization and ethnisation of the conflicts, and diverse responses from both state and non-state actors, including the over securitization of its management.

III. **Triggers and Drivers**

Conflicts between herders and farmers were found to be a product of many complex and interconnected factors. These include power, history, citizenship rights and access to and use of land—all of which are charged and potentially explosive in most African countries. These factors can be grouped into there: (a) environment-related factors, including climate change; (b) social-related factors such as ethno-religious considerations, c) political-related factors, especially the seeming political powerlessness of pastoralists in the post-colonial state, including their 'landlessness' (Omotola, et al, 2019; Shettima and Tar 2008: 170–174).

More specifically, the various chapters in this book underscore some of the most salient triggers of herder-farmer conflicts to include political ecology and environmental factors such as resource scarcity, climate change and desertification, leading to increased migration and competition for natural resources such as land, pastures and water. Other factors highlighted include weakening of customary/traditional institutions and cultural intolerance, land tenure problem, defective policy frameworks, rapid population growth, change in land use and land rights, weak state capacity/state failure manifesting in the pervasiveness of ungoverned spaces and ineffective regulation. Yet, issues such as the disconnect between national laws and community regulations, failure of resource governance, privatisation and/or commercialisation of land, extinction and/or encroachment of grazing reserves/routes, stereotyping of herders as jihadists in media outlets to justify ethnic killings, social ostracism, ethnicity and official partisanship, increased availability of deadly weapons, non-adherence to established laws by herders and farmers, transition from migrant to settler communities of herders, as well as contradictions inherent in regional protocols, particularly ECOWAS, were also stressed.

From the findings of the book, the root causes of the conflicts are located in different domains. While environmental factors are deeply implicated, other considerations like state capacity, power and politics, including identity politics (ethnicity, religion, gender, generational—youth), and the management of the problem, also matter (on state capacity in Nigeria, see Omotola and Alumona, 2016). These factors are universal across the case studies. If anything is different, it is only in degree, not of kind. Again, there may be variations in the ordering of each factor across geographies. In other words, while factor A, let us assume it to be environmental factors may take precedent as the most salient factor in a particular case, factor B, let us say power and politics or mismanagement of the problem may be the overriding consideration elsewhere. But this does not eliminate the presence of these other factors elsewhere. However, it is important to note that environmental factors are implicated across cases.

IV. **Consequences of Herder-Farmer Conflicts**

Studies have shown that herder-farmer conflicts have had devastating effects on both state and society (Omotola, 2024b, 2021a, 2021b, 2021c). These effects manifest in diverse forms: national and human security, economic costs, political instability, national integration and social cohesion, among others (Omotola and Oyewole 2024; International Crisis Group 2017). More specifically, the conflicts have been responsible for several deaths in their thousands arguably on the same pedestrian as the Boko Haram insurgency, kidnapping for various purposes, huge number of refugees and IDPs, food insecurity, loss of sources of livelihood, including land for framing, destruction of farm crops, killing of cattle, loss of revenue, complication of existing fault lines of cleavages, as well as rising tensions and associated psychological implications such as trauma and stress (Adams, et al. 2023; Yakubu et al. 2021; Benjaminsen and Ba 2021; Benjaminsen et al. 2009, Mercy Corp 2015). All the chapters in the book stressed these points in varying degrees.

Various contributions to this book highlight different dimensions of these effects based on their case studies. All the chapters underscore the effects of the conflicts on national and human security in their various forms. The gender dimensions of the conflicts came out very powerfully across the book (notably Chapters 7 by Babatunde, 8 by Ibnouf and 6 by Omotola) and to a lesser degree by others. Ibnouf (Chapter 8) extends the gender question to accommodate social inclusion where all critical stakeholders, apart from women and men, such as young people—boys and girls-would be included in the peacebuilding process. Issues of deaths, arson, humanitarian emergencies, food and other dimensions of human security were also stressed (Chapters 3 by Bontogho, 4 by Ngalim, 5 by Akachi, 9 by Alemdjrodo—virtually all the chapters).

V. **Management of the Problem: Gaps in Official and Unofficial Responses**

Both state and non-state actors have devised different ways of responding to the problem. At the official level, responses include the development of institutional, legal and policy frameworks, including the creation of, grazing routes and grazing reserve and policy of expulsion. Others include the establishment and management of IDP camps, resort to securitization approach through the deployment of the military and other paramilitary agencies to road blocks, patrol and surveillance, and in the extreme the launching of military offensives against violent and hot spots. Non-state actors have, on their parts, played important roles in peacebuilding through sensitization, advocacy, provision of relief materials, monitoring and evaluation of official responses, providing platforms for dialogue between conflict parties, and involvement in post-conflict resettlement and reintegration efforts, including the safe return of refugees and IDPs (all the chapters in the book address different aspects of these responses).

Despite these advances, most contributions to this book found, in agreement with extant studies (Maiangwa 2017;Omotola 2017; Olaniyan et al. 2015), that these responses have not been adequate in addressing the menace of herder-farmer conflicts. Some of the gaps adduced for the inadequacy of these responses include lack of or insufficient space for environmental peacebuilding, low level of social inclusion, politicization and ethnicisation, the over reliance on securitsation/militarization, existence of weak regulatory frameworks, inadequate attention to the important role of informal institutions, and poor synergy between formal and informal institutions in the peacebuilding process. These gaps, virtually all the chapters contend, must be addressed for sustainable peacebuilding in herder-farmer conflicts in Africa.

Lessons for Sustainable Security, Development and Peacebuilding

The findings of this book have revealed, in bold relief, some of the most critical lessons for sustainable security, development and peacebuilding in relations to herder-farmer conflicts in Africa. In this section, I tease out some of these critical lessons.

a. **Peacebuilding is Perpetual. It Entails Short and Long-Term Agenda**

   One important lesson from the study is that peacebuilding has short and long term components (Omotola, 2024b). Any successful peacebuilding initiative must always be conscious of this point. The import of this is that it has to be progressive, always evolving in response to everyday realities on the ground, including political, economic and social situations. Actors and stakeholders must design and execute their agenda in line with these considerations. This demand adjustments and readjustments based on new realities, including continuous dialogue and negotiations among all stakeholders. Otherwise, peacebuilding outputs may not lead to positive and sustainable outcomes.

b. **Mainstreaming Environmental Peacebuilding**

   One of the key lessons of the book for effectively managing herder-farmer conflicts is the need to mainstream environmental peacebuilding into the management of herder-farmer conflicts. There are many justifications for this. In the first place, environmental factors were deeply implicated in the escalation of herder-farmer conflicts across all the case studies. Environmental solutions are, therefore, inevitable. Unfortunately, such an approach has been largely missing. The poor attention to environmental peacebuilding is partly responsible for the failures of other interventions. Moreover, studies and experiences have shown elsewhere that environmental peacebuilding offers prospects of addressing environmental-based conflicts, including herder-farmer conflicts. Again, it is a perspective that is gaining rapid recognition and acceptability among various actors, with a lot of scholarly attention in environmental, conflict, peace and security, as well as development studies (Ide, et al. 2021a, 2021b; Bruch, et al. 2019; Hardt and Scheffran 2019).

The advantages of environmental peacebuilding are many. Apart from the opportunity of confronting one of the root causes of the problem (environmental problems), it also has the potential to contribute to the reduction of uncertainty or resource inequality; facilitate repeated interaction between conflict parties, which can foster a habit of cooperation and build trust. Environmental cooperation can, in turn, reduce perceived inequalities related to natural resource access and distribution, thereby laying the roots of sustainable peace. Chapter two of this book carefully highlights these salient issues.

c. **Beyond Gender: Social Inclusion also Matters**

Another important lesson learnt is the fact that gender matters for sustainable peacebuilding (Wilien, 2022). This is because herder-farmer conflicts affect men and women, boys and girls in differently. While all are actors in the conflict and peacebuilding process, with varying degrees of agency, variations also abound in the level of injury, damages or losses that they incur. Why the mainstream literature mainly underscores the victimhood of women, many of the contributions to this book, particularly Chapters 6, 7 and 8 (by Omotola, Babatunde, Ibnouf respectively), reveal that effect of the conflicts on women transcend physical, material and financial losses. They also suffer psychologically through rape, torture, assault, loss of loved ones and abuse of their children in different ways. Women were also found to be emerging as key players in the conflict process as underlined by some of the chapters. Any attempt at post-conflict peacebuilding must, by deliberate design, accommodate the agency of women in the peace process. Excluding or marginalising women in peacebuilding, as studies have shown, can be counterproductive.

Beyond mainstreaming women into peacebuilding, social inclusion is also of critical importance. This demands the involvement of all social categories or groupings, irrespective of gender, in the peace process. Important constituencies in this regard include the youth, male and female (who are also victims and actors in conflict), People with Disability (PWD), other minority groups (ethnic or religious) and interest groups that may be affected by herder-farmer conflicts one way or the other. Ibnouf's Chapter 8 made the strongest case in this respect.

d. **Imperative of Synergy between Formal and Informal Institutions of Peacebuilding**

   Formal and informal institutions were established as critical actors in the management of herder-farmer conflicts across all the case studies. While each has invested a lot of resources into the peacebuilding process, notable limitations persist, which account for their underperformance and below par achievements. Formal, state actors would appear to still dominate the peacebuilding arenas. Another notable limitation is the lack of or poor state of synergy between formal and informal institutions. Successful peacebuilding initiatives benefit from partnerships and collaborations between state and non-state actors. Without necessarily encroaching on each other's space, defined in terms of each ascribed or perceived roles in peacebuilding, they can complement and reinforce each other through knowledge and information sharing, joint programme/project execution, evaluation and monitoring, dispute settlement and conflict resolution, joint security committees and patrol teams, and community policing. They can also complement each other in terms of socialization and advocacy on conflict and peacebuilding.

e. **Recognizing the 'Local' as Important Foundation of Peacebuilding**

   The question of the 'local' has continued to gain increasing attention and respectability in the literature on peacebuilding (Hirblinger and Simons 2015; Omotola and Hassan, 2015; Emah and Kwaja 2020; Ebiede and Kwaja 2024; Medina et al. 2023; Hachmann et al. 2023). Such a development represents an indirect admission of the fact that all conflicts are first and foremost 'local' in most respects—actors, issues, consequences, through often with broader ramifications. The search for sustainable solution must therefore be sufficiently local in its orientation, contents and approaches.

   Entrenching the 'local' in peacebuilding is beneficial in many ways. As a bottom-up approach, it empowers and gives a sense of belonging to 'marginalized and vulnerable communities who lack seats at decision-making tables and suffer from the 'slow violence' of rampant destruction of their livelihoods and ecosystems'. Furthermore, localizing peacebuilding draws on local knowledge and expertise. It also creates a genuine sense of ownership and empowerment and heightens prospects for sustainability. It is a powerful foundation for peacebuilding legitimacy. This resonates with the popular progressive peacebuilding advocated by Bereketeab (2021). Most of the chapters allude to this salient point.

f. **Acknowledging the Overlapping Boundaries of Security, Development and Peacebuilding**

Security, development and peacebuilding, though distinct in certain ways, also share overlapping boundaries in many respects. While each can stand alone, they are also intricately interconnected. Above all else, the three cohabit in the same spaces and are concerned with related themes, with overlapping actors. The question of ordering, or sequencing in terms of which one comes first, is therefore untenable. The three are important in post-conflict settings in dire need for security, development and peacebuilding. None can stand alone sustainably in the absence of the other. It then follows, logically, that the three must be pursued concurrently/simultaneously without discrimination. The tendency to focus on 'peacebuilding' in post conflict arenas, in its strict sense, remains one of the main undoing of peacebuilding. Going forward, it is critical that all actors, state and non-state, local, national, regional and international, must begin to inculcate this reality into their peacebuilding interventions and initiatives. It offers a unique mechanism for addressing the root causes of the conflicts.

g. **Other Important Lessons**

Many other key lessons came across from the various chapters. These include:

- Governments at all levels need to show more commitment to the effective implementation of the legal frameworks for natural resource governance, including regional protocols.
- Contradictions between national and regional laws should be addressed by all affected governments. Synergy between national and regional actors is important to attain this.

- The need for adequate training of both traditional and religious leaders and institutions on conflict management/resolution and peacebuilding. This will help build their capacities for utilization of relevant local/indigenous knowledge system for peacebuilding.
- Peace education is helpful. This can be done in diverse ways, including introducing conflict and peacebuilding into academic curriculum across different levels of education. Such can help to develop better understanding of the issues and how best to deal with them. The media and SCOs can also be involved in promoting peace messaging and education on herder-farmer conflicts.
- There is need to foster community dialogue and strengthen traditional conflict prevention mechanisms to resolve herder-farmer disputes.
- Best practices that promote peaceful coexistence and cooperation between farmers and herders should be encouraged and replicated. These include alliance farming, dialogue platforms, night paddocking, and pasture improvement programs.
- Curb the spread of fake news on social media platforms is important. Misinformation and disinformation can rapidly inflame tensions and derail peacebuilding efforts. Such should be averted through fact-checking of information before disseminating.
- The need to pay attention to the question of late deployment, early withdrawal or reduction in the number of security agents deployed for peacekeeping in affected areas. The question of the accountability of security agents is also important.
- Better management of returnees matters, including issues of their safety, resettlement and reintegration is critical. Reconstruction, rehabilitation, security, empowerment, confidence buildings are also important.
- Better management of IDP camps is pertinent. Both state and non-state actors need to do more in their management of the IPD camps.
- Greater investment in demilitarisation, especially of society is critical. This is important in the wake of not just the massive proliferation and use of SALWs in these conflicts, but also the escalating rate of crimes across the state.

- There is need for sustainable peace education through CSOs, media, religious houses (Churches and Mosques) and schools. The peace message should emphasise the need to eschew violence and embrace peaceful coexistence.

References

Adams, E. I., Thill, A., Kuusaana, E. D. and Mittag, A. 2023. 'Farmer–herder Conflicts in Sub-Saharan Africa: Drivers, Impacts, and Resolution and Peacebuilding Strategies', *Environmental Research Letters*, 18(12), pp. 1–18. https://doi.org/10.1088/1748-9326/ad0702.

Benjaminsen, T. A. and Ba, B. 2021. 'Fulani-Dogon Killings in Mali: Farmer-herder Conflicts as Insurgency and Counterinsurgency', *African Security*, 14, pp. 4–26.

Benjaminsen, T. A., Maganga, F. P. and Abdallah, J. M. 2009. 'The Kilosa Killings: Political Ecology of a Farmer–Herder Conflict in Tanzania', *Development and Change*, 40, pp. 423–445.

Bereketeab, Redie, 2021. 'Peacebuilding in Africa: Popular Progressive versus Neoliberal Peacebuilding', in Adetula, Victor, Bereketeab, Redie and Obi, Cyril. Eds. *Regional Economic Communities and Peacebuilding in Africa: Lessons from ECOWAS and IGAD*. London and New York: Routledge, pp. 35–54.

Brottem, L. 2021. 'The Growing Complexity of Farmer–Herder Conflict in West and Central Africa' *Africa Security Brief* 39. Washington, DC: Africa Center for Strategic Studies.

Bruch, C., Jensen, D., Nakayama, M., and Unruh, J. 2019. 'The Changing Nature of Conflict, Peacebuilding, and Environmental Cooperation', *Environmental Law Report: News & Analysis*, 49.

Bukari, K. N. and Schareika, N. 2015. 'Stereotypes, Prejudices and Exclusion of Fulani Pastoralists in Ghana', *Pastoralism*, 5, pp. 1–12.

Chukwuma, K. H. 2020. 'Constructing the Herder–Farmer Conflict as (in)Security in Nigeria', *African Security*, 13(1), pp. 54–76. https://doi.org/10.1080/19392206.2020.1732703

Ebiede,T. M. and Kwaja, C. M. A. (eds.), 2024. *Policy Levers for Peace: Sub-National and Local Peacebuilding Mechanisms in Nigeria*. Conflict Research Network West Africa.

Eke, S. 2020. 'Nomad Savage' and Herder–Farmer Conflicts in Nigeria: The (Un) Making of an Ancient Myth', *Third World Quarterly*, 41, pp. 745–763.

Emah, E. B. and Kwaja, C. M. A., 2020. 'The Effectiveness of Peace-building Efforts and the Legitimacy of Actors: An Exegesis and Reflection of "The

Local" in Myanmar and Nigeria', *Journal of African-Centered Solutions in Peace and Security*, 3(1), pp. 86–126.

Hachmann, S., Löhr, K., Morales-Muñoz, H., Eufemia, U., Sieber S. and Bonatti, M. 2023. 'Conceptualizing Community-based Environmental Peacebuilding in Cesar, Colombia', *Human Ecology*, 51, pp. 221–235.

Hardt, J. N and Scheffran, J. 2019. 'Environmental Peacebuilding and Climate Change: Peace and Conflict Studies at the Edge of Transformation', *Policy Brief No. 68*: Toda Peace Institute, https://toda.org/assets/files/resources/policy-briefs/t-pb-68_hardt-and-scheffran_environmental-peacebuilding-and-climate-change.pdf.

Hirblinger and Simons, 2015. 'The Good, the Bad, and the Powerful: Representations of the Local in Peacebuilding', *Security Dialogue*, pp. 1–18.

Hussein, K., Sumberg, J. and Seddon, D. 1999. 'Increasing Violent Conflict between Herders and Farmers in Africa: Claims and Evidence', *Development Policy Review*, 17, pp. 397–418.

Ide, T., Bruch, C., Carius, A., Conca, A., Dabelko, G. D., Matthew, R., and Weinthal, W. 2021a. 'The Past and Future(s) of Environmental Peacebuilding', *International Affairs*, 97 (1), pp. 1–16.

Ide, T., Palmer, L. R., & Barnett, J. 2021b. 'Environmental Peacebuilding from Below: Customary Approaches in Timor-Leste', *International Affairs*, 97(1), pp. 103–117.

International Crisis Group, 2017, Herders against farmers: Nigeria's expanding deadly conflict. https://www.crisisgroup.org/africa/westafrica/nigeria/252-herders-against-farmers-nigerias-expanding-deadlyconflict.

Kendrich, C. and Sanders, L. 2024. 'Don't Call It Farmer-Herder Conflict', *The SAIS Review of International Affairs*, 9 February, available at https://saisreview.sais.jhu.edu/dont-call-it-farmer-herder-conflict/

Kwaja, C.M. and Ademola-Adelehin, B.I. 2017. 'The Implications of the Open Grazing Prohibition and Ranches Establishment Law on Farmer–Herder Relations in the Middle Belt of Nigeria', Washington, DC: Search for Common Ground, available at www.sfcg.org/wp-content/uploads/2018/02/Open-Grazing-Prohibition-Law-in-BenueState-December-2017.pdf

Maiangwa, B. 2017, '"Conflicting Indigeneity" and Farmer–Herder Conflicts in Postcolonial Africa', *Peace. Review 29*, no. 3 (2017), pp. 282–288.

Medina, L., Ensor, M.O., Schapendonk, F., Sieber, S., Pacillo, G., Laderach, P., Hellin, J. and Bonatti, M. 2023. 'Community Voices on Climate, Peace and Security: A Social Learning Approach to Programming Environmental Peacebuilding', *Environment and Security*, 2(1), pp. 75–104.

Mercy Corps. 2015. *The Economic Costs of Conflict and the Benefits of Peace: Effects of Farmer-Pastoralist Conflict in Nigeria's Middle Belt on Households*. Available at https://www.mercycorps.org/sites/default/files/Mercy%20Corps%20Nigeria%20Household%20Costs%20of%20Conflict%20Policy%20Brief%20July%202015.pdf

Olaniyan, A., Francis, M. and Okeke-Uzodike, U. 2015. 'The Cattle are 'Ghanaians' but the Herders are Strangers: Farmer-Herder Conflicts, Expulsion Policy, and Pastoralist Question in Agogo, Ghana', *African Studies Quarterly*, 15(2), March, pp. 53–67.

Omotola, J. S. 2024a. 'Traditional Institutions and the Management of Herders-Farmers Conflicts in Nasarawa State, Nigeria', in D. Ehrhardt, S. Umar and D. Alao eds. *Traditional Authority and Security in Contemporary Nigeria*, London: Routledge, pp. 169–190.

Omotola, J. S. 2024b. 'SADC and Peacebuilding in the Southern African Region', in R. Bereketeab ed., *Supranational Institutions and Peacebuilding in Africa: The African Union and Regional Economic Communities*, London: Routledge.

Omotola, J. S. 2021a. *The Embattled Trinity: Elections, Democracy and Development in Nigeria*, Inaugural Lecture, Federal University, Oye Ekiti, Nigeria, 12 December.

Omotola, J. S. 2021b. 'Nigeria: Has this House Truly Fallen?',Text of paper presented at the 4th Annual Democracy Lecture Day, 12 June.

Omotola, J. S. 2021c. 'Insurgency, Armed Banditry and Ethno-Religious Conflicts in Central Nigeria', Text of a Lead Paper presented at a National Conference Organised by the Department of History and International Studies, Federal University Lokoja in Honour of Professor Toyin Falola, as Part of the 5th Convocation Ceremony of the University, 10 November.

Omotola, J. S. 2017. 'Cattle Herding in Nigeria: Problems and Prospects', Commissioned Lead paper presented at the Annual National Conference of Nigerian Society of Animal Production, Landmark University, Omu-Aran, Kwara State, July 2017.

Omotola, J. S. and Oyewole, S. eds. 2024. *The Political Economy of Kidnapping and Insecurity in Nigeria*, Cham, Switzerland: Springer.

Omotola, J. S., Odoemene, A., Babatunde, A., Alemdjrodo, R., Ibnouf, F., Ngalim, A. and Bontogho, P. 2019. Herder-farmer Conflicts in Africa: Historical Trajectories, "New" Issues, Responses and Lessons for Peacebuilding, Research Report of the Collaborative Working Group Research Grants, 2018–2020 Submitted to the African Peacebuilding Network (APN) of the Social Science Research Council (SSRC), New York.

Omotola, J. S. and Alumona, I. M. eds. 2016, *The State in Contemporary Nigeria: Issues, Perspectives and Challenges (Essays in Honour of Professor Ben Nwabueze),* Ibadan, NG: John Archers Publishers.

Omotola, J. S. and Hassan, I. 2015. 'Herders and Farmers' Associations and Social Conflicts in Northern Nigeria', in: M. J. Kuna and J. Ibrahim, eds. Rural Banditry and Conflict in Northern Nigeria, Abuja: Centre for Democracy and Development (CDD), pp. 217–256.

Shettima, A. G. and Tar, U. A. 2008, 'Farmer-pastoralist conflict in West Africa: Exploring the causes and consequences', *Information, Society and Justice* 2(1), 163–184.

Wilén, N. 2022, 'Women, Gender and Peacebuilding in Africa', in B. Charbonneau and M. Ricard (eds.), *Routledge Handbook of African Peacebuilding*, London: Routledge.

Yakubu, S. M., Musa, M. W., Bamidele, T. E., Ali, M. B., Bappah, M. T., Munir, R. T. and Manuwa, A. 2021, 'Effects of farmer-herder conflicts on rural households food security in Gombe State, Nigeria', *Journal of Agricultural Extension, 25*, pp. 11–20.

Index

J. S. Omotola (ed.), *Herder-Farmer Conflicts in Africa*, https://doi.org/10.1007/978-3-031-80821-0

B

E

F

G

M

O

P

S

T

The manufacturer's authorised representative in the EU is Springer Nature Customer Service Centre GmbH, Europaplatz 3, 69115 Heidelberg, Germany. If you have any concerns regarding our products, please contact ProductSafety@springernature.com

Printed and bound by CPI Group (UK) Ltd, Croydon, CR0 4YY
30/09/2026
02225591-0005